ESSENTIAL
Writer's Handbook

William E. Messenger
Jan de Bruyn
Judy Brown
Ramona Montagnes

OXFORD
UNIVERSITY PRESS

Oxford University Press is a department of the University of Oxford.
It furthers the University's objective of excellence in research, scholarship,
and education by publishing worldwide. Oxford is a registered trade mark
of Oxford University Press in the UK and certain other countries.

Published in the United States of America by Oxford University Press
198 Madison Avenue, New York, NY 10016, United States of America.

© 2020 by Oxford University Press

CIP data is on file at the Library of Congress

ISBN: 978-0-19-093213-8

Printing number: 9 8 7 6 5 4 3 2 1

Printed by LSC Communications, Inc.
United States of America

Contents

Contents

Contents

Important Topics for English Language Learners

Several sections throughout this handbook provide information of particular importance to students whose first language is not English, or English language learners (ELL). The following list is a quick and convenient guide to those sections. Whether you are relatively new to writing in English or are more experienced and looking to master the finer points of the written language, these sections of the text—in combination with a dictionary—will help you improve your writing skills. Note that the entries in this list correspond to the ELL symbols found throughout the text: ELL .

Preface

Essential Writer's Handbook is designed to help you work on your writing skills. Improving written communication is an ongoing—even lifelong—project. Whether you are a long-time writer of English seeking to refine your abilities or a writer whose home or first language is not English or who is new to this country, the suggestions, examples, and guidelines in this handbook will help you to write with greater confidence and communicate with greater clarity.

Overview

Each of the six parts in this book addresses an essential aspect of the writing process. Part I provides practical guidance on planning and composing two larger units of communication, the essay and the paragraph. We start here because we have found that students who are beginning a written assignment usually want help with the more global aspects of composition before they move on to consider the more local concerns of sentence structure or word choice. In Part II and Part III, we explore the essentials of grammar and style, first by examining how sentences work, then by looking at how the parts of speech come together to form meaning. In Part IV we discuss the importance of punctuation, and in Part V we address issues of mechanics and spelling. Part VI offers valuable information on conducting research and citing sources in an essay. Appendix A provides a checklist that will help you revise, edit, and proofread your work, while Appendix B offers a sample research paper in MLA style.

How to Use This Handbook

We encourage you to use this handbook as a reference tool that you can consult as you approach college writing assignments as well as any other writing situations. We suggest that you begin by familiarizing yourself with this text by seeing what each part has to offer. Browse through the Table of Contents and the index. Look up some topics that you find challenging or might want to learn more about. Flip through the pages, pausing now and then for a closer look.

You may want to start at the beginning of Part I and proceed carefully through each section in sequence. Note that some points in later sections might not be clear to you unless you understand the material in the early sections. Or, if you are struggling with a particular problem, you may want to skip to the relevant section and then consult other sections as your needs change.

The book is subdivided into sections and subsections that are numbered consecutively throughout. Note how the running heads and the color-coded tabs on each page—together with the part index that follows the acknowledgments—can help you find things quickly.

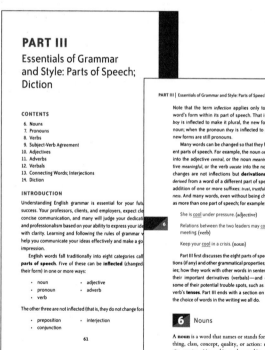

PART III
Essentials of Grammar
and Style: Parts of Speech;
Diction

CONTENTS

INTRODUCTION

Understanding English grammar is essential for your fut[ure] success. Your professors, clients, and employers, expect cle[ar,] concise communication, and many will judge your dedicati[on] and professionalism based on your ability to express your ide[as] with clarity. Learning and following the rules of grammar w[ill] help you communicate your ideas effectively and make a go[od] impression.

English words fall traditionally into eight categories call[ed] **parts of speech**. Five of these can be **inflected** (changed [in] their form) in one or more ways:

- noun
- pronoun
- verb
- adjective
- adverb

The other three are not inflected that is, they do not change for[m]:

- preposition
- conjunction
- interjection

61

PART III | Essentials of Grammar and Style: Parts of Speech; Diction

Note that the term *inflection* applies only to the change of a word's form within its part of speech. That is, when the noun *boy* is inflected to make it plural, the new form, *boys*, is still a noun; when the pronoun *they* is inflected to *them* or *theirs*, the new forms are still pronouns.

Many words can be changed so that they function as different parts of speech. For example, the noun *centre* can be made into the adjective *central*, or the noun *meaning* into the adjective *meaningful*, or the verb *vacate* into the noun *vacation*. Such changes are not inflections but **derivations**; a word can be *derived* from a word of a different part of speech, often by the addition of one or more suffixes: *trust, trustful, trustfully, trustfulness*. And many words, even without being changed, can serve as more than one part of speech; for example:

She is <u>cool</u> under pressure. (adjective)

Relations between the two leaders may <u>cool</u> after the meeting. (verb)

Keep your <u>cool</u> in a crisis. (noun)

Part III first discusses the eight parts of speech—their inflections (if any) and other grammatical properties; their subcategories; how they work with other words in sentences; and some of their important derivatives (verbals)—and calls attention to some of their potential trouble spots, such as **agreement** and a verb's **tenses**. Part III ends with a section on **diction**, which is the choice of words in the writing we all do.

6 Nouns

A **noun** is a word that names or stands for a person, place, thing, class, concept, quality, or action: *woman, character, city, country, citizen, ship, garden, machine, silence, vegetable, road, freedom, beauty, river, spring.* **Proper nouns** are names of specific persons, places, or things and begin with a capital letter: *Dorothy, Rumpelstiltskin, Pacific Ocean, Native American, Florida*, the *Titanic*. All other nouns, called **common nouns**, are capitalized only if they begin a sentence:

62

Help with Polishing Your Work

When you finish a piece of writing, go through the check-list in Appendix A. If you find you're not sure about something, follow the cross-references to the sections that will give you the help you need.

Help with Correcting and Revising Your Work

When you get a piece of writing back with marks and comments, look it over alongside the list of commomly used editing symbols and abbreviations on this handbook's inside back cover. The information there may be enough to help you make the appropriate changes. But if you need more than a reminder about a specific issue or pattern, look up the relevant topic and study the sections that discuss and illustrate those principles in greater detail. You should then be able to edit and revise your work with understanding and confidence.

Key Terms

Throughout the text, you will find important terms set in boldface. Pay attention to these terms, which make up the basic vocabulary of grammar, syntax, and style.

For English Language Learners

Our experience as university instructors has given us the opportunity to work with a number of writers whose home language is not English, who are engaged in the challenging project of reading and writing in English. At several points in this handbook, we offer information and direction of particular importance to those of you who are approaching English as a relatively new language, and we have designated those relevant sections with the symbol ELL .

Up-to-Date Documentation Guidelines

Part VI offers guidelines that cover the three most popular citation styles used in college classrooms today: MLA style, APA style, and Chicago style. To illustrate each method of documentation, we offer an array of examples modeled on the recommendations set out in the most recent edition of each style guide.

The components of each example are color-coded to help you identify and compare similar components across different examples. The color key is found at the bottom of relevant pages, as shown below.

integrity and indefatigable attention to public business" and "perpetually occupied by the affairs of his country" (Shelley 31).

Here the student writer has incorporated select words and phrases. The ellipsis indicates that material has been omitted in the interests of the student's own sentence str

37 Documentation

To be effective, documentation must be complete, ate, and clear. Completeness and accuracy depend o ful recording of necessary information as you d research and take notes. Clarity depends on the w present that information to your reader. You will b only if your audience can follow your method of mentation. Before you begin your research project, i gate the method of documentation you need to us section presents three frequently used styles:

1. Modern Language Association (**MLA**), which wide use in the humanities
2. American Psychological Association (**APA**), w used in some of the social and other sciences as in education studies
3. The *note* method recommended by *The Chicago of Style*, which is used in various disciplines

Which method you choose will depend on what dis (field of study) you are writing in and on the wi your audience.

Note: Each example on the following pages has col ing to help you recognize the common elements the in-text and reference citations, so that you ca struct them more easily. The color key is found at t tom of each page.

37a MLA Style

As detailed in the eighth edition of the *MLA Ha* (2016), MLA style uses internal citations within a

to attribute quotations, paraphrases, or summaries. In MLA, internal citations consist of the author's last name and where relevant, a page reference. Using this method, you provide a short parenthetical reference in the text, and you list all sources in a list titled Works Cited at the end of your paper. The entries in the list of works cited contain full bibliographic information, and they are alphabetized by the last names of authors, editors, or other creators (or by title, when no author, editor, or other creator is named).

The pages that follow illustrate examples of the most common patterns of MLA documentation: each in-text parenthetical reference is accompanied by its works-cited entry. Note that parenthetical references are usually placed at the end of the sentence in which the citation occurs. Note also that in an actual paper, the examples that follow would be double-spaced.

A note on number ranges: When you give a number range (e.g., a range of page numbers) in MLA style, provide the first and second numbers in full for numbers up to 99 (e.g., 5–88, 97–99). For larger numbers, give the first number in full but only the last two digits of the second number, unless additional digits are required for clarity (e.g., 122–28 for a range from 122 to 128, but 385–460 for a range from 385 to 460).

A Book by One Author (or Editor)
In-Text Citation

> A survey revealed that many North American cities "did not provide pedestrian amenities at all, and only half, in any way, encouraged their citizens to reach their destinations by foot" (Friedman 136).

When you don't mention the author by name in your sentence, the parenthetical reference includes the author's surname and a page reference, with *no intervening punctuation*. If you can include the author's name and credentials in your text, however, the parenthetical reference will be

Acknowledgments

Essential Writer's Handbook owes much to the contributions of reviewers, colleagues, friends, fellow writers, and talented and committed editors.

For their determination to strengthen and polish their work and their commitment to grow and change as thinkers and writers, we thank our students. We are especially grateful for their generosity in allowing us to use their questions and insights about writing in this book.

We would also like to thank Jen Coleman (Dabney S. Lancaster Community College), Tommie Delaney (Columbus State University), Larnell Dunkley, Jr. (Harold Washington College), Nancy Fox (University of West Florida), Julie Funderburk (Queens University of Charlotte), Lindsy Mason (Minnesota State University, Mankato), Karen S. Wilson (John Carroll University), and all of the other reviewers whose comments and suggestions have helped to shape all previous versions of *Essential Writer's Handbook*.

We deeply appreciate the encouragement, advice, and support we have received from the talented and enthusiastic staff at Oxford University Press—especially from Tracey MacDonald, Marianne Paul, and Liz Geist. Special appreciation goes out to Anne Stameshkin, our meticulous editor whose input and examples helped to shape this text.

To all of you, many thanks.

PART I
Essentials of Composition

INTRODUCTION

Writing is paradoxical, when you think about it. It is, on the one hand, the most commonplace of activities—something many of us do every day of the week, every week of the year. On the other hand, writing is one of the most astonishing and complex acts of communication any of us is asked to undertake in the course of getting an education, doing a job, or living a life.

Writing calls upon us to exercise creativity in generating ideas out of our own experience; it asks us to practice synthesis in entering the world of ideas and in discovering and integrating the ideas of others with insights of our own; it expects us to develop our powers of communication in shaping and presenting our arguments to different audiences of readers; it challenges us to demonstrate our talents for organization, reflection, and revision in working through the entire writing process, from having that first idea to printing the final draft.

Part I investigates the principles of unity, coherence, and emphasis that apply to the larger units of communication, the essay and the paragraph.

The Writing Process: Planning, Writing, and Revising the Whole Essay

A piece of writing is the result of a process. The usual steps that a writer takes, whether consciously or not, fall into three major stages:

Stage I: Planning
- Finding a subject and formulating questions about it
- Limiting the subject
- Determining audience and purpose
- Gathering reliable data
- Classifying and organizing the data
- Outlining

Stage II: Writing
- Writing the first draft
- Integrating evidence
- Commenting on the significance of the evidence

Stage III: Revising
- Revising the first draft
- Preparing the final draft
- Editing and proofreading

Often several parts of the process will be going on at the same time; for example, there is often a good deal of interaction among the activities in the planning stage. Sometimes the order will be different; for example, you may not be clear about your purpose until you have finished gathering and then classifying and organizing data. And sometimes in the revising stage, you may want to go back and rethink your purpose, dig up more material, or even further limit or expand your topic.

1a Finding and Limiting a Subject

1. For writing situations that are discipline-specific

Develop topics around researchable questions of current interest in the field, and narrow them to fit the time allotted to the assignment and the length expected by your reader.

Consider some of the following ideas to help you find a topic that will interest both you and your audience:

- A question of definition, a key term with a history of changing denotations over time (for a cultural geography course, "What is gendered space?")
- A central debate in the discipline's scholarly writing (for a feminist studies course, "How do scholars of the 1970s and those of today differ on the evaluation of Sylvia Plath's poetry?")
- A review of scholarly literature surrounding a particular question in the field (for an environmental literature course, "How can theories of ecocriticism be applied to the reading of American frontier fiction?")
- A cross-disciplinary question or issue, for example, a question preoccupying linguists and sociologists, or economists and geographers (for a human geography course, "How will global climate change affect birth rates in Central and South America?")
- An idea raised during one of your classes that deserves further investigation (for a film studies course, "Do the portrayals of children in recent Hollywood films provide clues to the way contemporary American culture has constructed ideas of childhood?")

Such possibilities should make it possible for you to produce a paper that is distinctive in its approach and that highlights your own perspectives—something more and better than a summary of the views of two or three major sources.

As you plan for the paper, devise a reasonable timeline for research, planning, writing, revising, and editing. Consider the expectations of your audience and the availability of a variety of electronic and non-electronic sources that are both scholarly and current.

2. For writing situations that are not discipline-specific

If you are enrolled in a writing course that involves writing papers in a variety of forms and for a range of audiences, you may be working outside a particular discipline or area of study. In such circumstances, a specific subject area or discipline will not likely be attached to your writing assignments, and you will be seeking one for yourself. A few minutes of free-associating, jotting down and playing around with any questions or ideas that pop into your head, will usually lead you at least to a subject area if not to a specific subject. Scanning the pages of a magazine, a newspaper, a credible website or blog, or a journal is another way to stimulate a train of thought; such sources are full of interesting subjects to write about, perhaps to argue about. Or think about the questions you may have about the course for which you are writing the essay. Often the very thing that puzzles you provides a good topic. The possibilities are almost endless.

Try to find a subject that interests you, one that you will enjoy working with and living with for an extended period of time. Formulate a question or series of questions worth investigating and researching. If you are assigned a topic that doesn't particularly interest you, try to make it a learning experience. Immerse yourself in it; you may be surprised at how interesting it can become.

Whether your assignment is discipline-specific or more general, consider taking notes to organize your thoughts and make sure your topic is a good fit for the assignment. Consider sharing your notes with your instructor or a peer editor to get feedback before you start writing. On the opposite page is a preliminary statement of purpose for a 3–5 page paper on nineteenth-century American writers.

3. Limiting the subject

Once you have a subject, limit it: narrow it to a topic you can develop adequately within the length of the essay you are writing. More often than not, writers start with subjects too big to handle. To save both time and energy, to avoid frustration, and to plan for a more focused essay, be sure to narrow your topic now. If anything, overdo the narrowing, for at a later stage it may be easier to broaden than it is to cut.

For example, let's say you wanted to write about "traveling"; that's obviously far too broad. "National travel"

Kevin Cheung   English 222/010
10 September 2018

Paper is due: 8 November 2018 (approximately
                 two months)

Target length: 3–5 pages

Audience: Fellow students and my instructor, all
                 with an interest in the subject

Subject: Poets' depictions of the American dream

Topic: Langston Hughes's poem "Let America Be
                 America Again"

Questions: What does this poem's speaker think of
                 the American dream? Who is the dream
                 for? Who speaks the italicized lines in the
                 poem asking the speaker who he is?

                 What does the line "America was never
                 America to me" mean?

                 Is this poem cynical, hopeful, or both
                 about America?

Sources so far:

                 Jabari Asim's "The Politics and Prose of
                 Langston Hughes," from *The Washington
                 Post*

                 Meta DuEwa Jones's "Listening to What the
                 Ear Demands: Langston Hughes and His
                 Critics," from *Callaloo*

                 Cindy Dyson's *Langston Hughes*

                 James Presley's "The American Dream of
                 Langston Hughes," from *Southwest Review*

or "international travel" is narrower, but still too broad.
"Traveling in Asia?" Better, but still too large, for where
would you begin? How thorough could you be in a mere
three or even five pages? When you find yourself narrowing your subject to something like "How to survive

on \$20.00 a day in Tokyo" or "What to do if you have only twenty-four hours in Hong Kong," then you can confidently look forward to developing your topic with sufficient thoroughness and specificity.

1b Considering Audience and Purpose

1. Audience

The sharper the focus you can get on who you're writing for, your audience, the better you can control your writing to make it effective for them. Try to define your audience for a given piece of writing as precisely as possible.

Some writing you do may have only one reader: the instructor. But some assignments may ask you to address some specific audience; sometimes an instructor will ask you to write "for an audience of your peers." In the absence of any other guideline, writing for your peers is not a bad idea. Your choice of the right tone and language to use and of what definitions and explanations to provide will often be appropriate if you keep an interested and serious but not expert audience in mind.

2. Purpose

All writing has the purpose of communicating ideas. In a college course, you write for the special purpose of demonstrating your ability to communicate your knowledge to your audience. But you will write more effectively if you think of each essay as having one or more of the following purposes:

1. To inform
2. To argue or persuade
3. To enter into discussion or debate with others who have explored the topic

Usually one of the three purposes will dominate, but one or both of the others will often be present as well.

The clearer your idea of what you want to do in an essay, and why, and for whom, the better you will be able to make effective rhetorical choices. You may even want to begin by writing down, as a note to yourself, a detailed description of your audience and as clear a statement of your purpose as you can formulate. Tape this note to the wall over your desk. If your ideas become clearer as the work proceeds, you can refine these statements.

1c Gathering and Organizing Evidence

An essay can't be built solely on generalizations and unsupported statements and opinions; it must contain specifics: facts, details, data, examples. Whatever your subject, gather material by reading and researching, conducting formal interviews, talking to others, or thinking about your personal experience. Collect as much information as you can within the time available for gathering evidence, even two or three times what you can use; you can then select the best and save the rest for future use.

Gathering the Evidence

1. Brainstorming

If you are expected to generate material from your own knowledge and experience (instead of through formal research), sit down for a few minutes with your phone or computer or with a pencil and a sheet of paper, write your topic at the top of the page, and begin recording your ideas. Put down everything that comes into your head about your topic. Let your mind run fast and free. Don't bother with sentences; don't worry about spelling; don't even pause to wonder whether the words and phrases are going to be of any use. Just keep writing. It shouldn't be long before you've filled the page with possible ideas, questions, facts, details, names, and examples. It may help if you also brainstorm your larger subject area, not just the narrowed topic, since some of the broader ideas could prove useful.

2. Using questions

Another way to generate material is to ask yourself questions about your subject or topic and write down the answers. Start with what we call the journalist's questions—*Who? What? Where? When? Why? How?*—and customize these questions for your specific purpose: *What is it? Who is associated with it? In what way? Where and when is it, or was it, or will it be? How does it work? Why is it? What causes it? What does it cause? What are its parts? What is it a part of? Is it part of a process? What does it look like? What is it like or unlike? What is its opposite? What if it didn't exist?* Such questions and the answers you develop will make you think of more questions, and so on; soon you'll have more than enough material that is potentially useful. You may even find yourself writing consecutive sentences, since some questions prompt certain kinds of responses. For example, asking *What is it?* may lead you to begin defining your subject; *What is it like or unlike?* may lead you to begin comparing and contrasting it, classifying it, thinking of analogies and metaphors; *What causes it?* and *What does it cause?* may lead you to begin exploring cause-and-effect relations; *What are its parts?* or *What is it a part of?* could lead you to analyze your subject; *How does it work?* or *Is it part of a process?* may prompt you to analyze and explain a process.

Organizing the Evidence

1. Classifying

As you brainstorm a subject and jot down notes and answers, you'll begin to see connections between ideas. Try putting them in groups or drawing circles around them and lines and arrows between them. Do this kind of classification when you have finished gathering material. You should end up with several groups of related items, which means that you will have classified your material according to some principle that arose naturally. During this part of the process, you will find yourself discarding the weaker or less relevant details, keeping only those that best suit the topic; that is, you will have selected the strongest ideas for your purpose.

For a tightly limited topic and a short essay, you may have only one group of details, but for an essay of even moderate length, say three pages or more, you will probably have several groups.

The map on the opposite page was created by a student to classify and organize her ideas for a four to five page

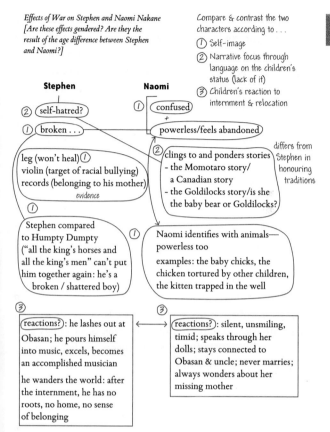

Effects of War on Stephen and Naomi Nakane
[Are these effects gendered? Are they the result of the age difference between Stephen and Naomi?]

Compare & contrast the two characters according to . . .
① Self-image
② Narrative focus through language on the children's status (lack of it)
③ Children's reaction to internment & relocation

Stephen

② self-hatred?

① broken . . .

Naomi

① confused
+
powerless/feels abandoned

leg (won't heal) ①
violin (target of racial bullying)
records (belonging to his mother)
evidence

② clings to and ponders stories
- the Momotaro story/ a Canadian story
- the Goldilocks story/is she the baby bear or Goldilocks?

differs from Stephen in honouring traditions

①

Stephen compared to Humpty Dumpty ("all the king's horses and all the king's men" can't put him together again: he's a broken / shattered boy)

① Naomi identifies with animals—powerless too
examples: the baby chicks, the chicken tortured by other children, the kitten trapped in the well

③

reactions?): he lashes out at Obasan; he pours himself into music, excels, becomes an accomplished musician

he wanders the world: after the internment, he has no roots, no home, no sense of belonging

③

reactions?): silent, unsmiling, timid; speaks through her dolls; stays connected to Obasan & uncle; never marries; always wonders about her missing mother

paper on the effects of war on the child characters in Joy Kogawa's novel *Obasan*.

2. Organizing after classifying

Once you have classified your material into groups, put the groups into a meaningful order. Don't necessarily accept the first arrangement that comes to mind; consider as many different arrangements as the material will allow, and then select the best one for your purpose and audience. The order should be logical rather than accidental or arbitrary.

1d Crafting a Thesis Statement

A crucial part of the planning or prewriting stage is developing a **thesis statement**.

1d

During the early stages of a project, you gradually increase your control over your proposed essay: you find and narrow a subject, you think about audience and purpose, you gather evidence and generate ideas, and you classify and arrange your material. At some point while you are doing all this, you will probably formulate a tentative thesis, a statement that identifies your topic and points the way to what you want to say about it.

1e Crafting an Outline

Create an **outline** to plan your essay's structure. Begin by writing your thesis statement, the foundation of your essay, at the top. The ordered groups become *main headings*, and the details that make up each group become subdivisions of the main heading in various levels of *subheadings*. On the opposite page is an example, a student's outline for a short essay. Note the layout of this outline: numerals and letters are used to indicate different levels of headings, and each subheading is indented a few spaces further than the heading it follows. Few outlines will need to go beyond one or two levels of subheading, but if further subdivision is necessary, here is how to indicate successive levels:

I.
II.
  A.
  B.
    1.
    2.
      a.
      b.
        (1.)
        (2.)
          (a.)
          (b.)

Creating an outline before you begin drafting a major essay will save you time and effort at later stages. Writing the draft will likely be a smoother process because it follows a plan: you know where you're going. You can avoid such pitfalls as unnecessary repetition, digression, and illogical or

Sonia's Outline

THESIS STATEMENT: Students who have a social life are happier, smarter, and better prepared for the workforce than are students who concentrate only on their studies.

I. They are happier.
   A. develop friendships
   B. develop maturity and a more balanced perspective toward life

II. They are smarter.
   A. receive academic support in study groups
   B. receive academic support from friends who are strong in certain subjects

III. They are better prepared for life after college.
   A. develop an effective network of contacts
   B. develop interpersonal skills
   C. develop communication skills

otherwise incoherent organization. In other words, a good outline can be like a map that keeps the writer from taking wrong turns, wandering in circles, or getting lost altogether.

Keep in mind, too, that an outline is not binding. If as you write and revise you think of a better way to organize a part of your essay, or if some part of the outline proves clumsy when you try to put it into paragraphs, or if you suddenly think of some new material that should be included, go with your instincts and revise accordingly. And as you proceed, you may also want to refine your thesis to reflect any major changes in your ideas.

1f Writing a First Draft

Once you have a good outline to follow, drafting becomes smoother and more purposeful. With the shape of the whole essay laid out, you can concentrate on the main tasks of drafting: finding the best way to convey your ideas, generating effective paragraphs that support

1f

your paper's thesis, and constructing good transitions and relationships between those paragraphs.

As you transition from your outline to your draft, keep the following in mind:

1. Sometimes a main heading and its subheading from the outline will become a single paragraph in the essay; sometimes each subheading will become a paragraph; and so on. The purpose and scope of your material will determine its treatment.

2. It may be possible to transfer the thesis statement from your outline to the essay unchanged, but you may want to change it (perhaps several times) to fit the actual essay. The thesis is the statement of your purpose or of the position you intend to defend in the essay, so it should be as polished as possible, and it can evolve as you write and learn more about what you want to say. The kind of basic or mechanical statement suitable in an outline may be inappropriate in the essay itself.

1g Beginnings

1. Postponing the beginning

Starting the actual writing can be a challenge: most writers have had the experience of staring at a computer screen or a blank sheet of paper while trying to think of a good way to begin. The good news is that you don't have to draft your paper in the order that your audience will read it. If you have no ideas for your paper's introduction at this point, plunge right into the body of the essay. Once you have finished writing the first draft, you'll have a better idea of what it is that needs to be introduced; you can then go back and write the beginning with relative ease.

2. Beginning directly

Just as it's rarely a good idea to begin your final paragraph with "In conclusion," avoid opening an essay with empty statements like "In this essay I will discuss" or "This essay is concerned with." On occasion, such as when your essay is unusually long or complicated or when you are presenting it as part of a research seminar, conference, or panel, it may be helpful to announce in advance what

12

your essay is about, to provide readers with what amounts to a brief outline. But most essays don't require this kind of beginning and won't engage an audience with such a stiff introduction. Begin by talking about your topic. Rather than inform readers of what you are going to say (and then remind them of what you have said), start with something substantial and, if possible, attention-getting. Try to end your essay with something similarly sharp and definitive.

3. Determining subject and thesis

However you begin, it is necessary to identify your subject and to state your thesis somewhere near the beginning of your essay. For example, even if your title is something like "Imagery in Shakespeare's Sonnet 65," you should still, within the first paragraph, mention both the author and the title of the poem. Do so even if your title includes this information. Remember that the title of your essay is not part of the essay's content; the essay should be able to stand on its own.

In certain types of essays or for certain purposes, you may decide to delay the full statement of your thesis to near the end. This could be for the purpose of building to a climax, or of answering a question in an essay whose purpose is to explore. Even then, you will probably provide at least some indication of your thesis near the beginning, perhaps in general terms or as a question.

4. Being direct, smooth, economical: some examples

Begin as directly, smoothly, and economically as you can. Here, for example, are three ways an essay with the title "Imagery in Shakespeare's Sonnet 65" might begin; note how differences in order, punctuation, and wording make each succeeding one better and shorter than the one before:

(1) In Sonnet 65 by William Shakespeare, there is a great deal of imagery.

(2) William Shakespeare in his Sonnet 65 uses imagery to . . .

(3) The imagery in Shakespeare's Sonnet 65 . . .

Here is the beginning of an essay on Shakespeare's Sonnet 65. The writer can't seem to focus or get to the point:

1g

> William Shakespeare, famous English poet and writer of plays, has always been known for the way he uses imagery to convey the point he is making in a particular piece of work. Shakespeare's Sonnet 65 is no exception to this, and this is one of the better examples of his work that I have studied, for illustrating his use of imagery.
>
> The best example in the sonnet comes in lines five and six, where Shakespeare compares a "summer's honey breath" and a "wrackful siege of battering days."

Compare this with another student's beginning on the same topic:

> In Sonnet 65, Shakespeare appeals to a person's knowledge of visible properties in nature in an attempt to explain invisible properties of love and time.

The second writer takes control of the material immediately. Even without yet mentioning a particular image or line from the poem, the second writer accomplishes more with one crisp sentence than the first does in two paragraphs.

1h Revising, Editing, and Proofreading

Even professional writers can't write a polished, finished essay in one draft. So even if you are happy with your first draft, consider ways to improve it before handing it in. To do so, you will need to carefully revise, edit, and proofread what you have written.

1. Revising

Revision (re-vision, literally "scrutinizing again") is an extremely important stage of writing. Experienced writers revise a piece of writing at least two or three times before they consider it to be finished.

Revise carefully and slowly, looking for ways to improve what you've written. Don't aim just to correct errors made in haste, but also to remove clutter and improve unity, coherence, transitions, support, effective selection of details, organization, and so on. Many writers find that going through a draft for one thing at a time is effective—for example, going through it looking only at paragraphing, then going through it again looking only at the structure and variety of sentences, then at punctuation, and so on. Focus on the big picture first. Most writers consider sentence-level and stylistic concerns as part of the editing phase.

Adopt the role of an observant and alert reader looking for strengths and pinpointing weaknesses and errors. To do this effectively, try to allow yourself a cooling-off period; wait as long as possible between the drafting and the revising—at least two or three days—so that you can look at your own work objectively, as another reader would. If you're having trouble, you may find the checklist in Appendix A helpful during your revisions. You can also ask one of your classmates or a tutor at your campus writing center to give you feedback.

2. Editing and proofreading

Editing and proofreading may take place throughout the writing process, but you should focus on them with even more precision after you finish revising any larger issues in your paper.

During editing, look carefully at each sentence and consider how your sentences work together in each paragraph. Find ways to improve your diction (word choice) and sentence structure, to edit for concision, and to fix grammatical issues. At this point, also look for errors in spelling, mechanics, and punctuation. This final proofreading will prove worthwhile; despite earlier careful scrutiny, you may discover not only typographical errors but also previously unnoticed slips in spelling, punctuation, and grammar.

Do your proofreading and editing with exaggerated care. Read each sentence, as a sentence, slowly (and aloud whenever possible); but also read each word as a word and check each punctuation mark. You might consider starting at the end of your work and reading backward, one word at a time, so that you won't get caught up in the flow of a sentence and overlook an error.

Do not put full trust in any of the spelling, grammar, and style checks that are part of word-processing programs. They can't possibly cover all the matters that require attention. Remember that spell-checkers can't spot a misspelled word that happens to be the same as some other correctly spelled word—for example, *form* instead of *from*, or *through* instead of *though*; nor can they tell you that you've mistaken, say, *your* for *you're*, or *principal* for *principle*.

1i Preparing the Final Draft

When you are through revising, editing, and proofreading a piece of writing, carefully prepare the final draft, the one that will be presented to your reader or readers. Once the work is out of your hands, it will be too late to change anything, so make sure it's in good shape when it leaves your hands. Be sure that the final project is in the appropriate format and file type for its genre and purpose. Follow your instructor's directions for submission; do not email a paper when the instructions are to post it somewhere or to provide a printed copy. Don't wait until the last minute to post, print, or email a paper, as technology may fail you at just the wrong moment. For most of your academic writing, heed the requirements of your particular audience, and follow carefully the manuscript conventions listed and discussed in #26.

2 Paragraphs

To be effective, all paragraphs, but especially body paragraphs, require **unity**, **coherence**, and well-controlled **emphasis**. Writing a paragraph involves designing the best possible package to contain and convey your ideas. You have a sense of what point you wish to convey (your topic), and, usually early in the process, you have an array of items to include as well (your supporting ideas and evidence). You arrange your ideas, explanations, and evidence in the package by ordering them logically, linking them to one another using strategies for coherence. You may well spend some time rearranging to make the package look the way you want it to—to give each item the appropriate emphasis.

 ## Unity

An effective body paragraph ordinarily deals with one main idea; its singleness of purpose engages its readers by focusing their attention on that main idea. If a paragraph is disrupted by irrelevant digressions or unnecessary shifts in point of view or focus, readers may lose the thread of the discourse and become confused. A paragraph is unified when every sentence in it contributes to its purpose.

 ## Organizational Coherence

Another essential quality of a successful paragraph is coherence. Coherence can be defined as the connection of ideas. Simply placing one sentence after another doesn't guarantee coherence. In fact, coherence is achieved only by carefully packing the contents of a paragraph and linking the ideas to one another. You can ensure coherence in your writing in two ways:

- By carefully organizing your material
- By using a variety of transitional devices that create structural coherence.

A body paragraph has a *beginning*, a *middle*, and an *ending*. Good organization means rational order. Typically, the beginning introduces the main idea; the middle clearly and logically follows from and develops the statement of that idea, and the ending is a natural conclusion that closes the discussion or provides a transition to the next paragraph.

1. The beginning: topic sentences

Body paragraphs typically open with a statement of the main idea, called a **topic sentence**.

2b

Functions of topic sentences

A good topic sentence indicates what the paragraph will be about. It is a promise that the rest of the paragraph fulfills. If the paragraph is part of a larger context, such as an essay, the topic sentence will usually perform two other functions:

- It will refer to the subject of the essay and at least suggest the relation of the paragraph to that subject.
- It will provide a transition so that the new paragraph flows smoothly from the preceding paragraph.

Efficiency of topic sentences

Since it has so much to do, a good topic sentence, even more than other sentences, should be efficient. Here is one that is not:

> The poet uses a great deal of imagery throughout the poem.

This sentence indicates the topic—the poem's imagery—but promises nothing more than to show that the poem contains a lot of it. Further thought might lead to a revision like this, a topic sentence that not only has more substance in itself, but also suggests the approach the paragraph will take:

> The poem's imagery, most of it drawn from nature, helps to create not only the poem's mood, but its themes as well.

The same essay also contains the following inefficient topic sentence:

> In the second stanza, the poet continues to use images.

What is needed is something sharper, more specific, such as an assertion that provides a significant idea that can be usefully developed. For example:

> The imagery in the second stanza contrasts vividly with that in the first.

> *or*

> In the second stanza, images of death begin the process that leads to the poem's ironic conclusion.

A good topic sentence should be more than just a table of contents; it should be a significant part of the contents of the paragraph. Pay close attention to the formulation of your topic sentences, for they can help you achieve both unity and coherence not only in individual paragraphs, but also in a whole essay.

Placement of topic sentences

Often a paragraph's development fulfills the promise made in its topic sentence. Or, by conscious design, a writer may place a topic sentence at the end or elsewhere in a paragraph. Sometimes delaying a topic sentence can increase readers' interest by creating a little mystery to get them to read on. And stating a topic at the end of a paragraph takes advantage of that most emphatic position.

A paragraph's topic, though focused, may consist of more than one part. Similarly, it need not be stated all in one sentence. In this paragraph, for example, note that not until the end of the second sentence is the topic fully clear. It is fairly common for a paragraph to have a second topic sentence, one that partly restates the topic and partly leads into the body of the paragraph.

In select cases, writers may choose to clearly imply, rather than explicitly state, a paragraph's topic. Paragraphs with implied topic sentences occur most often in narratives, where paragraphs begin in such a way that their relation to the preceding paragraph is sufficiently clear—perhaps indicated by no more than an opening *Then* or *When*.

See also #1g.

2. The middle

Coherence through orderly development

A well-developed body paragraph fulfills the promise of its beginning. After considering the different possibilities, choose a way of presenting your material. The order you choose to follow should be one that makes sense; one idea should lead logically to another until you reach your goal. Then your paragraph will be coherent.

Patterns of development

Orderly development sometimes occurs automatically as one works through one's ideas in composing paragraphs

2b

and essays. But most writers must give some conscious thought to how a particular paragraph (or essay) can best be shaped. The most common *patterns of development* writers use to make paragraphs orderly and coherent are the following:

- *spatial* (moving through space, such as top to bottom or left to right; used in describing physical space)
- *chronological* (moving through time; used in narration and process analysis)
- *climactic* (moving from the least important to the most important point; often used in academic writing)
- *inverse pyramid* (moving from the most important to the least important point; often used in journalism)
- *inductive* (moving from data to assertions; often used in writing for sciences and social sciences)
- *deductive* (moving from assertions to supporting data or premises; often used in writing for the humanities)
- *block* (in a comparison of two items, a full discussion of the first item followed by a full discussion of the second item)
- *alternating* (in a comparison of two items, a back-and-forth discussion of the first and second items)

These patterns are often used in combination within a paragraph or an essay.

3. The ending

As you compose and revise drafts, the endings of paragraphs will sometimes come naturally. But they are likely to do so only if, when you begin a paragraph, you know just where it is going. The final sentence of a paragraph, like all the others, should be a part of the whole: it will most often be a statement growing out of the substance of the paragraph, a sentence that rounds off the paragraph in a satisfying way.

Some advice for ending paragraphs

If a paragraph doesn't seem to be ending naturally, you may have to stop and think consciously about it. Here are a few pointers to help you do that:

- A good ending may point back to the beginning but not merely repeat it; if it repeats something, it will do so in order to put it in the new light made possible by the development of the paragraph.

- A good ending sentence doesn't usually begin with a stiff *In conclusion* or *To conclude*. Sometimes the best way to end a paragraph is simply to let it stop, once its point is made. A too-explicit conclusion might damage the effectiveness of an otherwise good paragraph that has a natural quality of closure at its end.

- A good ending might provide forward-looking material to help with the transition to the next paragraph, but only if this material flows naturally from the preceding sentences. Forcing transitional material into a paragraph's final sentence may diminish that paragraph's integrity and effectiveness.

- A good ending might have a slight stylistic shift that marks a paragraph's closing, perhaps no more than an unusually short or long sentence. Or an ending might be marked by an allusion or brief quotation, as long as it is relevant and to the point and not there simply for its own sake.

- A good paragraph usually doesn't end with an indented (block) quotation, or even a shorter full-sentence quotation that isn't set off. Even if you carefully introduce such a quotation, it will leave a feeling that you have abandoned your paragraph to someone else. If you use a quotation near the end of a paragraph, follow it with a brief comment that explains, justifies, or re-emphasizes it in your own words.

2c Structural Coherence

Careful organization and development go a long way toward achieving coherence. But you will sometimes need to use other techniques, providing links that ensure a smooth flow of thought from one sentence to another.

The main devices for structural coherence are parallelism, repetition, pronouns and demonstrative adjectives,

2c

and transitional words and phrases. Like the patterns of development, these devices are not mutually exclusive: two or more may work together in the same paragraph, sometimes even in the same words and phrases.

1. Parallelism (see also #5h)

Parallel sentence structure is an effective way to correct successive sentences. Similar structural patterns in clauses and phrases (see #3d–f) work like a call and its echo. But don't try to maintain a series of parallel elements for too long. If the echoes remain obvious, they will be too noticeable and will become less powerful as they get farther from the original.

2. Repetition

Like parallelism, repetition of words and phrases effectively links successive sentences. But take care not to overdo it. Repetition carefully chosen for rhetorical effect can be powerful (as in Martin Luther King's famous "I Have a Dream" speech), but repetition, especially on paper, can also suggest a limited vocabulary or lack of ingenuity. Structure and space out your repetitions, and use the device sparingly.

3. Pronouns and demonstrative adjectives

By referring to something mentioned earlier, a pronoun (e.g., *him, her, he, she, they, them, it, you*; see #7) or a demonstrative adjective (*this, that, these, those*; see #10a.1) constructs a bridge within the paragraph between itself and its antecedent or referent (that is, the word it is replacing or referring to).

It is also possible to use pronouns and demonstrative adjectives to create links between paragraphs, but avoid doing so when the antecedent is ambiguous or too distant to be clear (see #7d).

Make it a point to use demonstrative adjectives rather than demonstrative pronouns (see #7a.5). While demonstrative adjectives are clear and can add emphasis, demonstrative pronouns are often weak and ambiguous.

4. Transitional terms

In your writing, use transitional words and phrases strategically to create a logical flow from one part or idea to another. Most transitional expressions appear at or near the beginning of sentences and paragraphs. Here are some of the more common and useful transitions:

- Showing addition of one point to another

and	also	another	in addition
further	besides	moreover	

- Showing similarity between ideas

again	equally	in other words
in the same way	likewise	similarly

- Showing difference between ideas

but	although	conversely
despite	even though	however
yet	though	in contrast
whereas	nevertheless	in spite of
still	otherwise	on the contrary
on the other hand		

- Showing cause and effect

as a result	because	consequently	for
of course	since	then	
therefore	thus		

- Introducing examples or details

for example	in particular	namely	specifically
for instance	to illustrate	that is	

- Expressing emphasis

chiefly	especially	more important
indeed	mainly	primarily

- Showing relations in time and space

after	afterward	at the same time
before	earlier	in the meantime

later	meanwhile	simultaneously
then	while	subsequently
behind	beyond	farther away
here	nearby	in the distance
next	there	to the left

These and other transitional words and phrases are the glue that helps hold paragraphs together. But if the paragraph isn't unified or its parts haven't been arranged to fit with one another, even the most explicit transitional terms can't create structural coherence by themselves.

Note: Don't overuse transitional terms. Adding a transitional word or phrase to nearly every sentence can make your writing sound stiff and mechanical.

2d Emphasis and Variety

1. Emphasis

In a paragraph, as in a sentence, the most emphatic, or important, position is its ending, and the second most emphatic position is its beginning (see #4f). That is another reason the opening or topic sentence is such an important part of a paragraph.

Structure and diction (word choice) are also important. Parallelism and repetition create emphasis. Independent clauses are more emphatic than subordinate clauses and phrases (see #3d–f). Precise, concrete, and specific words are more emphatic than vague, abstract, and general ones (see #14b). A long sentence will stand out among several shorter ones; a short sentence will stand out among longer ones. Keep these points in mind as you draft and revise your paragraphs; let emphasis contribute to the effectiveness of your writing.

2. Variety

Try to ensure that any longer piece of writing you produce contains a variety of paragraph lengths: long, short, medium. Reading can become repetitive if most of an essay's paragraphs are too similar in length. (The same is true of sentences of similar length: see #4b.) You should also try to use various patterns of development in your paragraphs. For example, alternating between two topics, however admirable an approach, would likely lose its impact if it were the only pattern used in several successive paragraphs.

Normally, then, the paragraphs that make up an extended piece of writing will vary in length. Ensure that each of your paragraphs is as long or as short as it needs to be to achieve its intended purpose. There is no optimal length for a paragraph. Determine a paragraph's length requirements by the particular job it is doing. In a narrative essay, a single sentence or word may constitute a paragraph. In a complex argument essay, a paragraph may go on for a full page—though such long paragraphs are rare in contemporary academic writing. Most body paragraphs consist of at least three or four sentences, and seldom more than nine or ten. Transitional paragraphs are usually short, sometimes only one sentence. Introductory and concluding paragraphs will be of various lengths, depending on the complexity of the material and on the techniques of beginning and ending that the writer is using.

PART II
Essentials of Grammar and Style: Sentences

CONTENTS

INTRODUCTION

Part II introduces the basic elements and patterns of English sentences and defines and classifies different kinds of sentences. It also examines how the various elements work together in sentences. When you have finished Part II, you will better understand how sentences work and how to avoid common problems when writing your own sentences.

3 Sentence Elements and Patterns

All sentences have this purpose: to communicate ideas and/or feelings. We know how to interpret different kinds of expression because we understand and accept the *conventions* of the way sentences communicate. Sentences are classified according to their purposes, which include:

Declarative: This class deals with the effects of globalization on education. (states a fact)

Interrogative: Is this your phone? (asks a question)

Imperative: Please print the essay. (gives a command, makes a request)

Exclamatory: That was an unforgettable trip! (exclaims, expresses strong feeling or emphasis)

A sentence may fall into more than one category:

"Should the voting age be lowered?" the candidate asked. (interrogative and declarative)

Please contact me about your project: I have information that's relevant. (imperative and declarative)

Slow down! (imperative and exclamatory)

Your awareness of the *conventions* guides you in understanding the purposes of sentences you hear, read, speak, or write: you know almost instinctively how to frame a sentence to make it do what you want.

A more conscious grasp of the way sentences work will help you frame them even more effectively. It will help you when you're in doubt. And it will help you not only to avoid weaknesses and errors but also to revise and correct them when they do occur.

Since most sentences in written and academic discourse are *declarative*, we'll focus on their patterns first. Most of the rest of this section deals with the basic elements and patterns of declarative sentences. (See #4a for an expanded discussion of basic sentence elements and their modifiers.)

3a Subject and Predicate, Noun and Verb

A standard declarative sentence consists of two parts: a **subject** and a **predicate**. The subject is what acts or is talked about; the predicate is what the subject does or what is said about it. The essential element of the subject is a noun or a pronoun. (Nouns name persons, places, things, classes, concepts, qualities, or actions; see #6.) Pronouns stand in place of and refer to nouns; see #7.) The essential element of the predicate is a verb. (Verbs express actions, occurrences, processes, conditions, or states of being; see #8.)

subject	predicate
Birds	fly.
I	disagree.

3b Modifiers

Both the subject and the predicate often include **modifiers**, words that change or limit the meaning of nouns and verbs. Nouns are modified by **articles** (*a, an, the*; see #6c) and other **adjectives**, which generally answer the questions *Which? What kind of? How many?* and *How much?* (see #10):

subject	predicate
The young child	babbled.
A caged bird	will sing.

Verbs are modified by **adverbs**, which generally answer the questions *How? When? Where? Why?* and *To what degree?* (see #11):

subject	predicate
The young child	babbled happily.
They	flew south.

3c Structure Words

Subjects, **verbs**, **modifiers**, **objects**, and **complements** make up the substance of all sentences. (See #4 for more on these sentence elements.) But many sentences also include words like *and*, *but*, *for*, *of*, *under*, and *with*. Such words connect other elements in various ways, and they are sometimes called **structure** or **function words**. Most of these structure words belong to two other classes of words, or parts of speech: **conjunctions**, which join words, phrases, and subordinate and independent clauses (see #13b), and **prepositions**, which link their object (a noun or a pronoun) to other words in the sentence to clarify a relationship (see #13a). (Note that the parts of speech are discussed at greater length in Part III.)

3d-f Phrases and Clauses

To master sentence structure and punctuation, first consider the differences between **phrases** and **clauses**. Phrases and clauses are groups of words that function as grammatical units or elements *within* sentences but (with the exception of **independent clauses**) cannot stand alone as sentences.

3d Phrases

A **phrase** is a group of words lacking a subject and/or predicate but functioning as a grammatical unit within a sentence.

A **verb phrase** (see #8d) acts as the verb in this sentence:

> Most of the wedding guests <u>will be arriving</u> in the morning.

A **prepositional phrase** (see #13a) can function as an adjective (here modifying a relative pronoun):

> Most <u>of the wedding guests</u> will be arriving in the morning.

or as an adverb (here modifying a verb phrase):

> Most of the wedding guests will be arriving <u>in the morning</u>.

The words *Most of the wedding guests* constitute a **noun phrase** functioning as the subject of the sentence. Any noun or pronoun along with its modifiers—so long as the group doesn't contain a subject–predicate combination—can be thought of as a noun phrase.

A **gerund phrase** (which begins with a gerund—a verb form that ends in *ing* and functions a noun; see #12c) can function as a subject:

> Bungee jumping can be risky.

3d

or as a direct object:

> She tried bungee jumping.

A **participial phrase** (which is always adjectival and begins with a past or present participle; see #12b) can modify a subject:

> Trusting her instincts, Ashaki gave the candidate her support.

or a direct object:

> I am reading an article discussing human cloning.

An **infinitive phrase** (which begins with an infinitive—a verb form that consists of *to* followed by the basic form of a verb; see #12a) can function as a direct object (noun):

> This organization wants to eradicate poverty.

or as a subject (noun):

> It may be impossible to eradicate poverty.

It can also function as an adjective, for example one modifying the subject:

> Their desire to eradicate poverty is idealistic.

or it can function as an adverb, for example one modifying the verb:

> They arranged the agenda to highlight the anti-poverty campaign.

Adverbial infinitive phrases can also act as **sentence modifiers** (see #11a and #11c.3), modifying not the verb or any other single word but rather all the rest of the sentence:

To be honest,

To tell the truth,

the meeting ended shortly after you left.

3d Two other kinds of phrases you should be familiar with are the **appositive** and the **absolute**.

An **appositive** is a word or group of words that renames or restates, in other terms, the meaning of a neighboring word. For example, if you start with two simple sentences,

Marc is our neighbor. He sometimes stops by to watch a game.

you can turn the first into an appositive by reducing it and combining it with the second:

Marc, our neighbor, sometimes stops by to watch a game.

The noun phrase *our neighbor* is here **in apposition to** *Marc*.

Most appositives are nouns or noun phrases that redefine, usually in more specific terms, the nouns they follow. Following are several other appositive patterns:

A skillful lawyer, Julia navigated the custody case.
   (appositive precedes the noun)

Searching frantically, tossing books and papers everywhere, they failed to find the missing passport.
   (participial phrase functions as an appositive)

Document (provide details of your sources for) this argument. (verb phrase functions as an appositive)

My sister, Pei, starts college next year.
   (a single word, a proper noun, functions as
   an appositive)

How she traveled—whether she journeyed alone or not—remains a mystery. (subordinate clause
   functions as an appositive)

(For the punctuation of appositives, see #15d.2.)

An **absolute phrase** has no direct grammatical link with what it modifies; it depends simply on juxtaposition, modifying the rest of the sentence like an umbrella. Most absolute phrases consist of a sentence with the verb changed to a participle (see #12b). Instead of using two sentences, you can reduce the first to an absolute phrase modifying the second.

Two Sentences:

> The intermission had ended. The last act finally began.

Sentence with Absolute Phrase:

> <u>The intermission having ended</u>, the last act finally began.

If the original verb is a form of *be,* the participle can sometimes be omitted:

> <u>The thunderstorm (being) over</u>, the picnic resumed.

Sometimes, especially with certain common expressions, the participle isn't preceded by a noun:

> There were a few rough spots, but <u>generally speaking</u>, the rehearsal was a success.

And sometimes infinitive phrases function as absolutes:

> <u>To say the least</u>, the campaign was not a success.

You can also think of many absolutes as *with*-phrases from which the preposition has been dropped:

> <u>(With) the thunderstorm over</u>, the picnic resumed.

3e Independent (Main) Clauses

A clause is a group of words containing both a *subject* and a *predicate.* An **independent clause** can stand by itself as a sentence.

An independent clause can also function as only part of a sentence. For example, if you start with two separate independent clauses—that is, two simple sentences:

> The exam ended.

> The students handed in their test booklets.

you can combine them to form a **compound sentence** (see #3g):

> The exam ended; the students handed in their test booklets.

> The exam ended, and the students handed in their test booklets.

> The exam ended; therefore the students handed in their test booklets.

3e

3f Subordinate (Dependent) Clauses

A **subordinate clause**, unlike an independent clause, usually cannot stand by itself. Even though, as a clause, it contains a subject and a predicate, it is by definition *subordinate*, *dependent* on another clause—an *independent* one— for its completion or meaning. In the following examples, the subordinate clauses are underlined; these sentences are called **complex sentences** (see #3g):

> When the exam ended, the students handed in their test booklets.

> The students handed in their test booklets as the exam ended.

> The students handed in the essays that they had written for their exam.

> The exam ended, which meant that the students had to turn in their test booklets.

Subordinate clauses often begin with such words as *when*, *as*, *that*, and *which*, called **subordinators**, which clearly signal the presence of a subordinate clause (see #13b.3).

Like a phrase, a subordinate clause functions as a grammatical unit in its sentence. It can take on several of the functions discussed in #3d and in #4.

A **noun clause** can serve as the subject of a sentence:

> That free speech matters is evident.

as a direct object:

Azin knows <u>what she is doing</u>.

or as a predicate noun:

The question is <u>what we should do next</u>.

Adjective clauses (also called **relative clauses**; see #7a.4) modify nouns or pronouns, such as a direct object:

The reporter questioned the police officer <u>who had found the missing child</u>.

or a subject:

The project <u>that I am working on</u> is proceeding smoothly.

Adverb clauses usually modify main verbs:

We left <u>because we were very tired</u>.

3g Kinds of Sentences: Grammatical Types

Sentences can be classified grammatically as **simple, compound, complex**, and **compound-complex**.

1. Simple sentences

A **simple** sentence has one subject and finite verb unit, and therefore it contains only one clause, an independent clause:

   s   v
<u>The boat</u> <u>leaks</u>.

      s   v
<u>The new museum</u> <u>opened</u> on the weekend.

The subject or the verb, or both, can be compound—that is, consist of more than one part—but the sentence containing them will still be simple:

<u>Jordan and Kim</u> left early. (compound subject)

She <u>watched and waited</u>. (compound verb)

<u>The sergeant and her troops</u> <u>moved</u> down the hill <u>and crossed</u> the river. (compound subject, compound verb)

2. Compound sentences

A **compound** sentence consists of two or more simple sentences—that is, independent clauses—linked by coordinating conjunctions (see #13b.1), by punctuation, or by both:

s   V   s   V

The conductor's baton fell, and the concert ended.

s   V

The clouds massed thickly against the hills; soon

s   V

the rain fell in torrents.

s V   s   V

We wanted to hear jazz, but they played bluegrass
instead.

s   V   s

Gabriel's patience and persistence paid off; he not only

V   V

won the prize but also earned his competitors' respect.

s   V   s   V   s

The day was mild, the breeze was warm, and everyone

V

went for a swim.

3. Complex sentences

A **complex** sentence consists of one independent clause and one or more subordinate clauses; in the following examples, the subordinate clauses are underlined:

We believe that we have some original plans for the campaign. (noun clause as direct object)

The strike was averted before we reported to the picket line. (adverb clause modifying *was averted*)

This course is the one that requires the most field research. (adjective clause modifying *one*)

Marco Polo, who left his native Venice as a teenager, returned home after twenty-five years of adventure. (adjective clause modifying *Marco Polo*)

When the film ended, the audience burst into
applause that lasted several minutes. (adverbial
clause modifying *burst*, adjective clause
modifying *applause*)

Although it seems premature, the Senate is planning to
confirm the nominee.
(adverbial clause of concession, in effect
modifying the rest of the sentence)

3g

Note that when the meaning is clear, the conjunction *that*
introducing a noun clause, or the relative pronouns *that* and
which, can be omitted:

He claimed he was innocent.

. . . the suitcase he had brought with him.

4. Compound-complex sentences

A **compound-complex** sentence consists of two or more
independent clauses and one or more subordinate clauses:

Because the architect knows that the preservation of
historical landmark buildings is vital, she is consulting
widely, but as delays have developed, she has grown
impatient, and therefore she is thinking of pulling out of a
project that represents everything important to her.

We can analyze this example as follows:

Because the architect knows (adverb clause)

that the preservation of historical landmark buildings is vital
(noun clause)

she is consulting widely (independent clause)

but (coordinating conjunction)

as delays have developed (adverb clause)

she has grown impatient (independent clause)

and (coordinating conjunction)

therefore (conjunctive adverb)

she is thinking of pulling out of a project
(independent clause)

that represents everything important to her
(adjective clause)

4 Working with Sentence Elements to Create Variety and Emphasis

4a Basic Sentence Elements and Their Modifiers

To achieve variety and emphasis in your writing, you will need to recognize and manipulate basic sentence elements and their modifiers.

1. Subject

The subject is what is talked about. It is the word or phrase answering the question *Who?* or *What?* before the verb.

> <u>Osman</u> watched the performance. (*Who* watched? Osman. Osman is the source of the action of watching.)

The subject of a sentence will ordinarily be one of the following: a basic noun (see #6), a pronoun (see #7), a gerund or gerund phrase (see #12c), an infinitive or infinitive phrase (see #12a), or a noun clause:

> <u>Ohio</u> became a state in 1803. (noun)

> <u>He</u> is an American historian. (pronoun)

> <u>Skydiving</u> is a risky activity. (gerund)

> <u>Visiting the website</u> is part of our daily routine. (gerund phrase)

> <u>To travel</u> is to enjoy life. (infinitive)

> <u>To order tofu</u> is to make a healthy choice. (infinitive phrase)

> <u>That Ohio became a state in the early 1800s</u> is common knowledge. (noun clause)

2. Finite verb

The **finite verb** is the focal point of the clause or the sentence. It indicates both the nature and the time of the action (see #8a):

> The mayor <u>will respond</u> during the press conference.
> (action: responding; time: the future)

> Lewis Carroll <u>invented</u> the adventures of Alice for a child named Alice Liddell. (action: inventing; time: past)

> Appalachia's fiddlers <u>have</u> a distinctive musical style.
> (action: having, possessing; time: present)

3. Object

If a verb is transitive, it will have a **direct object**. (Transitive verbs *make* a *transition* or *convey* a *movement* from their subject to their object; see #8a.) Like the subject, the direct object may be a noun, a pronoun, a gerund or gerund phrase, an infinitive or infinitive phrase, or a noun clause:

> The price includes <u>admission</u>. (noun)

> The increase in fuel taxes worried <u>us</u>. (pronoun)

> Our economy needs <u>farming</u>. (gerund)

> He enjoys <u>writing reports</u>. (gerund phrase)

> We wanted <u>to participate</u>. (infinitive)

> You need <u>to define your terms</u>. (infinitive phrase)

> The reporter revealed <u>that his source feared retaliation</u>.
> (noun clause)

Along with a direct object, there may also be an **indirect object** or an **objective complement**:

> We gave <u>you</u> a blank check. (*you*: indirect object; *check*: direct object)

> She found the situation <u>untenable</u>. (*situation*: direct object; *untenable*: objective complement)

4. Subjective complement

Similarly, a *linking verb* typically requires a **subjective complement**. (Linking verbs *connect* or *link* their subject to its complement; see #8a.) This complement will usually be either a *predicate noun* or a *predicate adjective*. A predicate noun may be a noun or a pronoun, or (especially after *be*) a gerund or gerund phrase, an infinitive or infinitive phrase, or a noun clause:

4a

> We are <u>friends</u>. (noun)
>
> Was he the <u>one</u>? (pronoun)
>
> His passion is <u>traveling</u>. (gerund)
>
> His passion is <u>traveling abroad</u>. (gerund phrase)
>
> My first impulse was <u>to run</u>. (infinitive)
>
> Our next challenge will be <u>to take action</u>. (infinitive phrase)
>
> She remains <u>what she has long been</u>: a loyal friend. (noun clause)

A predicate adjective will ordinarily be a descriptive adjective, a participle, or an idiomatic prepositional phrase:

> His music has become <u>joyful</u>. (descriptive adjective)
>
> The novel's plot is <u>intriguing</u>. (present participle)
>
> They seem <u>dedicated</u>. (past participle)
>
> The government is <u>out of ideas</u>. (prepositional phrase)

The linking verb *be* (and sometimes others) can also be followed by an adverbial word or phrase (I am *here*; he is *in his office*).

These elements—**subject**, **finite verb**, and **object** or **complement**—are the core elements of major sentences. They are closely linked in the ways indicated above, with the verb as the focal and uniting element.

5. Modifiers

Modifiers add to the core grammatical elements. They limit or describe other elements so as to modify—that is, to change—a listener's or reader's idea of them. The two principal kinds of modifiers are *adjectives* (see #10) and *adverbs* (see #11). Also useful, but less frequent, are *appositives* and *absolute phrases* (see #3d). An adjective or adverb may even be part of the core of a sentence. For example, an adjective is essential if it completes the predicate after a linking verb (Recycling is *vital*). An adverb is essential if it modifies an intransitive verb that would otherwise seem incomplete (Peter lives *in a condominium*). But generally modifiers do their work by adding to—enriching—a central core of thought.

4a

Adjective modifiers *(see #10)*

Adjective modifiers modify nouns, pronouns, and phrases or clauses functioning as nouns. They commonly answer the questions *Which? What kind of? How many?* and *How much?* An adjective modifier may be a single-word adjective, a series of adjectives, a participle or participial phrase, an infinitive or infinitive phrase, a prepositional phrase, or a relative clause:

> <u>Early</u> settlers of the <u>western</u> United States encountered <u>sudden</u> floods, <u>prolonged</u> droughts, and <u>early</u> frosts. (single words modifying nouns immediately following)

> We are <u>skeptical</u>. (predicate adjective modifying the pronoun *We*)

> That the author opposes globalization is <u>evident</u> in his first paragraph. (predicate adjective modifying the noun clause *That the author opposes globalization*)

> <u>Four ambitious young</u> reporters are competing to work on this story. (series modifying *reporters*)

> The <u>train</u> station is filled with commuters and tourists. (noun functioning as adjective, modifying *station*)

> <u>Grinning</u>, he replied to her text. (present participle modifying *he*)

<u>Brimming with confidence</u>, they began their performance.
(present participial phrase modifying *they*)

They continued the climb toward the summit, <u>undaunted</u>.
(past participle modifying *they*)

Lijuan applied for the position, <u>having been encouraged to do so by her advisor</u>. (participial phrase, perfect tense, passive voice, modifying *Lijuan*)

They prepared a meal <u>to remember</u>. (infinitive modifying *meal*)

Our tendency <u>to favor jazz</u> is evident in our album collection.
(infinitive phrase modifying *tendency*)

The report <u>on the evening news</u> focused on forest fires in northern Oregon. (prepositional phrase modifying *report*)

The soccer team, <u>which was traveling to a tournament in Mexico</u>, filed slowly through airport security. (relative clause modifying *team*)

Adverb modifiers (see #11)

Adverb modifiers modify verbs, adjectives, other adverbs, and whole clauses or sentences. They commonly answer the questions *How? When? Where?* and *To what degree?* An adverb modifier may be a single word, a series, an infinitive or infinitive phrase, a prepositional phrase, or an adverbial clause:

Mix the chemicals <u>thoroughly</u>. (single word modifying the verb *mix*)

As new students, we are <u>completely</u> happy. (single word modifying the adjective *happy*)

They planned their future together <u>quite</u> enthusiastically. (single word modifying the adverb *enthusiastically*)

<u>Apparently</u>, the experiment is being delayed. (single word modifying the rest of the sentence)

He loves her <u>truly</u>, <u>madly</u>, <u>deeply</u>. (series modifying
the verb *loves*)

<u>To succeed</u>, you must work well with others. (infinitive
modifying the verb *must work*)

She was lucky <u>to have been selected</u> for the exchange
program. (infinitive phrase modifying the predicate
adjective *lucky*)

The passenger ship arrived <u>at the port</u>. (prepositional
phrase modifying the verb *arrived*)

We disagreed <u>because we were taking different theoretical</u>
<u>approaches to the text</u>. (clause modifying
the verb *disagreed*)

The election results trickled in slowly <u>because the ballots</u>
<u>were being counted by hand</u>. (clause modifying
the adverb *slowly* or the whole preceding clause,
The election results trickled in slowly.)

Shut down your computer <u>when you leave on vacation</u>.
(clause modifying the preceding independent clause)

4b-i Sentence Length, Variety, and Emphasis

To create emphasis and to avoid monotony, vary the lengths
and kinds of your sentences. This is a process to practice
when revising a draft to strengthen its style. Examine
some pieces of writing that you particularly enjoy or that
you find unusually clear and especially readable: you will
likely discover that they contain both a pleasing mixture
of short, medium, and long sentences and a similar variety
of kinds and structures.

4b Variety in Lengths

A sentence may, in rare cases, consist of one word, or it
may go on for a hundred words or more. There are no strict
guidelines to tell you how long to make your sentences. If

you're curious, do some research to determine the average sentence length in several pieces of writing you have handy. You'll probably find that the average is somewhere between 15 and 25 words per sentence, that longer sentences are more common in formal and specialized writing, and that shorter sentences are more frequent in informal and popular writing, in email, and in narrative and dialogue.

A string of short sentences will sound choppy and fragmented; avoid the staccato effect by interweaving some longer sentences. On the other hand, a succession of long sentences may make your ideas hard to follow; give your readers a break—and your prose some sparkle—by using a few short, emphatic sentences to change your pace occasionally. Even a string of medium-length sentences can bore readers into inattention. Impart some rhythm, some shape, to your paragraphs by varying sentence length.

4b

1. Short sentences

If you receive feedback that you're writing too many short sentences, try the following strategies to lengthen some of them:

- Build a sentence up by elaborating its elements with modifiers, including various kinds of phrases and clauses.
- Combine sentences and parts of sentences to form compound subjects, predicates, and objects or complements.
- Combine two or more sentences—especially if they are simple sentences—into a compound, complex, or compound-complex sentence.

2. Long sentences

If you find yourself writing too many long sentences, check them for three possible problems:

1. You may be rambling or trying to pack too much into a single sentence, possibly making it less unified and more difficult to read. Try breaking it up into more unified or more easily manageable parts.
2. You may be using too many words to make your point. Try cutting out any wordiness (see #14f).
3. You may have slipped into what is called "excessive subordination"—too many loosely related details

obscuring the main idea, or confusing strings of subordinate clauses modifying each other. Try removing some of the clutter, reducing clauses to phrases and phrases to single words.

4c Variety in Kinds

A string of simple and compound sentences risks coming across to a reader as simplistic. In some narratives and in certain technical and business documents, successive simple and compound sentences may be appropriate for recounting a sequence of events, but in academic writing, let the complexity of your ideas be reflected in complex and compound-complex sentences. However, be aware that a string of similarly structured complex and compound-complex sentences may also become oppressive. Give your readers a more varied and interesting experience by changing pace.

4d Variety in Structures

Avoid an unduly long string of sentences that use the same syntactical structure. For example, though the standard order of elements in declarative sentences is subject–verb–object or subject–verb–complement, consider varying that order occasionally for emphasis. Use an occasional interrogative sentence, whether a rhetorical question (a question that doesn't expect an answer) or a question that you proceed to answer as you develop a paragraph.

In particular, try not to begin a string of sentences with the same kind of word or phrase or clause—unless you are purposely setting up a controlled succession of parallel structures for emphasis or coherence (see #2c). Imagine the effect of several sentences beginning with such words as *Similarly, Especially, Consequently,* and *Nevertheless.* Whatever else the sentences contained, the sameness would be distracting. Or imagine a series of sentences all starting with a subject-noun, or with a present-participial phrase. To avoid such undesirable sameness, take advantage of the way modifiers of various kinds can be moved around in sentences.

4e Emphasizing a Whole Sentence

To make sure your readers perceive the relative importance of your ideas the same way you do, learn to control emphasis.

You can emphasize whole sentences in several ways:

- Set a sentence off by itself, as a short paragraph. (Use this strategy judiciously.)
- Put an important sentence at the beginning or, even better, at the end of a paragraph.
- Put an important point in a short sentence among several long ones, or in a long sentence among several short ones.
- Shift the style or structure of a sentence to make it stand out from those around it (see #2d). In particular, a stylistically enhanced sentence—for example, a periodic sentence, a sentence with parallel or balanced structure, or a richly metaphorical or allusive sentence—stands out beside plainer sentences.

 ### Emphasis Within a Sentence

You can also emphasize important parts of individual sentences. The principal devices for achieving emphasis *within* sentences are position and word order, repetition, stylistic contrast, and syntax. In addition, you can add emphasis by effective use of punctuation (see Part IV).

 ### 4f Emphasis by Position and Word Order

The most emphatic position in a sentence is its ending; the second most emphatic position is its beginning. The longer the sentence, the stronger the effect of emphasis by position. Consider the following:

a. The best teacher I've ever had was my tenth grade chemistry teacher, a brilliant woman who left a job at NASA to teach high school.
b. A brilliant woman who left a job at NASA to teach high school, my tenth grade chemistry teacher was the best teacher I've ever had.

   c.   My tenth grade chemistry teacher, a brilliant woman who left a job at NASA to teach high school, was the best teacher I've ever had.

   d.   The best teacher I've ever had was a brilliant woman who left her job at NASA to teach high school, and who taught me tenth grade chemistry in high school.

Each sentence contains the same three ideas, but each distributes the emphasis differently. In each the last part is the most emphatic, the first part next, and the middle part least.

Loose sentences and periodic sentences

A *loose, cumulative,* or *"right-branching"* sentence makes its main point in an early independent clause and then adds modifying subordinate elements:

> The concert began modestly, with the performers sitting casually onstage and taking up their instruments to play their first piece.

In contrast to the loose is the *periodic* (or "*left-branching*") sentence, which wholly or partly delays its main point, the independent clause, until the end:

> With the performers sitting casually onstage and taking up their instruments to play their first piece, the concert began modestly.

Full periodic sentences are usually the result of careful thought and planning. However, they can sometimes sound contrived, less natural, and therefore should not be used without forethought.

Using the expletive and the passive voice for emphasis

Two basic sentence patterns, the *expletive* and the *passive voice*, can be weak and unemphatic in most contexts. Used sparingly and strategically, however, they can enable you to emphasize who or what is being acted upon in a sentence rather than who or what is acting. For example:

> Passive voice can be used to move a certain word or phrase to an emphatic place in a sentence.

Here, putting the verb in the passive voice (*can be used*) makes *Passive voice* the subject of the sentence and enables this important element to come at the beginning; otherwise, the sentence would have to begin less strongly (for example, with *You can use passive voice*). This next example makes strategic use of the expletive pattern:

> There are advantages to using the expletive pattern for a deliberate change of pace in your writing.

In this case, opening the sentence with *There* is preferable to opening with long and unwieldy alternatives.

Use expletives and passive voice when you need to delete or delay mention of the agent or otherwise shift the subject of a sentence.

4g Emphasis by Repetition

Repeat an important word or idea to emphasize it, to make it stay in your readers' minds. Unintentional repetition can be wordy and tedious; but intentional, controlled repetition—used sparingly—can be very effective, especially in sentences with balanced or parallel structures:

> If you have the courage to face adventure, the adventure can sometimes give you courage.

> If it's a challenge they seek, it's a challenge they'll find.

4h Emphasis by Contrast

A word or phrase that differs in style or tone from those that surround it may stand out in contrast:

> The chef—cautious as her behavior sometimes appears—dazzles the kitchen staff with her gutsy culinary experiments.

> My grandmother may be almost ninety years old, but she approaches each day with a child's *joie de vivre*.

4i Emphasis by Syntax

Put your most important claims in independent clauses; put lesser claims in subordinate clauses and phrases.

Sometimes you have more than one option, depending on what you want to emphasize:

Reading the menu, she frowned at the high prices.

Frowning at the high prices, she read the menu.

But more often the choice is determined by the content. Consider the way subordination affects emphasis in the following pairs of sentences:

5b

original: I was strolling into the laboratory when my attention was drawn by the pitter-pattering of a little white rat in a cage.

revised: When I strolled into the laboratory, my attention was drawn by the pitter-pattering of a little white rat in a cage.

5 Common Sentence Problems

Here we define some common problems that can affect the clarity of sentences, and we suggest ways to avoid or correct them.

The three sentence errors that can most impede clear communication in your writing are the *fragment*, the *comma splice*, and the *run-on sentence*. Edit closely to identify and correct them.

5a Sentence Fragments

A **fragment** is a group of words that is not a complete sentence but is punctuated as if it were a sentence. It is missing either a subject or a predicate, and/or it does not express a complete idea.

frag: We looked for sources. <u>For example, statistics, case studies, and government reports.</u>

revised: We looked for sources such as statistics, case studies, and government reports.

5b Comma Splices

A **comma splice** occurs when two independent clauses are joined inadequately with only a comma, rather than with a semicolon or with a comma and a coordinating conjunction. The error usually stems from a misunderstanding of sentence structure.

>*cs:* The team lost the series, the coach lost her job.

>*revised:* The team lost the series; the coach lost her job.

5c Run-on (Fused) Sentences

5b

A **run-on sentence**, sometimes called a **fused sentence**, is in fact not a single sentence but two sentences run together without the necessary punctuation. An error most likely to occur when a writer is rushed, it can sometimes, like the comma splice, result from a problem in understanding how sentences work.

>*fs:* We left the museum they entered as we exited.

>*revised:* We left the museum, and they entered as we exited.

5d Misplaced Modifiers

1. Modifier placement

Part of the meaning in English sentences is conveyed by the position of words in relation to each other. And though there are certain standard or conventional arrangements, a good deal of flexibility is possible, particularly for the placement of adverb modifiers. Because of this flexibility, writers sometimes put a modifier where it conveys an unintended or ambiguous meaning, or where it is linked by juxtaposition to a word it can't logically modify. To say precisely what you mean, you have to be careful in placing your modifiers—especially adverbs. The following sentence demonstrates how a misplaced modifier can suggest an absurd misunderstanding:

>*mm:* While testifying before the court, the Department of Homeland Security officer denied allegations heatedly concerning targeted and excessive passenger screening reported in a recent PBS documentary at JFK airport.

The adverb *heatedly* belongs before *denied*, the verb it modifies. The adjective phrase *reported in a recent PBS documentary* belongs after *allegations*, the noun it modifies. And the adverbial phrase *at JFK airport* belongs after the phrase *concerning targeted and excessive passenger screening*.

Usually it is best to keep modifiers and the words they modify as close together as possible:

> ***mm:*** Love is a <u>difficult</u> emotion to express in words.
>
> ***clear:*** Love is an emotion (that is) difficult to express in words.

2. *Only*, *almost*, etc.

Pay particular attention to such adverbs as *only*, *almost*, *just*, *merely*, and *even*. In speech, we often place these words casually, but in writing we should put them where they clearly mean what we want them to:

> ***mm:*** Hardy <u>only</u> wrote novels as a sideline; his main interest was poetry.
>
> ***clear:*** Hardy wrote novels <u>only</u> as a sideline; his main interest was poetry.

> ***mm:*** The students <u>almost</u> washed fifty cars last Saturday.
>
> ***clear:*** The students washed <u>almost</u> fifty cars last Saturday.

3. Squinting modifiers

A **squinting modifier** is a word or phrase put between two elements either of which it could modify:

> ***squint:*** It was so warm <u>for a week</u> we barely left the apartment.

Which clause does the adverbial phrase modify? It is ambiguous. A speaking voice could impart clarifying emphasis to such a sentence, but a writer must substitute words or structures for the missing vocal emphasis. Here, adding *that* removes the ambiguity:

> ***clear:*** It was so warm that for a week we didn't need to wear coats.
>
> ***clear:*** It was so warm for a week that we didn't need to wear coats.

Dangling Modifiers

Like a pronoun without an antecedent (see #7), a **dangling modifier** has no word in the rest of the sentence to attach to; instead it is left dangling, grammatically unattached, and so it often tries to attach itself, illogically, to some other word. Most dangling modifiers are *verbal phrases*; be watchful for them in editing drafts of your work.

1. Dangling participial phrases

> *dm:* Strolling casually beside the lake, my eyes fell upon two children chasing a pair of geese.

Since the adjectival phrase wants to modify a noun, it tries to link with the subject of the adjacent clause, *eyes*. Eyes can scarcely be said to "stroll." To avoid the unintentionally humorous dangler, simply change the participial phrase to a subordinate clause:

> *revised:* As I strolled casually beside the lake, my eyes fell upon two children chasing a pair of geese.

Or, if you want to keep the effect of the opening participial phrase, rework the clause so that its subject is the logical word to be modified:

> *revised:* Strolling casually beside the lake, I let my gaze fall upon two children chasing a pair of geese.

2. Dangling gerund phrases

When a gerund phrase is the object of a preposition, it can dangle much like a participial phrase:

> *dm:* After being informed of the correct procedure, our attention was directed to the next steps.

It isn't "our attention" that was "informed." The passive voice contributes to the confusion here.

> *revised:* After informing us of the correct procedure, the instructor directed our attention to the next steps.

3. Dangling infinitive phrases

> *dm:* To reach the other side of the lake, a ferry must be taken.

Ineffective passive voice is the issue, depriving the infinitive phrase of a logical word to modify.

> *revised:* To reach the other side of the lake, travelers must take a ferry.

4. Dangling elliptical clauses

An **elliptical clause** is an adverbial clause abridged so that its subject and verb are implied rather than stated; the subject of the independent clause then automatically serves also as the implied subject of the elliptical clause. If the implied subject is different from the subject of the independent clause, the subordinate element will dangle, sometimes illogically.

> *dm:* Once in disguise, the hero's conflict emerges.

It isn't "the hero's *conflict*" that is in disguise, but the *hero*. Either supply a logical subject and verb for the elliptical clause, or retain the elliptical clause and make the other subject logically agree with it:

> *revised:* Once the hero is in disguise, his conflict emerges.
> *revised:* Once in disguise, the hero begins to reveal his conflict.

5. Dangling prepositional phrases and appositives

A prepositional phrase can also dangle. In this example, an indefinite *it* (see #7d.5) is the issue:

> *dm:* Like a child in a toy shop, it is all she can bear not to touch everything.
> *revised:* Like a child in a toy shop, she can hardly bear not to touch everything.

And so can an appositive prove to be problematic:

> **dm:** A superb racing car, a Ferrari's engine is a
> masterpiece of engineering.

The phrase seems to be in apposition with the noun *engine*, but it is illogical to equate an engine with an entire car (the possessive *Ferrari's* is adjectival). Revise it:

> **revised:** A superb racing car, a Ferrari has an engine that
> is a masterpiece of engineering.

5f Mixed Constructions

ELL Avoiding mixed constructions can be especially challenging for anyone whose first language has a different sentence structure than English has. When writing in English, avoid beginning a sentence with one construction and then shifting into another. Even an inadvertent shift can cause confusion for readers.

> **mix:** Eagle Creek is a small community is located
> near Wells Gray Provincial Park.

The writer here sets up two clauses beginning with *is* but then omits a subject for the second occurrence of *is*. Either drop the first *is* and add commas around the resulting appositive phrase (*a small community*), or add *that* or *which* before the second *is*.

> **mix:** Since the pool is used for swimming lessons all
> day, therefore we have to swim laps at night.

Here the writer begins with a subordinating *Since* but then uses *therefore* to introduce the second clause, which would be correct only if the first clause were independent. Fix this by dropping either the *therefore* or by removing *since* and correctly connecting two independent clauses.

> **revised:** Since the pool is used for swimming lessons all
> day, we have to swim laps at night.

> **revised:** The pool is used for swimming lessons all day,
> so we have to swim laps at night.

5g Shifts in Perspective: Inconsistent Point of View

Be consistent in your point of view within a sentence and, except in special cases, from one sentence to the next. Avoid illogical shifts in the *tense*, *mood*, and *voice* of verbs, and in the *person* and *number* of pronouns.

1. Shifts in tense

shift: The professor <u>explained</u> what she expected of us and then she <u>sits</u> in her chair and <u>tells</u> us to begin.

All of the events described in this sentence occurred at a particular time in the past. So, change *sits* and *tells* to the past tense to coincide with *explained*.

2. Shifts in mood

shift: If it <u>were</u> Sunday and I <u>was</u> through with my work, I would go running with you.

This sentence begins and ends in the subjunctive, but *was* is indicative. Correct this by changing indicative *was* to subjunctive *were*.

3. Shifts in voice

shift: Readers should not ordinarily have to read instructions a second time before some sense <u>can be made</u> of the details.

In this case, stay with active voice (and the same subject):

revised: Readers should not ordinarily have to read instructions a second time before <u>they can make</u> sense of the details.

4. Shifts in person of pronoun

Shifts in person from words such as *one*, *a person*, *somebody*, or *someone* to the second-person *you*, while common in informal conversation, are likely to be questioned in print, and particularly in more formal academic writing. Edit to produce consistency in person.

> ***shift:*** If <u>a person</u> wants to be a cautious investor, <u>you</u> should not invest in the stock market.

> ***revised:*** If <u>you</u> want to be a cautious investor, <u>you</u> should not invest in the stock market.

> ***revised:*** If <u>a person</u> wants to be a cautious investor, <u>he or she</u> should not invest in the stock market.

5g

5. Shifts in number of pronoun

> ***shift:*** If the committee wants <u>its</u> recommendations followed, <u>they</u> should have written <u>their</u> report more carefully.

The committee changed from a collective unit (*it*) to a collection of individuals (*they, their*); the committee should be either singular or plural throughout.

5h Faulty Parallelism

Parallelism, the balanced and deliberate repetition of identical grammatical structures (words, phrases, clauses), can be a strong stylistic technique. It makes for vigorous, balanced, and rhythmical sentences. Like any other device, parallelism can be overdone. However, more commonly writers underuse it. In most writing, some parallel structure is appropriate. Build parallel elements into your sentences, and now and then try making two or three successive sentences parallel with each other. Here is a sentence from a paper on computer crime. Note how parallelism (along with alliteration) strengthens the first part, thereby helping to set up the second part:

> Although they can distinguish <u>the malicious from the mischievous</u> or <u>the harmless hacker from the more dangerous computer criminal</u>, security officials may still penalize anyone who breaks into company files.

Be careful as you experiment, for it is easy to set up a parallel structure and then lose track of it. Study the following examples of **faulty parallelism (fp).**

1. With coordinate elements

Coordinate elements in a sentence should have the same grammatical form. If they don't, the sentence will lack parallelism and therefore be ineffective.

> *fp:* Reading should be <u>engrossing</u>, <u>active</u>, and <u>a challenge</u>.

The first two complements are predicate adjectives, the third a predicate noun. Change *a challenge* to the adjective *challenging* so that it will be parallel.

    The coordinate parts of compound subjects, verbs, objects, and modifiers should be parallel in form.

> *fp:* <u>Eating huge meals</u>, <u>too many sweets</u>, and <u>snacking frequently</u> can lead to obesity.

This sentence can be corrected either by beginning each of the three parts of the subject with a gerund:

> *revised:* <u>Eating huge meals</u>, <u>eating too many sweets</u>, and <u>snacking frequently</u> can lead to obesity.

or by using only the first gerund and following it with three parallel objects:

> *revised:* Eating <u>huge meals</u>, <u>too many sweets</u>, and <u>frequent snacks</u> can lead to obesity.

Another example:

> *fp:* He talks about his computer in terms <u>suggesting a deep affection for it</u> and <u>that also demonstrate a thorough knowledge of it</u>.

Simply change the participial phrase (*suggesting . . .*) to a relative clause (*that suggest . . .*) so that it will be parallel with the second part.

    It is particularly easy for a writer to produce faulty parallelism by omitting a second *that*:

> *fp:* Marvin was convinced <u>that the argument was unsound</u> and <u>he could profitably spend some time analyzing it</u>.

A second *that*, before *he*, corrects the error and clarifies the meaning.

2. With correlative conjunctions

5h

Check for parallel structure when using correlative conjunctions:

> *fp:* Whether <u>for teaching a young child the alphabet</u> or <u>in finding the quickest route to the park</u>, smartphone apps can be extremely useful.

The constructions following the *whether* and the *or* should be parallel: change *in* to *for*.

The correlative pair *not only . . . but also* can be particularly troublesome:

> *fp:* She not only <u>corrected my grammar</u>, but also <u>my spelling</u>.

The error can be corrected either by repeating the verb *corrected* (or using some other appropriate verb, such as *criticized* or *repaired*) after *but also*:

> *revised:* She not only <u>corrected my grammar</u>, but also <u>corrected my spelling</u>.

or by moving *corrected* so that it occurs before *not only* rather than after it:

> *revised:* She corrected not only <u>my grammar</u>, but also <u>my spelling</u>.

3. In a series

In any series of three or more parallel elements, make sure that little beginning words like prepositions, pronouns, and the *to* of infinitives precede either the first element alone or each of the elements. And don't omit needed articles:

> *fp:* The new library offers <u>a large auditorium</u>, <u>state-of-the-art computer lab</u>, <u>an impressive collection of journals</u>, and <u>brilliant, hard-working staff</u>.

The article *a* is missing before the second and fourth items and should be added to make the items parallel. Another way to fix this would be to remove the articles and insert the possessive pronoun *its* before the first item.

> *fp:* She urged her teammates <u>to obey the rules</u>, <u>to think positively</u>, and <u>ignore criticism</u>.

5h

Tip: Check your work by jotting down the items in such a series in a vertical list after the word that introduces them: any slips in parallelism should then be clearer to you.

> *correction:* She urged her teammates to obey the rules,
> to think positively,
> and **to** ignore criticism.

PART III
Essentials of Grammar and Style: Parts of Speech; Diction

CONTENTS

INTRODUCTION

Understanding English grammar is essential for your future success. Your professors, clients, employers, and coworkers expect clear, concise communication, and many will judge your dedication and professionalism based on your ability to express your ideas with clarity. Learning and following the rules of grammar will help you communicate your ideas effectively and make a good impression.

English words fall traditionally into eight categories called **parts of speech**. Five of these can be **inflected** (changed in their form) in one or more ways:

- noun
- pronoun
- verb
- adjective
- adverb

The other three are not inflected (that is, they do not change form):

- preposition
- conjunction
- interjection

Note that the term *inflection* applies only to the change of a word's form within its part of speech. That is, when the noun *boy* is inflected to make it plural, the new form, *boys*, is still a noun; when the pronoun *they* is inflected to *them* or *theirs*, the new forms are still pronouns.

Many words can be changed so that they function as different parts of speech. For example, the noun *center* can be made into the adjective *central*, or the noun *meaning* into the adjective *meaningful*, or the verb *vacate* into the noun *vacation*. Such changes are not inflections but **derivations**; a word can be *derived* from a word of a different part of speech, often by the addition of one or more suffixes: *trust, trustful, trustfully, trustfulness*. And many words, even without being changed, can serve as more than one part of speech; for example:

> She is <u>cool</u> under pressure. (adjective)

> Relations between the two leaders may <u>cool</u> after the meeting. (verb)

> Keep your <u>cool</u> in a crisis. (noun)

Part III first discusses the eight parts of speech—their inflections (if any) and other grammatical properties; their subcategories; how they work with other words in sentences; and some of their important derivatives (verbals)—and calls attention to some of their potential trouble spots, such as **agreement** and a verb's **tenses**. Part III ends with a section on **diction**, which is the choice of words in the writing we all do.

6 Nouns

A **noun** is a word that names or stands for a person, place, thing, class, concept, quality, or action: *woman, character, city, country, citizen, ship, garden, machine, silence, vegetable, road, freedom, beauty, river, spring.* **Proper nouns** are names of specific persons, places, or things and begin with a capital letter: *Dorothy, Rumpelstiltskin, Pacific Ocean, Native American, Florida,* the *Titanic.* All other nouns, called **common nouns**, are capitalized only if they begin a sentence:

Freedom is a precious commodity.

or form part of a proper noun:

Spring Garden Road

or are personified or otherwise emphasized, for example in poetry:

Our noisy years seem moments in the being
Of the eternal Silence....

(Wordsworth)

One can also classify nouns as either **concrete**, for names of tangible items (*doctor, elephant, utensil, book, barn*), or **abstract**, for names of intangible things or ideas (*freedom, honor, happiness, history*).

Collective nouns are names of collections or groups often considered as units: *army, committee, family, herd, flock.*

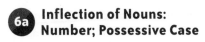

6a Inflection of Nouns: Number; Possessive Case

ELL Nouns can be inflected in two ways: for **number** and for **possessive case**.

1. For number

Most common concrete nouns that stand for countable things are either **singular** or **plural**. Most singular nouns are inflected to indicate the plural by the addition of *s* or *es*: *girl, girls*; *box, boxes*. But some are made plural in other irregular ways: *child, children*; *stimulus, stimuli*. All nouns that can be singular or plural are called **count nouns**.

However, some concrete nouns, called **non-count** nouns, name materials that are measured, weighed, or divided, rather than counted—for example, *gold, oxygen, rice, sand,* and *pasta*. As **non-count** nouns, these are not inflected for the plural. Also uncountable are **abstract** nouns and nouns that stand for ideas, activities, and states of mind or being; for example, *honor, journalism, dancing, happiness.*

Some nouns, however, can be either count or non-count, depending on the context in which they are used. For example:

Plants need <u>soil</u> to grow. (non-count)

Gardeners should know the properties of various <u>soils</u>. (count, equivalent to *kinds of soil*)

They insisted on telling the truth as a matter of <u>honor</u>. (non-count)

Many <u>honors</u> were heaped upon the returning hero. (count)

For detailed information on countable and uncountable nouns, consult a dictionary such as the *Oxford Advanced Learner's Dictionary* (OALD).

6a

2. For possessive case

Whether a noun is a *subject* (**subjective** case) or an *object* (**objective** case) is shown by word order rather than inflection. But nouns are inflected for **possessive** case. By adding an apostrophe and an *s*, or sometimes only an apostrophe, you inflect a noun so that it shows possession or ownership: *my mother's job*, *the children's toys*, *the students' grades*.

6b Grammatical Functions of Nouns

Nouns function in sentences in the following ways:

- as the subject of a verb:

  <u>Students</u> work hard.

- as the direct object of a verb:

  Our team won the <u>championship</u>.

- as the indirect object of a verb:

  We awarded <u>Yoko</u> the prize.

- as the object of a preposition:

We gave the prize to <u>Yoko</u>.

- as a predicate noun after a linking verb:

  Tamika is an <u>accountant</u>.

- as an objective complement:

  The judges declared Yoko the <u>winner</u>.

- as an appositive to any other noun:

  Andre, the <u>chef</u>, stopped Roger, the <u>dishwasher</u>.

Nouns in the *possessive case* function as adjectives:

<u>Maria's</u> coat is beautiful. (Which coat? Maria's.)

I did a <u>day's</u> work. (How much work? A day's.)

or as predicate nouns, after a linking verb:

The beautiful coat is <u>Maria's</u>.

Even without being inflected for possessive case, many nouns can also function as adjectives within noun phrases: the *school* paper, a *wedding* gown, the *automobile* industry, the *dessert* course, and so on.

A noun (or pronoun) referring to someone being directly addressed, as in dialogue or in a letter, is called a *noun of address*. Such nouns, usually proper names, are not directly related to the syntax of the rest of the sentence and are set off with punctuation:

Soon, <u>Steve</u>, you'll see what I mean.

6c Nouns and Articles: *a*, *an*, and *the*

ELL Articles modify nouns. They are also sometimes called *determiners* because an article indicates that a noun will soon follow.

The definite article (*the*) and the indefinite articles (*a* and *an*) are used idiomatically; therefore, they often challenge people whose first language doesn't include articles. An English dictionary can be invaluable in helping you decide which article, if any, to use. If you are having difficulty proofreading for articles, keep your dictionary handy.

Here are some guiding principles for the use of articles.

1. Using the indefinite article

The form *a* of the indefinite article is used before words beginning with a consonant (*a dog, a building, a computer, a yellow orchid*), including words beginning with a pronounced *h* (*a horse, a historical event, a hotel, a hypothesis*) and words beginning with a *u* or an *o* whose initial sound is that of *y* or *w* (*a useful book, a one-sided contest*). The form *an* is used before words beginning with a vowel sound (*an opinion, an underdog, an ugly duckling*) and words beginning with an unpronounced *h* (*an honor*).

Generally, a person or thing designated by the indefinite article is not specific:

> He wants to buy <u>a</u> car.

The indefinite article *a* is like *one*: it is often used before singular countable nouns.

2. Using the definite article

Generally, the definite article designates one or more particular persons or things whose identity is established by context (familiarity) or a modifier (clauses, phrases, superlative adjectives, ordinal numbers). In the following examples, the definite article is used because the **context** is understood or the reader is familiar with the noun being modified:

> Go to <u>the</u> bookstore (the one we both know about)
> and get <u>the</u> required textbook (the one that is unique to
> the course).

> <u>The</u> black horse is in <u>the</u> barn.

If the noun is followed by a **modifying clause** or **phrase**, the definite article is often used:

> My parents gave me <u>the</u> bike I wanted. (*bike* is
> particularized by the modifying clause *I wanted*)

The definite article can also be used to indicate exclusiveness;

6c

the is then equivalent to *the only* or *the best*. In fact, we often use *the* in front of **superlative adjectives**:

> He is <u>the</u> happiest person I know.

We also can indicate exclusiveness with the use of **ordinals**. Ordinals are numerical adjectives such as *first*, *second*, and *third*:

> <u>The</u> first act of the play takes place in Vienna.

> <u>The</u> third sequel appealed to adolescent tastes.

3. Using the definite article with proper nouns

Definite articles go with some **proper nouns** but not with others. Strangely, *the* often goes with place names that are plural or have modifying phrases that begin with *of*.

We say	But also
America	the United States
Mackinac Island	the San Juan Islands
Mount Hood	the Rockies
Texas State University	the University of Iowa

4. Using articles (art) with non-count nouns or plural nouns

Non-count nouns, including abstract nouns, take no article if the non-count sense governs:

> *art:* The poem features a praise of nature.

Here *a* must be removed because *praise* in this context is non-count. But notice the difference if the concrete noun *hymn* is inserted:

> *revised:* The poem features a hymn of praise to nature.

Also avoid using *a* or *an* with plural count nouns:

> *art:* She wanted a writing notebooks.

> *revised:* She wanted writing notebooks.

However, you can use *the* with plural nouns if they are particularized by a modifier.

6c

> *revised:* She wanted the writing notebooks that are
> made in Italy. (Here *notebooks* is particularized
> by *that are made in Italy*.)

5. Using articles with abstract nouns

If a usually abstract noun is used in a count but not particularized sense, the indefinite article precedes it; if in a
particularized way, the definite article:

> This is <u>an</u> honor. (count)

> He did me <u>the</u> honor of inviting me. (non-count, specific)

6. Using the definite article in front of nouns that represent groups

The definite article usually precedes an adjective functioning as a noun that represents a group:

> <u>The</u> young should heed the advice of <u>the</u> elderly.

This rule can also be applied to species of animals or inven-
tions when emphasizing the class.

> <u>The</u> smartphone is a prominent feature of our lives.

7. Using the definite article with titles of artistic works

Titles of artistic works are not usually preceded by articles,
but usage is inconsistent, and some idiomatically take the
definite article. It would be incorrect to say:

> *art:* Donne's poetic power is evident in the
> Sonnet X, "Death Be Not Proud."

Either omit *the* or change *the* to *his*. However, it would be
correct to refer to "the *Adventures of Huckleberry Finn*."

8. Using articles with names of academic fields and courses

With names of academic fields and courses, whether proper
nouns or abstract common nouns, no article is used:

> She is enrolled in Psychology 301.
> He reads books on psychology.

7 Pronouns

A pronoun is a word that *stands for* or *in place of* a noun, or functions like a noun in a sentence. Most pronouns refer to nouns that come earlier, their **antecedents**:

> Joshua offered an opinion, but <u>he</u> didn't feel confident about <u>it</u>.

7a Pronoun Types

There are eight different pronoun types:

- personal
- impersonal
- interrogative
- relative
- demonstrative
- indefinite
- reflexive (or intensive)
- reciprocal

Like nouns, pronouns can function as subjects of verbs, direct and indirect objects, and objects of prepositions; some can also function as appositives and predicate nouns. Some pronouns are inflected much more than nouns, and some require close proofreading for case, reference, and agreement.

1. Personal pronouns

Personal pronouns refer to specific persons or things. They are inflected in four ways:

For person
- **First-person** pronouns (*I*, *we*, etc.) refer to the person or persons doing the speaking or writing.
- **Second-person** pronouns (*you*, *yours*) refer to the person or persons being spoken or written to.
- **Third-person** pronouns (*he*, *she*, *it*, *they*, etc.) refer to the person(s) or thing(s) being spoken or written about.

For number
- **Singular** pronouns (*I*, *she*, etc.) refer to individuals.

  <u>I</u> am writing. <u>She</u> is writing.

- **Plural** pronouns (*we*, *they*, etc.) refer to groups.

  <u>We</u> are writing. <u>They</u> are writing.

For gender (second- and third-person pronouns)

- **Masculine** pronouns (*he*, *him*, *his*) refer to males.
- **Feminine** pronouns (*she*, *her*, *hers*) refer to females.
- The **neuter** pronoun (*it*) refers to ideas or things, and sometimes to animals. Note: It is becoming increasingly common for professional and student writers to use *they* as a gender-neutral or non-binary singular pronoun. Discuss this option with your instructor before using it in your writing.

  (In the plural forms—*we*, *you*, *they*, etc.—there is no indication of gender.)

For case

- Pronouns that function as **subjects** must be in the **subjective** case:

  <u>I</u> paint. <u>She</u> paints. <u>They</u> are painting.

- Pronouns that function as **objects**—whether direct or indirect—must be in the **objective** case:

  The idea hit <u>them</u>. Give <u>her</u> the book. Give <u>it</u> to <u>me</u>.

- Pronouns that indicate possession or ownership must be in the **possessive** case:

  That turtle is <u>his</u>. This turtle is <u>mine</u>. Where is <u>yours</u>?

  (Note that pronouns in the possessive case—*yours*, *theirs*, *its*, *hers*, etc.—do not take an apostrophe before the *s* to indicate possession.)

The following chart shows all the inflections of personal pronouns:

	Subject	Object	Possessive Pronoun	Possessive Adjective
singular				
1st person	I	me	mine	my
2nd person	you	you	yours	your
3rd person	he	him	his	his
	she	her	hers	her
	it	it		its

7a

	Subject	Object	Possessive Pronoun	Possessive Adjective
plural				
1st person	we	us	ours	our
2nd person	you	you	yours	your
3rd person	they	them	theirs	their

Possessive (or **pronominal**) **adjectives** always precede nouns (*My* car is in the shop); **possessive pronouns** may function as subjects, objects, and predicate nouns (Let's take *yours*).

2. Impersonal pronouns

In some very formal contexts, the **impersonal pronoun** *one,* meaning essentially "a person," serves in place of a first-, second-, or third-person pronoun:

7a

One must keep one's priorities straight.

The pronoun *it* is also used as an impersonal pronoun, usually as the subject of some form of *be* and usually referring to time, weather, distance, and the like:

It is getting late. It's almost four o'clock.

It's warm. It feels warmer than it did yesterday.

It is two miles from here to the station.

3. Interrogative pronouns

Interrogative pronouns are *question words* used usually at or near the beginning of *interrogative sentences. Who* is inflected for objective and possessive case, *which* for possessive case only:

Subjective	Objective	Possessive
who	whom	whose
which	which	whose
what	what	

Who refers to persons, *which* and *what* to things; *which* sometimes also refers to persons, as in *Which of you is going?*

The compound forms *whoever* and *whatever*, and sometimes even *whichever* and *whomever*, can also function as interrogative pronouns. Here are some examples showing interrogative pronouns functioning in different ways:

- as a subject:

  <u>Who</u> said that?

  <u>Which</u> of these experts are you citing?

- as the direct object of a verb:

  <u>Whom</u> do you suggest for the position?

- as the object of a preposition:

  To <u>whom</u> did you recommend the restaurant?

- as an objective complement:

  <u>What</u> did you call me?

In front of a noun, an interrogative word functions as an **interrogative adjective**:

  <u>Whose</u> book is this?

4. Relative pronouns

A **relative pronoun** usually introduces an *adjective clause*—called a **relative clause**—in which it functions as subject, object, or object of a preposition. The pronoun links, or *relates*, the clause to an antecedent in the same sentence, a noun or pronoun that the whole clause modifies.

The principal relative pronouns are *who*, *which*, and *that*. *Who* and *which* are inflected for case:

Subjective	Objective	Possessive
who	whom	whose
which	which	whose
that	that	

Who refers to persons (and sometimes to animals thought of as persons), *which* to things, and *that* to either persons or things. Consider some examples of how relative pronouns function:

Natalia, <u>who</u> is leaving in the morning, will call us later tonight. (*who* as subject of verb *is*; clause modifies *Natalia*)

Joel contacted the reporter <u>whom</u> he had met at the crime scene. (*whom* as direct object; clause modifies *reporter*)

At midnight Sula began to revise her essay, <u>which</u> was due in the morning. (*which* as subject of verb *was*; clause modifies *essay*)

She avoided working on the annual report <u>that</u> she was having trouble with. (*that* as object of preposition *with*; clause modifies *report*)

A relative clause is either **restrictive** and unpunctuated, or **nonrestrictive** and set off with punctuation. It is **restrictive** if it gives us information that is essential to identifying the antecedent (e.g., *whom he had met at the crime scene*); it is **nonrestrictive** if the information it gives us is not essential to identifying the antecedent and could be left out of the sentence (e.g., *which was due in the morning*). Any of the three relative pronouns (*who, which, that*) can be used to introduce a restrictive relative clause, but only *which* and *who* can introduce a nonrestrictive relative clause. If the relative pronoun in a restrictive clause is the object of a verb or a preposition, it can usually be omitted:

She avoided working on the annual report [<u>that</u> or <u>which</u>] she was having trouble with.

But if the preposition is placed before the pronoun (e.g., *with which*), the pronoun cannot be omitted:

She was working on the annual report with <u>which</u> she was having trouble.

And don't omit the relative pronoun when it is necessary to prevent misreading:

> *incorrect:* Different varieties of tea shops sell are medicinal.

A *that* or a *which* after *tea* prevents misreading the subject of the verb as "different varieties of tea shops."

When *whose* precedes and modifies a noun in a relative clause, it functions as what is called a **relative adjective**:

> Jana was the one <u>whose</u> advice he most valued.

And sometimes a **relative adverb**, often *when* or *where*, introduces a relative clause:

> Here's an aerial photo of the town <u>where</u> I live. (The clause *where I live* modifies the noun *town*.)

> My parents told me about the time <u>when</u> I learned to walk. (The *when*-clause modifies the noun *time*.)

Sometimes *what* and the *ever*-compounds (*whatever, whoever, whomever, whichever*) are also considered relative pronouns, even though they introduce noun clauses (e.g., "Remember *what I said.*" "Take *whichever one you want.*"). *Who, whom,* and *which* may also introduce such noun clauses.

5. Demonstrative pronouns

Demonstrative pronouns, which can be thought of as pointing to the nouns they refer to, are inflected for *number*:

Singular	Plural
this	these
that	those

This and *these* usually refer to something nearby or something just said or about to be said; *that* and *those* usually refer to something farther away or more remote in time or longer in duration:

> The clerk was helpful; <u>this</u> was what pleased her the most.

> <u>These</u> are the main points I will cover in today's class.

> <u>That</u> was the story he told us the next morning.

> <u>Those</u> were his exact words.

These pronouns also often occur in prepositional phrases with *like* and *such as*:

Anyone who wears a shirt like <u>that</u> is my fashion hero.

I need more close friends like <u>those</u>.

A cute house such as <u>this</u> will sell immediately.

Note: Useful as demonstrative pronouns can be, employ them sparingly in writing, for they are often vague in their reference. If you think a demonstrative pronoun is too vague, follow it with a noun to turn it into a *demonstrative adjective*: *this* belief, *that* statement, *these* buildings, *those* arguments.

6. Indefinite pronouns

ELL **Indefinite pronouns** refer to indefinite or unknown persons or things, or to indefinite or unknown quantities of persons or things. The major issue with these words is whether they are *singular* or *plural*. Think of indefinite pronouns as falling into four groups:

7a

- Group 1: compounds ending with *body*, *one*, and *thing*. These words function like nouns—that is, they need no antecedents—and they are almost always considered *singular*:

anybody	everybody	nobody	somebody
anyone	everyone	no one	someone
anything	everything	nothing	something

- Group 2: a few other indefinite pronouns that are almost always *singular*:

| another | each | either | much |
| neither | one | other | |

- Group 3: a few that are always *plural*:

| both | few | many | several |

- Group 4: a few that can be either *singular* or *plural*, depending on context and intended meaning:

| all | any | more | most |
| none | some | | |

Only *one* and *other* can be inflected for number, by adding *s* to make them plural: *ones, others*. Several indefinite pronouns can be inflected for possessive case; unlike personal pronouns, they take *'s*, just as nouns do (or, with *others'*, just an apostrophe):

anybody's	anyone's	everybody's	everyone's
nobody's	no one's	somebody's	someone's
one's	other's	another's	others'

The remaining indefinite pronouns must use *of* to show possession; for example:

That was the belief <u>of many</u> who were present.

When in the possessive case, indefinite pronouns function as adjectives. In addition, all the words in groups 2, 3, and 4, except *none*, can also function as adjectives:

<u>any</u> boat	<u>some</u> people	<u>few</u> people
<u>more</u> money	<u>each</u> day	<u>either</u> direction

The adjective expressing the meaning of *none* is *no*:

Send <u>no</u> attachments.

Sometimes the cardinal numbers (*one, two, three*, etc.) and the ordinal numbers (*first, second, third*, etc.) are also classed as indefinite pronouns:

How many ducks are on the pond? I see <u>several</u>. I see <u>seven</u>.

Do you like these stories? I like <u>some</u>, but not <u>others</u>.
I like the <u>first</u> and the <u>third</u>.

7. Reflexive and intensive pronouns

Reflexive and intensive pronouns are formed by adding *self* or *selves* to the possessive form of the first- and second-person personal pronouns, to the objective form of third-person personal pronouns, and to the impersonal pronoun *one*.

Singular	Plural
myself	ourselves
yourself	yourselves
himself	themselves
herself	themselves
itself	
oneself	

A **reflexive pronoun** is used as an object when that object is the same person or thing as the subject:

He treated <u>himself</u> to bubble tea. (direct object)

She gave <u>herself</u> a treat. (indirect object)

We kept the idea to <u>ourselves</u>. (object of preposition)

These pronouns are also used as **intensive pronouns** to emphasize a subject or object. An intensive pronoun comes either right after the noun it emphasizes or at the end of the sentence:

Although he let the others choose their positions, Angelo <u>himself</u> is going to pitch.

The professor told us to count up our scores <u>ourselves</u>.

They are also used in prepositional phrases with *by* to mean "alone" or "without help":

I can do this job by <u>myself</u>.

Note: Do not use this form of pronoun as a substitute for a personal pronoun:

The team and I [not *myself*] played a great game tonight.

8. Reciprocal pronouns

ELL Like a reflexive pronoun, a **reciprocal pronoun** refers to the subject of a sentence, but this time the subject is always plural. The two reciprocal pronouns themselves are singular and consist of two words each:

each other (referring to a subject involving two)

one another (referring to a subject involving three or more)

They can be inflected for possessive case by adding *'s*:

each other's   one another's

These pronouns express mutual interaction between or among the parts of a plural subject:

The president and the prime minister praised each other's policies.

The computers in this office speak to one another, even though the employees never do.

7b Case

7a

Determining the correct case of personal, interrogative, and relative pronouns is sometimes challenging. If you know how a pronoun is functioning grammatically, you will know which form to use. Here are some guidelines to help you with the kinds of sentences that sometimes cause problems:

1. A pronoun functioning as the *subject* should be in the *subjective* case. Whenever you use a pronoun as part of a *compound subject*, make sure it is in the *subjective* case. Someone who wouldn't say "*Me* am going to the store" could slip and say something like "Sunil and *me* studied hard for the test" instead of the correct

   Sunil and I studied hard for the test.

If you're not sure, remove the other part of the subject; then you'll know which pronoun sounds right:

   [Sunil and] I studied hard for the test.

2. A pronoun functioning as a direct or indirect *object* should be in the *objective* case. When you use a pronoun as part of a compound object, make sure it's in the *objective* case. Again, test by removing the other part:

They asked [Ingrid and] me to take part in the play.

3. A pronoun functioning as the *object* of a preposition should be in the *objective* case:

    > *ca:* This information is between you and I.

    > *revised:* This information is between you and me.

The objective *me* is correct in this instance, for it is the object of the preposition *between*.

4. A pronoun functioning as a *predicate noun* after a linking verb should be in the *subjective* case. In other words, if the pronoun follows the verb *be*, it takes the subjective form:

    > It is they who must decide, not we.

If such usages sound stuffy and artificial to you—as they do to many people—find another way to phrase your sentences; for example:

    > They, not we, must decide.

Again, watch out for compound structures:

    > *ca:* The nominees are Yashmin and me.

    > *revised:* The nominees are Yashmin and I.

5. Pronouns following the conjunctions *as* and *than* in comparisons should be in the *subjective* case if they are functioning as subjects, even if their verbs are not expressed but left "understood":

    > Renee is as bright as they [are].

    > Aaron has learned less than I [have].

If, however, the pronouns are functioning as objects, they should be in the *objective case*:

    > I trust her more than [I trust] him.

6. Use the appropriate case of the interrogative and relative pronouns *who* and *whom*, *whoever* and *whomever*. Although *who* is often used instead of *whom* in speech

and informal writing, you should know how to use the two correctly when you want to write or speak more formally.

a. Use the *subjective* case for the *subject* of a verb in a question or a relative clause:

> <u>Who</u> is going?

> Dickens was a novelist <u>who</u> was extremely popular in his own time.

b. Use the *objective* case for the object of a verb or preposition:

> <u>Whom</u> do you prefer in that role?

> He is the mayoral candidate <u>whom</u> I most admire.

> She is the manager for <u>whom</u> the employees have the most respect.

7b

If such usages with *whom* seem to you unnatural and stuffy, avoid them by rephrasing:

> She is the manager that the employees respect most.

c. In noun clauses, the case of the pronoun is determined by its function in its clause, not by other words:

> How can you tell <u>who won</u>? (subjective case)

> I'll give the prize to <u>whomever the judges declare the winner</u>. (objective case, object of preposition)

7c Agreement of Pronouns with Their Antecedents

Any pronoun that refers to or stands for an *antecedent* must **agree** with—that is, be consistent with—that antecedent in **person** (first, second, or third), **number** (singular or plural), and **gender** (masculine, feminine, or neuter). For example:

Olivia wants to go to college so that she will be prepared to take her place in the world. (Pronouns are third person, feminine, and singular to agree with *Olivia*.)

The following sections point out the most common sources of trouble with pronoun agreement. Note that these errors all have to do with *number*—whether a pronoun should be *singular* or *plural*. Mistakes in gender and person also occur, but not as frequently.

1. Antecedents joined by *and*

When two or more singular antecedents are joined by *and*, use a *plural* pronoun:

Both Jennifer and Chinmoy contributed their expertise.

If such a compound is preceded by *each* or *every*, however, the pronoun should be *singular*:

Each article and editorial has its own title.

7c

2. Antecedents joined by *or* or *nor*

When two or more antecedents are joined by *or* or *nor*, use a *singular* pronoun if the antecedents are singular:

Either David or Jonathan will bring his car.

Neither Maylin nor her mother gave her consent to borrow the car.

If one antecedent is masculine and the other feminine, rephrase the sentence.

Use a *plural* pronoun if the antecedents are plural:

Neither the players nor the coaches did their jobs properly.

If the antecedents are mixed singular and plural, a pronoun should agree with the nearest one. But if you move from a plural to a singular antecedent, the sentence will almost inevitably sound awkward; try to construct such sentences so that the last antecedent is plural:

awk: Neither the actors nor the director could control his temper.

revised: Neither the director nor <u>the actors</u> could control <u>their</u> tempers.

For more information on agreement of verbs with compound subjects joined by *or* or *nor*, see #9b.2.

3. Indefinite pronoun as antecedent

If the antecedent is an *indefinite pronoun*, you'll usually use a *singular* pronoun to refer to it. The indefinite pronouns in Group 1 (the compounds with *body*, *one*, and *thing*) are singular, as are those in Group 2 (*another, each, either, much, neither, one, other*):

<u>Each</u> of the boys worked on <u>his</u> own project.

<u>Either</u> of these women is likely to buy that motorcycle for <u>herself</u>.

<u>Everything</u> has <u>its</u> proper place.

Indefinite pronouns from Group 3 (*both, few, many, several*) are always plural:

Only a <u>few</u> returned <u>their</u> ballots.

The indefinite pronouns in Group 4 (*all, any, more, most, none, some*) can be either singular or plural; the intended meaning is usually clearly either singular or plural:

<u>Some</u> of the food on the menu could be criticized for <u>its</u> lack of nutrients.

<u>Some</u> of the ships in the fleet had been restored to <u>their</u> original beauty.

Confusion sometimes arises with the indefinite pronoun *none*. Although *none* began by meaning *no one* or *not one*, it now commonly has the plural sense:

<u>None</u> of the boys knew how to fix <u>their</u> bicycles.

With a mass noun, or if your intended meaning is "not a single one," treat *none* as singular:

<u>None</u> of the food could be praised for <u>its</u> quality.

<u>None</u> of the boys knew how to fix <u>his</u> bicycle. (In this
sentence you could perhaps even change *None*
to *Not one*.)

When any of these words function as *adjectives*, the same
principles apply:

<u>Each</u> boy worked on <u>his</u> own project.

<u>Either</u> woman is likely to buy that motorcycle for <u>herself</u>.

Only a <u>few</u> people returned <u>their</u> ballots.

<u>Some</u> food can be praised for <u>its</u> nutritional value.

<u>Some</u> ships had been restored to <u>their</u> original beauty.

Note: The word *every* used as an adjective requires a
singular pronoun:

<u>Every</u> boy has <u>his</u> own project.

7c

4. Collective noun as antecedent

If the antecedent is a *collective noun*, use either a singular
or a plural pronoun to refer to it, depending on context
and desired meaning. If the collective noun stands for the
group seen as a unit, use a *singular* pronoun:

The <u>team</u> worked on <u>its</u> power play during the practice.

If the collective noun stands for the members of the group
seen as individuals, use a *plural* pronoun:

The <u>team</u> took up <u>their</u> starting positions.

5. Agreement (agr) with demonstrative adjectives

Demonstrative adjectives agree in number with the nouns
they modify (nouns such as *kind* or *kinds* often cause the
most difficulty):

agr: <u>These kind</u> of doctors work especially hard.

revised: <u>This kind</u> of doctor works especially hard.

revised: <u>These kinds</u> of doctors work especially hard.

7d Pronoun Reference

A pronoun's **reference** to an antecedent must be clear. The pronoun or the sentence will be unclear if the antecedent is remote, ambiguous, vague, or missing.

1. Remote antecedent

An antecedent should be close enough to its pronoun to be unmistakable; your reader shouldn't have to pause and search for it. An antecedent should seldom appear more than one sentence before its pronoun within a paragraph.

> *ref:* People who expect to find happiness in material things may discover that the life of the mind is more important than the life filled with possessions. Material prosperity may seem fine at a given moment, but in the long run its delights fade into inconsequential boredom and emptiness. <u>They</u> then realize, too late, where true happiness lies.

The word *People* is too far back to be a clear antecedent for the pronoun *They*. If the second sentence had also begun with *They*, the connection would be clearer. Or the third sentence might begin with a more particularizing phrase, like "Such people . . ."

2. Ambiguous reference

A pronoun should refer clearly to only one antecedent:

> *ref:* When Lea's mother told her that <u>she</u> had won an award, <u>she</u> was obviously delighted.

Each *she* could refer either to Lea (*her*) or to Lea's mother. When revising, rephrase the sentence:

> *weak:* When Lea's mother told her that she (her mother) had won an award, she (Lea) was obviously delighted.

> *clear:* Lea was obviously delighted when her mother told her about winning an award.

> *clear:* Lea's mother had won an award, and she was
> obviously delighted when she told Lea about it.

> *clear:* Lea was obviously delighted when her mother
> said, "I won an award!"

Another example:

> *ref:* His second film was far different from his first. It
> was a war story set in Belgium.

Combine the two sentences, reducing the second to a subordinate element:

> *clear:* His second film, a war story set in Belgium, was
> far different from his first.

> *clear:* His second film was far different from his first,
> which was a war story set in Belgium.

3. Vague reference

Vague reference is usually caused by the demonstrative pronouns *this* and *that* and the relative pronoun *which*:

> *ref:* The doctors are overworked, and there are no
> beds available. This is an intolerable situation for
> the hospital.

> *clear:* The overworked doctors and the lack of available
> beds make for an intolerable situation for the
> hospital.

> *ref:* The doctors are overworked, and there are no
> beds available, which is an intolerable situation
> for the hospital.

> *clear:* The doctors are overworked, and there are no
> beds available. These two circumstances make
> for an intolerable situation for the hospital.

Don't catch the "this" virus; sufferers from it are driven to begin a large proportion of their sentences and other independent clauses with a *this*. Whenever you catch yourself beginning with a *this*, look carefully to see

- if the reference to the preceding clause, sentence, or paragraph is as clear on paper as it may be in your mind;
- if the *this* could be replaced by a specific noun or noun phrase, or otherwise avoided (for example, by rephrasing or subordinating);
- whether, if you decide to keep *this*, it is an ambiguous demonstrative pronoun; if so, try to make it a *demonstrative adjective*, giving it a noun to modify—even if the result is no more specific than "This idea," "This fact," or "This argument."

4. Missing antecedent

Sometimes a writer may have an antecedent in mind but fail to write it down:

> *ref:* In the early seventeenth century, the Renaissance attitude was concentrated mainly on the arts rather than on developing the scientific part of <u>their</u> minds.

The writer was probably thinking of "the people of the Renaissance." Simply changing *their* to *people's* would clear up the difficulty.

> *ref:* Whenever a student assembly is called, <u>they</u> are required to attend.

> *revised:* Whenever an assembly is called, students are required to attend.

5. Indefinite *you*, *they*, and *it*

In formal writing, avoid the pronouns *you*, *they*, and *it* when they are indefinite:

> *informal:* In order to graduate, <u>you</u> must have at least 120 course credits.

> *formal:* In order to graduate, a student must have at least 120 course credits.

> *informal:* In some cities <u>they</u> do not have enough recycling facilities.

> *formal:* Some cities do not have enough recycling facilities.

Although it is correct to use the expletive or impersonal *it* and say "*It* is raining," "*It* is seven o'clock," and so on, avoid such indefinite uses of *it* as the following:

> *informal:* It states in our textbook that we should be careful how we use the pronoun *it*.

> *formal:* Our textbook states that we should be careful how we use the pronoun *it*.

7e Pronouns and Inclusive Language

Several indefinite pronouns, as well as indefinite nouns like *person* and many other nouns used in a generalizing way, present an additional challenge: avoiding gender bias.

In centuries past, if a *singular antecedent* had no grammatical gender but could refer to one or more males or females, it was conventional to use the masculine pronoun *he* (*him, his, himself*) in a generic sense, meaning any person, male or female:

> *biased:* Everyone in the room raised his hand.

> *biased:* A writer should be careful about his diction.

Today this practice is regarded as inappropriate and inaccurate.

All of us should avoid using biased language. Colloquially and informally, many writers simply do so by using a plural pronoun:

> *agr:* Anyone who doesn't pay their taxes is asking for trouble.

Here are six solutions you can use when writing in a formal context:

1. If you are referring to a group or class consisting entirely of either men or women, use the appropriate pronoun, whether masculine or feminine:

   Everyone in the room raised his hand.

   Everyone in the room raised her hand.

If the group is mixed, try to avoid the problem, for example by using the indefinite article:

Everyone in the room raised a hand.

2. Make the antecedent itself plural: then the plural pronoun referring to it is grammatically appropriate, and no problem of gender arises:

All those in the room raised their hands.

Writers should be careful about their diction.

3. If your purpose and the formality of the context permit, you can use the impersonal pronoun *one* or the second-person pronoun *you*:

If one is considerate of others' feelings, one will get along better.

If you are considerate of others' feelings, you will get along better.

4. Revise so that no gendered pronoun is necessary:

Everyone's hand went up.

5. If a sentence doesn't lend itself to such changes, or if you want to keep its original structure for some other reason, you can still manage. Don't resort to strings of unsightly devices such as *he/she, him/her, her/his, him/herself*, or *s/he*. But an occasional *he or she* or *she or he* and the like is usually acceptable:

If anyone protests, he or she will be asked to leave.

A writer should be careful about her or his diction.

But don't do this too often, as such repetitions can become tedious and cluttering.

6. It is becoming increasingly common for writers to use *they* as a gender-neutral or non-binary singular pronoun.

Each student talked for five minutes about <u>their</u> influences.

If anyone needs more time, <u>they</u> should let the instructor know.

Check with your instructor before using this approach.

8 Verbs

Verbs are core parts of speech. A verb is the focal point of a clause or a sentence. Standard sentences consist of subjects and predicates: every subject has a predicate, and the heart of every predicate is its **verb**.

Verbs express not only *action* but also *occurrence*, *process*, and *condition* or *state of being*. All verbs *assert* or *ask* something about their subjects, sometimes by *linking* a subject with a complement. Some verbs are single words; others are phrases consisting of two or more words. Here are some sentences with the verbs underlined:

He <u>throws</u> curve balls.

Karen <u>is</u> a scientist.

By midnight, I <u>will have driven</u> two hundred miles.

<u>Are</u> you <u>listening</u>?

The two columns of figures <u>came out</u> even.

8a Transitive, Intransitive, and Linking Verbs

Verbs are classified according to the way they function in sentences.

A verb taking a *direct object* is considered **transitive**. A transitive verb makes a transition, conveys a movement, from its subject to its object:

He <u>introduced</u> me to his uncle.

She <u>expresses</u> her ideas eloquently.

A direct object answers the question consisting of the verb and *what* or *whom*: Introduced *whom*? Me. Expresses *what*? Ideas.

A verb without a direct object is considered **intransitive**:

> What <u>has happened</u> to the aquarium's whale?

> The earthquake <u>occurred</u> during the night.

Many verbs can be either transitive or intransitive, depending on how they function in particular sentences:

> I <u>ran</u> the business effectively. (transitive)

> I <u>ran</u> to the store. (intransitive)

A third kind of verb is called **linking** or **copulative**. The main one is *be* in its various forms. Some other common linking verbs are *become, seem, remain, act, get, feel, look, appear, smell, sound,* and *taste*. Linking verbs don't have objects but are yet incomplete; they need a **subjective complement**. A linking verb is like an equal sign in an equation: something at the right-hand (predicate) end is needed to balance what is at the left-hand (subject) end. The complement will be either a *predicate noun* or a *predicate adjective*.

> Angela <u>is</u> a lawyer. (predicate noun: *lawyer*)

> Angela <u>is</u> not well. (predicate adjective: *well*)

> Mikhail <u>became</u> a pilot. (predicate noun: *pilot*)

> Mikhail <u>became</u> uneasy. (predicate adjective: *uneasy*)

Verbs such as *act, sound, taste, smell,* and *feel* can also function as transitive verbs: She *acted* the part. He *sounded* his horn. He *smelled* the hydrogen sulfide. I *tasted* the soup. He *felt* the bump on his head.

Similarly, many of these verbs can also function as regular intransitive verbs, sometimes accompanied by *adverbial* modifiers (see #11): We *looked* at the painting. Arnab *is* on the stage. Teresa *is* at home. We *are* here. But whenever one of these verbs is accompanied by a predicate noun or a predicate adjective, it is functioning as a linking verb.

8b Inflection of Verbs: Principal Parts

ELL Verbs are the most complex, the most highly inflected, of the eight parts of speech. Verbs are inflected in the following situations:

- For **person** and **number**, in order to agree with a subject;
- For **tense**, in order to show an action's time—present, past, or future—and aspect—simple, perfect, or progressive;
- For **mood**, in order to show the kind of sentence—indicative, imperative, or subjunctive; and
- For **voice**, in order to show whether a subject is active (performing an action) or passive (being acted upon).

Every verb (except some auxiliaries; see #8d) has what are called its **principal parts**:

1. Its **basic** form (the form listed in a dictionary),
2. Its **past-tense** form,
3. Its **past participle**, and
4. Its **present participle**.

Verbs regularly form both the *past tense* and the *past participle* simply by adding *ed* to the basic form. If the basic form already ends in *e*, only *d* is added:

Basic Form	Past-tense Form	Past Participle
push	pushed	pushed
move	moved	moved

Present participles are regularly formed by adding *ing* to the basic form. Verbs ending in an unpronounced *e* usually drop that *e* before adding *ing*:

Basic Form	Present Participle
push	pushing
move	moving

In addition, some verbs double a final consonant before adding *ed* or *ing*:

grin	grinned	grinning

Good dictionaries list any irregular principal parts, ones not formed by simply adding *ed* or *ing*.

Note: The basic form of a verb is sometimes called the **infinitive**, meaning that it can be preceded by *to* to form an infinitive: *to be*, *to push*, *to agree*. Infinitives, participles, and gerunds are called **verbals** or **non-finite verbs** (see #12); they function not as verbs but as other parts of speech. **Finite verbs**, unlike verbal forms, are restricted or limited by person, number, tense, mood, and voice; finite verbs function as the main verbs in sentences.

8c Irregular Verbs

ELL Some of the most common English verbs are **irregular** in the way they make their past-tense forms and their past participles. Whenever you aren't certain about the principal parts of a verb, check your dictionary. If you're looking for a verb that is a compound or that has a suffix, look for the main verb: for *misread*, *proofread*, or *reread*, look under *read* instead.

8d Auxiliary Verbs

ELL Auxiliary or helping verbs go with other verbs to form verb phrases indicating tense, voice, and mood. The auxiliary *do* helps in forming questions, forming negative sentences, and expressing emphasis:

> <u>Did</u> you arrive on time?
>
> I <u>did not</u> arrive on time.
>
> I <u>did</u> wash my face!

Modal auxiliaries

There are also what are called **modal auxiliaries**. The principal ones are *can*, *could*, *may*, *might*, *must*, *should*, and *would.* They combine with main verbs and other auxiliaries to express such meanings as ability, possibility, obligation, and necessity.

The following chart illustrates the principal modal verbs currently in use in Standard English:

The Modal	Used to Express . . .
can	ability
could	ability, possibility
may	permission
might	possibility
ought to	obligation
should	
must	
shall	probability, prediction
will	
should	condition
would	

8d

Consider the following examples:

I <u>can</u> understand that.

There <u>could</u> be thunderstorms tomorrow.

I would tell you the answer if I <u>could</u>.

The instructor <u>may</u> decide to cancel the quiz.

The equivalent phrases *able to* (*can*), *ought to* (*should*), and *have to* (*must*) also function as modal auxiliaries.

Note that *could, might, would,* and *should* also serve as the past-tense forms of *can, may, will,* and *shall,* respectively. These past-tense forms appear most often when demanded by the sequence of tenses after a verb in the past tense:

He <u>was</u> sure that I <u>could</u> handle the project.

She <u>said</u> that I <u>might</u> watch the rehearsal if I <u>was</u> quiet.

Also note that *might* and *may* are sometimes interchangeable when expressing possibility:

> She <u>may</u> (<u>might</u>) challenge the committee's decision.

> He <u>may</u> (<u>might</u>) have finished the job by now.

But usually there is a difference, with *may* indicating a stronger possibility, *might* a somewhat less likely one. To express a condition contrary to fact, *might* is the right word:

> If you had edited your essay, you <u>might</u> [not *may*] have received a higher grade.

That is, you *didn't* edit carefully, and you *didn't* get a higher grade. *Might* is necessary for clear expression of a hypothetical as opposed to a factual circumstance.

8e Verb Tenses and Their Functions

8d

 A verb's **tense** indicates when an action, event, or condition occurs:

> *past tense:* Yesterday, I <u>practiced</u>.

> *present tense:* Today, I <u>practice</u>.

> *future tense:* Tomorrow, I <u>will practice</u>.

This section offers brief descriptions and illustrations of the main functions of each tense. Although these points are sometimes oversimplifications of very complex matters, and although there are exceptions and variations other than those listed, these guidelines should help you to use the tenses and to take advantage of the possibilities they offer for clear expression.

Tense		Verb Form
1. Simple Present	I/you	dance
	he/she/it	dances
	we/you/they	dance
2. Simple Past	I/you/he/she/ it/we/you/they	danced

3. Simple Future	I/you/he/she/ it/we/you/they	will dance
4. Present Perfect	he/she/it	has danced
	I/you/we/ you/they	have danced
5. Past Perfect	I/you/he/she/ it/we/you/they	had danced
6. Future Perfect	I/you/he/she/ it/we/you/they	will have danced
7. Present Progressive	I	am dancing
	you	are dancing
	he/she/it	is dancing
	we/you/they	are dancing
8. Past Progressive	I	was dancing
	you	were dancing
	he/she/it	was dancing
	we/you/they	were dancing
9. Future Progressive	I/you/he/she/ it/we/you/they	will be dancing
10. Present Perfect Progressive	I/you	have been dancing
	he/she/it	has been dancing
	we/you/they	have been dancing
11. Past Perfect Progressive	I/you/he/she/ it/we/you/they	had been dancing
12. Future Perfect Progressive	I/you/he/she/ it/we/you/they	will have been dancing

8e

1. Simple present

Generally, use this tense to describe an action or condition that is happening now, at the time of the utterance:

The pitcher <u>throws</u>. The batter <u>swings</u>. It <u>is</u> a high fly ball . . .

It can also indicate a general truth or belief:

> Bismarck, North Dakota, <u>is</u> one of the coldest capitals in the United States.

or describe a customary or habitual or repeated action or condition:

> I <u>paint</u> pictures for a living.

or describe the characters or events in a literary or other work, or what an author does in such a work:

> While he <u>is</u> away from Denmark, Hamlet <u>arranges</u> to have Rosencrantz and Guildenstern put to death. After he <u>returns</u> he <u>holds</u> Yorick's skull and <u>watches</u> Ophelia being buried. He <u>duels</u> with Laertes and <u>dies</u>. Without a doubt, death <u>is</u> one of the principal themes in the play.

> In *Pride and Prejudice*, Jane Austen <u>shows</u> the consequences of making hasty judgments of others.

8e

2. Simple past

Use this tense for a single or repeated action or condition that began and ended in the past:

> She <u>earned</u> a lot of money last summer.

> I <u>was</u> happy when I received my paycheck.

3. Simple future

The most common and straightforward way to indicate future time is to use the simple future, putting *will* or *shall* before the basic form of the verb:

> She <u>will arrive</u> tomorrow morning.

4. Present perfect

Use this tense for an action or condition that began in the past and that continues to the present; though commonly considered "completed" as of the moment, some actions or conditions referred to in this tense could continue after the present:

I <u>have earned</u> a lot of money this summer.

James Bond <u>has</u> just <u>entered</u> the casino.

You can use this tense for something that occurred entirely in the past, if you intend to imply the sense of "before now" or "so far" or "already":

I <u>have painted</u> a picture; take a look at it.

I <u>have visited</u> Greece three times.

5. Past perfect

Use this tense for an action completed in the past before a specific past time or event. Notice that there are at least two actions taking place in the past:

Though I <u>had seen</u> the film twice before, I watched it again last week.

8e

6. Future perfect

Use this tense for an action or condition that will be completed before a specific future time or event:

I <u>will</u> already <u>have eaten</u> when you arrive.

7. Present progressive

Use this tense for an action or condition that began at some past time and is continuing now, in the present:

Global warming <u>is causing</u> a significant rise in sea levels around the world.

Sometimes the simple and the progressive forms of a verb say much the same thing:

We <u>hope</u> for snow. We <u>are hoping</u> for snow.

But usually the progressive form emphasizes an activity, or the singleness or continuing nature of an action, rather than a larger condition or general truth:

A tax hike <u>hurts</u> many people.
The tax hike <u>is hurting</u> many people.

Stative verbs, verbs that express sense, cognitive, or emotional states, don't often appear in the progressive form. Unless the stative verb is expressing an action, do not use it in the progressive tense.

incorrect: After being sprayed by the skunk, the dog is smelling bad now. (condition)

correct: After having its nose injured, the dog is smelling poorly. (activity)

Here is a short list of some common stative verbs:

appear	appreciate	be	believe	dislike
feel	hear	imagine	know	like
look	love	remember	resemble	seem
smell	understand	want	wish	

8e

8. Past progressive

Use this tense for an action in progress during some past time, especially if you want to emphasize the continuing nature of the action:

I remember that I <u>was painting</u> a picture that day.

Sometimes the past progressive tense describes an interrupted action or an action during which something else happens:

When the telephone rang, I <u>was making</u> shrimp tempura.

9. Future progressive

Use this tense for a continuing action in the future or for an action that will be occurring at some specific time in the future:

I <u>will be painting</u> pictures as long as I can hold a brush.

10. Present perfect progressive

Use this tense to emphasize the continuing nature of a single or repeated action that began in the past and that has continued at least up to the present. This tense is suitable for showing trends in the sense of showing changes over time.

I <u>have been working</u> on this sketch for an hour.

The profits <u>have been increasing</u> in the last quarter.

11. Past perfect progressive

Use this tense to emphasize the continuing nature of a single or repeated past action that was completed before or interrupted by some other past action:

We <u>had been expecting</u> something quite different.

I <u>had been pondering</u> the problem for an hour when suddenly the solution popped into my head.

12. Future perfect progressive

This tense is seldom used in academic writing. Use it to emphasize the continuing nature of a future action before a specific time in the future or before a second future action:

If she continues to dance, by the year 2023 she <u>will have been dancing</u> for over half her life.

8f   Tense Sequence

ELL   When two or more verbs occur in the same sentence, they will sometimes be of the same tense, but often they will be of different tenses.

1. Compound sentences

In a compound sentence, the verbs can be equally independent; use whatever tenses the sense requires:

I <u>am leaving</u> [present progressive] now, but she <u>will leave</u> [future] in the morning.

The polls <u>have closed</u> [present perfect]; the clerks <u>will</u> soon <u>be counting</u> [future progressive] the ballots.

2. Past tense in independent clauses

In complex or compound-complex sentences, if the verb in an independent clause is in any of the past tenses, the verbs in any clauses subordinate to it will usually also be in one of the past tenses. For example:

I <u>told</u> her that I <u>was</u> sorry.

They <u>agreed</u> that this time the newly elected treasurer <u>would</u> not <u>be</u> a gambler.

Refer to a time *earlier* than that of the verb in the simple past tense by using the *past perfect* tense:

We <u>had left</u> the party before they <u>arrived</u>.

But there are exceptions. When the verb in the subordinate clause states a general or timeless truth or belief, or something characteristic or habitual, it stays in the present tense:

Einstein <u>showed</u> that space, time, and light <u>are</u> linked.

And the context of the sentence sometimes dictates that other kinds of verbs in subordinate clauses should not be changed to a past tense. If you feel that a tense other than the past would be clearer or more accurate, use it; for example:

I <u>learned</u> yesterday that I <u>will be able</u> to get into the new program in the fall.

The rule calls for *would*, but *will* is logical and clear. Notice that the adverbial marker "in the fall" tells us the action will occur in the future.

Here is another example of a sentence in which the "sequence of tenses" rule is best ignored:

The office assistant <u>told</u> me this morning that Professor Barnes <u>is</u> ill and <u>will</u> not <u>be teaching</u> class this afternoon.

8g Mood

English verbs are usually considered to have three moods. The most common mood is the **indicative**, which is used for statements of fact or opinion and for questions:

The weather forecast for tomorrow <u>sounds</u> promising.

The **imperative** mood is used for most commands and instructions:

<u>Put</u> the picnic basket in the trunk.

The **subjunctive** mood in English is less common, and it presents some challenges. It is fading from contemporary English; there are only two kinds of instances where the subjunctive still functions.

1. In a *that*-clause after verbs expressing demands, obligations, requirements, recommendations, suggestions, wishes, and the like:

   > The doctor recommended that she <u>take</u> a week off.
   >
   > I wish [that] I <u>were</u> in Canada.

2. Use the subjunctive to express conditions that are hypothetical or impossible—often in *if*-clauses or their equivalents:

   > He looked as if he <u>were</u> going to explode. (But he didn't explode.)
   >
   > If Lise <u>were</u> here, she <u>would</u> back me up. (But she isn't here.)

   An *as if*-or *as though*-clause almost always expresses a condition contrary to fact, but not all *if*-clauses do; don't be misled into using a subjunctive where it's not appropriate:

   > ***wrong:*** He said that if there <u>were</u> another complaint, he would resign.

   The verb should be *was*, for the condition could turn out to be true: there may be another complaint.

Since only a few subjunctive forms differ from those of the indicative, they are easy to learn and remember. The third-person-singular subjunctive form loses its *s*:

> ***indicative:*** I like the way she <u>paints</u>.
> ***subjunctive:*** I suggested that she <u>paint</u> my portrait.

The subjunctive forms of the verb *be* are *be* and *were*:

> ***indicative:*** He <u>is</u> friendly. (I <u>am</u>, you/we/they <u>are</u>)
> ***subjunctive:*** The judge asked that she <u>be</u> excused. (that I/you/we/they <u>be</u>)

> ***indicative:*** I know that I <u>am</u> in Columbus.
>
> ***subjunctive:*** I wish that I <u>were</u> in Florence.

Note that both *be* and *were* function with either singular or plural subjects. Note also that the past-tense form *were* functions in present-tense expressions of wishes and contrary-to-fact conditions. Other verbs also use their past tense as a subjunctive after a present-tense wish:

> I wish that I <u>shopped</u> less.

After a past-tense wish, use the standard past-perfect form:

> He wished that he <u>had been</u> more attentive.
>
> She wished that she <u>had played</u> better.

8h Voice

There are two voices, *active* and *passive*. The active voice is direct: *I made this toy boat.* The passive voice is less direct, reversing the normal subject–verb–object pattern: *This toy boat was made by me.* The passive-voice verb uses some form of *be* followed by a past participle (*was made*). What in active voice would be a direct object (*boat*) in passive voice becomes the subject of the verb. And passive constructions often leave unmentioned the agent of the action or state they describe: *The toy boat was made* (by whom isn't specified).

Using the passive voice, some people can promise action without committing themselves to perform it, and they can admit error without accepting responsibility:

> ***passive:*** Be assured [by whom?] that action will be taken [by whom?].
>
> ***active:*** I assure you that I will act.
>
> ***passive:*** It is to be regretted [by whom?] that an error has been made [by whom?].
>
> ***active:*** I am sorry that we made an error.

When possible, use the direct and more vigorous active voice.

Passive constructions can also lead to a *dangling modifier* (see #5e):

> ***passive:*** Mixing the chemicals, hydrogen sulfide <u>was formed</u>.

In this sentence, there is no subject to explain who is doing the mixing. The frequency of such errors is itself a good reason to be sparing with the passive voice. The active voice eliminates the grammatical error:

> ***active:*** By mixing the chemicals, the chemist produced hydrogen sulfide.

When to use the passive voice

Use the passive voice when the active voice is impossible or when the passive is for some other reason clearly preferable or demanded by the context. Generally, use the passive voice when

- the agent, or doer of the act, is indefinite or not known;
- the agent is less important than the act itself; or
- you want to emphasize either the agent or the act by putting it at the beginning or end of the sentence.

Note: Don't confuse passive constructions with the past tense just because the past participle is used. Passive constructions can appear in any of the tenses.

9 Subject-Verb Agreement

A verb should agree with its subject in number and person. Here are the main circumstances to pay attention to in your own writing.

9a Words That Come Between Subject and Verb

When something plural comes between a singular subject and its verb, the verb must still agree with the subject:

Far below, a <u>landscape</u> of rolling brown hills and small trees <u>lies</u> among the small cottages.

<u>Each</u> of the plans <u>has</u> certain advantages.

<u>Neither</u> of the parties <u>was</u> willing to compromise.

Similarly, don't let an intervening singular noun affect the agreement between a plural subject and its verb.

9b Compound Subjects

1. A compound subject made up of two or more singular nouns joined by *and* is usually plural:

   Careful thought and attention to detail <u>are</u> essential.

   There are occasional exceptions. If two nouns identify the same person or thing, or if two nouns taken together are thought of as a unit, the verb is singular:

   Macaroni and cheese <u>is</u> a student favorite.

   Note: Phrases such as *in addition to*, *as well as*, *along with*, and *together with* are prepositions, not conjunctions like *and*. A singular subject followed by one of them still takes a singular verb:

   The cat as well as the dog <u>comes</u> when I whistle.

   Ms. Hondiak, along with her daughters, <u>is</u> attending college this year.

   Compound subjects preceded by *each* or *every* take a singular verb:

   Each dog and cat <u>has</u> its own dish.

2. When the parts of a subject are joined by the coordinating conjunction *or* or by the correlative conjunctions *either . . . or*, *neither . . . nor*, *not . . . but*, *not only . . . but also*, or *whether . . . or*, the part nearest the verb determines whether the verb is singular or plural:

9a

> One or the other of you <u>has</u> the winning ticket. (both
> parts singular: verb singular; note that the
> subject is *one or the other, not you*)

> Neither I nor my parents <u>were</u> to blame. (first part
> singular, second part plural: verb plural)

9c Agreement with Indefinite Pronouns

Most indefinite pronouns are almost always singular,
while a few are always plural (see #7a.6). A few (namely *all,
any, more, most, none, some*) can be either singular or plural,
depending on whether they refer to a single quantity or to
a number of individual units within a group:

> <u>Some</u> of the pasta <u>is</u> eaten. (a single amount; *pasta* is
> singular, a mass noun)
> <u>Some</u> of the cookies <u>are</u> missing. (a number of cookies;
> *cookies* is plural)

> <u>All</u> of this novel <u>is</u> good. (a whole novel; *novel* is
> singular)
> <u>All</u> of his novels <u>are</u> well written. (a number of novels;
> *novels* is plural)

> <u>Most</u> of the champagne <u>was</u> drunk. (a single mass;
> *champagne* is singular)
> <u>Most</u> of the cases of champagne <u>have</u> been exported.
> (a number of cases; *cases* is plural)

> <u>None</u> of the work <u>is</u> finished. (a single unit; *work* is
> singular)
> <u>None</u> of the reports <u>are</u> ready. (a number of reports;
> *reports* is plural)

9d Subject Following Verb

When the normal subject–verb order is reversed, the verb
still must agree with the real subject, not some word that
happens to precede it:

> There <u>is</u> only one <u>answer</u> to this question.
> There <u>are</u> several possible <u>solutions</u> to the problem.

> Here <u>comes</u> the judge.
> Here <u>come</u> the clowns.

When compounded singular nouns follow an opening *there* or *here*, most writers make the verb agree with the first noun:

> There <u>was</u> <u>a computer</u> and <u>a scanner</u> in the next room.

But others find this kind of syntax awkward sounding. By rephrasing the sentence you can easily avoid the issue and save a few words as well:

> A computer and a scanner were in the next room.

9e   Agreement with Relative Pronouns

Whether a relative pronoun is singular or plural depends on its antecedent. Therefore when a relative clause has *who*, *which*, or *that* as its subject, the verb must agree in number with the pronoun's antecedent:

> Her success is partly due to her mother and father, who
> <u>have</u> overcome many obstacles. (The antecedent of
>   *who* is *mother and father*.)

Questions about agreement most often occur with the phrases *one of those . . . who* and *one of the . . . who*:

> He is one of those people who <u>have</u> difficulty presenting.

Have is correct, since the antecedent of *who* is the plural *people*, not the singular *one*.

10   Adjectives

An **adjective** modifies—limits, qualifies, particularizes—a noun or pronoun. Adjectives generally answer the questions *Which? What kind of? How many?* and *How much?*

> <u>The</u> <u>black</u> cat was <u>hungry</u>; he ate <u>five</u> sardines and drank
> <u>some</u> milk.

10a Kinds of Adjectives

Adjectives fall into two major classes: **non–descriptive** and **descriptive.**

1. Non-descriptive adjectives

The several kinds of non-descriptive adjectives include some that are basically *structure words*:

- **articles**: *a, an, the*

- **demonstrative adjectives**:

  <u>this</u> hat   <u>that</u> problem

  <u>these</u> women   <u>those</u> books

- **interrogative and relative adjectives**:

  <u>Which</u> book is best?   <u>What</u> time is it?

  <u>Whose</u> opinion do you trust?

  She is the one <u>whose</u> opinion I trust.

- **possessive adjectives**—the possessive forms of personal and impersonal pronouns and of nouns:

  <u>my</u> book   <u>her</u> car   <u>its</u> color

  <u>their</u> heritage   <u>one's</u> beliefs   a <u>man's</u> coat

  the <u>river's</u> mouth   <u>Omar's</u> job

- **indefinite and numerical adjectives**:

  <u>some</u> money   <u>any</u> time   <u>more</u> fuel

  <u>several</u> keys   <u>three</u> ducks   <u>thirty</u> ships

  the <u>fourth</u> act   <u>much</u> sushi

10a

2. Descriptive adjectives

Descriptive adjectives give information about such matters as the size, shape, color, nature, and quality of whatever a noun or pronoun names:

a <u>tempting</u> dessert   a <u>well-done</u> steak

a <u>once-in-a-lifetime</u> chance   <u>Canadian</u> literature

an <u>experimental</u> play   <u>composted</u> leaves

a <u>fascinating</u> place <u>to visit</u>   a <u>dictionary</u> definition looking refreshed, he . . .   the man <u>of the hour</u>

the festival <u>to exceed all others</u>

the rabbits <u>who caused all the trouble</u>

an <u>impressive</u> <u>three-story</u> <u>Victorian</u> house

a <u>large</u>, <u>unwieldy</u> knife

As these examples illustrate, adjectival modifiers can be single, in groups or series, or in compounds; they can be proper adjectives, formed from proper nouns; they can be words that are adjectives only or words that can also function as other parts of speech, including nouns functioning as adjectives; they can be present participles, past participles, or infinitives; they can be participial phrases, infinitive phrases, or prepositional phrases; or they can be relative clauses.

 10b **Comparison of Descriptive Adjectives**

Most descriptive adjectives can be inflected or supplemented for *degree* in order to make *comparisons*. The basic or dictionary form of an adjective is called its **positive** form: *high, difficult, calm.* Use it to compare two things that are equal or similar, or with qualifiers such as *not* and *almost* to compare two things that are dissimilar:

This assignment is <u>as difficult as</u> last week's.

It is <u>not nearly so difficult as</u> I expected.

To make the **comparative** form, add *er* or put *more* (or *less*) in front of the positive form: *higher, calmer, more difficult, less difficult.* Use it to compare two unequal things:

My grades are <u>higher</u> now than they were last year.

Your part is <u>more difficult</u> than mine.

For the **superlative** form, add *est* or put *most* (or *least*) in front of the positive form: *highest, calmest, most difficult, least difficult.* Generally, use it to compare three or more unequal things:

Whose talent is the <u>greatest</u>?

He is the <u>calmest</u> and <u>least pretentious</u> person I know.

You can usually follow these guidelines:

- For adjectives of one syllable, usually add *er* and *est*:

Positive	Comparative	Superlative
short	shorter	shortest

- For adjectives of *three or more* syllables, usually use *more* and *most* (or *less* and *least*):

beautiful	more beautiful	most beautiful
annoying	more annoying	most annoying

- For most adjectives of two syllables ending in *al*, *ect*, *ed*, *ent*, *ful*, *ic*, *id*, *ing*, *ish*, *ive*, *less*, or *ous* (and any others where an added *er* or *est* would sound wrong), generally use *more* and *most* (or *less* and *least*):

10b

formal	more formal	most formal
direct	more direct	most direct
polished	more polished	most polished
potent	more potent	most potent
tactful	more tactful	most tactful

- For other adjectives of two syllables, you usually have a choice; for example:

gentle	gentler, more gentle	gentlest, most gentle
lively	livelier, more lively	liveliest, most lively

When there is a choice, the forms with *more* and *most* will usually sound more formal and more emphatic than those with *er* and *est*.

Note: A few commonly used adjectives form their comparative and superlative degrees irregularly:

good	better	best
bad	worse	worst

far	farther; further	farthest; furthest
little	littler; less, lesser	littlest; least
much, many	more	most

Good dictionaries list all irregular forms after the basic entry, including those in which a spelling change occurs.

10c Placement and Ordering of Adjectives

1. Placement of adjectives

Adjectival modifiers usually come just before or just after what they modify. Articles always, and other determiners almost always, precede the nouns they modify, usually with either no intervening words or only one or two other adjectives:

> Trying to save <u>some</u> money, <u>the</u> manager decided to close <u>his</u> store early.

> <u>The wise</u> manager decided not to hire <u>his scatterbrained</u> nephew.

Predicate adjectives almost always follow the subject and linking verb:

> The forest is <u>cool</u> and <u>green</u> and <u>full of mushrooms</u>.

> Shortly after his operation he again became <u>healthy</u>.

Adjectives serving as *objective complements* usually follow the subject–verb–direct object:

> I thought the suggestion <u>preposterous</u>.

Most other single-word adjectives, and many compound adjectives, precede the nouns they modify:

> The <u>tall</u>, <u>dark</u>, and <u>handsome</u> hero lives on only in <u>romantic</u> fiction.

Compound adjectives and adjectives in phrases are often comfortable after a noun:

10b

Elfrida, <u>radiant and delighted</u>, left the room, <u>secure</u> in her victory.

Relative clauses and various kinds of phrases customarily follow the nouns they modify:

He is one detective <u>who believes in being thorough</u>.

The president <u>of the company</u> will retire next month.

The only adjectival modifier not generally restricted in its position is the participial phrase:

<u>Having had abundant experience</u>, Kenneth applied for the job.

Kenneth, <u>having had abundant experience</u>, applied for the job.

Kenneth applied for the job, <u>having had abundant experience</u>.

10c

2. Ordering of adjectives

ELL Adjectives usually follow an idiomatic order: a determiner (an article, possessive, or demonstrative) comes first, then numbers, then adjectives that express a general description, then physical-state adjectives (including age, size, shape, color, and temperature), then proper adjectives, and then noun adjuncts (including adjectives ending in *ic(al)* or *al*) before the main noun. The following examples illustrate this order:

the one brilliant young movie star

their third impractical expensive white lamp

a sophisticated small Indian restaurant

your four new large red coffee mugs

Sue's two funny, daring Swedish friends

Notice that *daring* and *funny* are separated by a comma because they are interchangeable in order (see #15b.3).

11 Adverbs

Adverbs are often thought of as especially tricky. This part of speech is sometimes called the "catch-all" category, since any word that doesn't seem to fit elsewhere is usually assumed to be an adverb. Adverbs, therefore, are a little more complicated than adjectives.

11a Kinds and Functions of Adverbs

Whereas adjectives can modify only nouns and pronouns, adverbs can modify *verbs*, *adjectives*, other *adverbs*, and *independent clauses* or whole *sentences*. Adverbial modifiers generally answer such questions as *How? When? Where? Why?* and *To what degree?* That is, they indicate such things as *manner* (How?); *time* (When? How often? How long?); *place* and *direction* (Where? In what direction?); *cause, result,* and *purpose* (Why? To what effect?); and *degree* (To what degree? To what extent?). They also express affirmation and negation, conditions, concessions, and comparisons. Here are some examples:

> Fully expecting to fail, he slumped disconsolately in his seat and began taking the test.

To what degree? *Fully*: the adverb of degree modifies the participial (verbal) phrase *expecting to fail*. How? *Disconsolately*: the adverb of manner modifies the verb *slumped*. Where? *In his seat*: the prepositional phrase functions as an adverb of place modifying the verb *slumped*.

> Because their budget was tight, they eventually decided not to buy a car.

Why? *Because their budget was tight*: the adverbial clause of cause modifies the verb *decided* or, in a way, all the rest of the sentence. When? *Eventually*: the adverb of time modifies the verb *decided*. The negating *not* modifies the infinitive (verbal) *to buy*.

> If you're tired, I will walk the dog.

The conditional clause modifies the verb (*will walk*).

> Although she dislikes the city *intensely*, she agreed
> to go there in order to keep peace *in the family*.

Intensely (degree) modifies the verb *dislikes*. *There* (place) modifies the infinitive *to go*. *Although she dislikes the city intensely* is an adverbial clause of concession. The prepositional phrase *in order to keep peace in the family* is an adverb of purpose modifying the verb *agreed*. The smaller adverbial prepositional phrase *in the family* modifies the infinitive phrase *to keep peace*, answering the question *Where*?

> Meredith was better prepared than I was.

The adverb *better* modifies the adjective *prepared*; it and the clause *than I was* express comparison or contrast.

Adverbs as condensed clauses

Some single-word adverbs and adverbial phrases, especially sentence modifiers, can be thought of as reduced clauses:

> Fortunately [It is fortunate that], the cut was not deep.

> When possible [When it is possible], let your writing sit before revising it [before you revise it].

Other kinds of adverbs: relative, interrogative, conjunctive

1. The **relative adverbs** *(where, when, and why)* are used to introduce relative (adjective) clauses:

   > She returned to the town where she had grown up.

   > Adam looked forward to the moment when it would be his turn.

2. The **interrogative adverbs** *(where, when, why,* and *how)* are used in questions:

   > Where are you going? Why? How soon? How will you get there? When will you return?

3. **Conjunctive adverbs** usually join whole clauses or sentences to each other and indicate the nature of the connection:

> Only fifteen people showed up. <u>Nevertheless</u>, the promoter didn't let his disappointment show.
>
> The tornado almost flattened the town; <u>however</u>, only Dorothy and her dog were reported missing.

If you aren't sure whether a particular word is a conjunctive adverb or a conjunction, remember that adverbs can move around in a sentence; conjunctions cannot:

> Only Dorothy and her dog, however, were reported missing.

11b Comparison of Adverbs

Like descriptive adjectives, most adverbs that are similarly descriptive can be inflected or supplemented for degree. The following are some guidelines on how adverbs are inflected:

- Some short adverbs without *ly* form their comparative and superlative degrees with *er* and *est*; for example:

Positive	Comparative	Superlative
fast	faster	fastest
hard	harder	hardest
high	higher	highest

Less and *least* also sometimes go with the positive form of these adverbs; for example:

> They still ran fast, but <u>less fast</u> than they had the day before.
>
> Students work <u>least hard</u> on the days following an exam.

- Adverbs of three or more syllables ending in *ly* use *more* and *most*, *less* and *least*; for example:

| happily | more happily | most happily |
| stridently | less stridently | least stridently |

- Most two-syllable adverbs, whether or not they end in *ly*, also use *more* and *most*, *less* and *least*, though a few can also be inflected with *er* and *est*; for example:

slowly	more slowly	most slowly
grimly	less grimly	least grimly
often	more often, oftener	most often, oftenest

- Some adverbs form their comparative and superlative degrees irregularly:

badly	worse	worst
well	better	best
much	more	most
little	less	least
far	farther, further	farthest, furthest

- A few adverbs of place use *farther* and *farthest*; for example:

down	farther down	farthest down
north	farther north	farthest north

- As with adjectives, the adverbs *much*, *far*, and *by far* serve as intensifiers in comparisons:

Angelo and Felipe live <u>much</u> more comfortably than they used to.

They flew <u>far</u> lower than they should have.

He practices harder <u>by far</u> than anyone else in the orchestra.

11c Placement of Adverbs

1. Adverbs modifying adjectives or other adverbs

An intensifying or qualifying adverb almost always goes just before the adjective or adverb it modifies:

<u>almost</u> always	<u>strongly</u> confident	<u>very</u> hot
<u>only</u> two	<u>most</u> happily	

2. Modifiers of verbs

Whether single words, phrases, or clauses, most modifiers of verbs are more flexible in their position than are any other part of speech. Often they can go almost anywhere in a sentence and still function clearly:

Proudly, he pointed to his photo in the paper.

He proudly pointed to his photo in the paper.

He pointed proudly to his photo in the paper.

He pointed to his photo in the paper proudly.

3. Sentence modifiers

Sentence modifiers usually come at the beginning, but they, too, can be placed elsewhere for purposes of emphasis or rhythm:

Fortunately, the groom was able to stand.

The groom, fortunately, was able to stand.

The groom was, fortunately, able to stand.

The groom was able to stand, fortunately.

11c

With longer or more involved sentences, however, a sentence modifier at the end loses much of its force and point, obviously; obviously it works better if placed earlier, as this sentence demonstrates. (See also #16b, on the placement and punctuation of conjunctive adverbs, and #5d, on misplaced modifiers.)

12 Verbals

Infinitives, participles, and gerunds are called **verbals**, forms that are derived from verbs but that cannot function as main or finite verbs. Verbals are **non-finite** forms, not restricted by person and number as finite verbs are. They function as other parts of speech yet retain some characteristics of verbs: they can have objects, they can be modified by adverbs, and they can express tense and voice. Verbals often introduce *verbal phrases*, groups of words that themselves function as other parts of speech. Verbals enable you to inject much of the strength and liveliness of verbs into your writing even though the words are functioning as adjectives, adverbs, and nouns.

12a Infinitives

An infinitive usually consists of the word *to* (often called "the sign of the infinitive") followed by the basic form: *to be*, *to live*. Infinitives can function as *nouns*, *adjectives*, and *adverbs*.

1. Infinitives as nouns

> <u>To save</u> the wolves was Farley Mowat's primary intention.

The infinitive phrase *To save the wolves* is the subject of the verb *was*. The noun *wolves* is the direct object of the infinitive *To save*.

> She wanted <u>to end</u> the game quickly.

The infinitive phrase *to end the game quickly* is the direct object of the verb *wanted*.

2. Infinitives as adjectives

> His strong desire <u>to be</u> a doctor made him studious.

The infinitive phrase *to be a doctor* modifies the noun *desire*. Since *be* is a linking verb, the infinitive is here followed by the predicate noun *doctor*.

> The cappuccino coupons are the ones <u>to save</u>.

The infinitive *to save* modifies the pronoun *ones*.

3. Infinitives as adverbs

> She was lucky <u>to have</u> such a friend.

The infinitive phrase *to have such a friend* modifies the predicate adjective *lucky*. The noun phrase *such a friend* is the direct object of the infinitive *to have*.

> He went to Croton-on-Hudson <u>to experience</u> the Clearwater Festival.

The infinitive phrase *to experience the Clearwater Festival* is an adverb of purpose modifying the verb *went*; *the Clearwater Festival* is the direct object of the infinitive *to experience*.

12a

12b Participles

The **past participle** and **present participle** work with various auxiliaries to form a finite verb's *perfect* and *progressive* tenses. But without the auxiliaries to indicate *person* and *number*, the participles are verbals and cannot function as verbs. Instead they function as *adjectives*, modifying nouns and pronouns:

> Beaming happily, Josef examined his freshly sanded bench.

Present participles always end in *ing*, regular past participles in *ed* or *d*. Irregular past participles end variously: *made, mown, broken*, etc. A regular past participle is identical to the past-tense form of a verb, but you can easily check a given word's function in a sentence. In the example above, the past-tense form *examined* clearly has *Josef* as its subject; the past participle *sanded*, with no subject, is an adjective modifying *bench*. More examples:

> Painted houses require more care than brick ones.

The past participle *painted* modifies the noun *houses*.

> Impressed, she recounted the film's more thrilling episodes.

The past participle *impressed* modifies the subject, *she*; the present participle *thrilling* modifies the noun *episodes* and is itself modified by the adverb *more*.

> The subject discussed most often was the message behind the song.

The past participle *discussed* modifies the noun *subject* and is itself modified by the adverbial *most often*.

> Suddenly finding himself alone, he became very flustered.

The present participle *finding* introduces the participial phrase *finding himself alone*, which modifies the subject, *he*; *finding*, as a verbal, has *himself* as a direct object and is modified by the adverb *Suddenly*. The past participle *flustered* functions as a predicate adjective after the linking verb *became*; it modifies *he* and is itself modified by the adverb *very*.

12c Gerunds

When the *ing* form of a verb functions as a noun, it is called a **gerund**:

> Jamaal gave himself a good <u>talking</u> to.
>
> <u>Moving</u> offices can be hard work.
>
> Min has a profound fear of <u>flying</u>.
>
> Careful preparation——<u>brainstorming</u>, <u>organizing</u>, and <u>outlining</u>——helps produce good essays.

The gerund *talking* is a direct object and is itself modified by the adjective *good*. The gerund *Moving* is the subject of the sentence and has *offices* as a direct object. The gerund *flying* is the object of the preposition *of*. In the final example, the three gerunds constitute an appositive or definition of the subject noun, *preparation*.

Note: In formal usage, a noun or a personal pronoun preceding a gerund will usually be in the possessive case:

> <u>His</u> cooking left much to be desired.
>
> She approved of <u>Bob's</u> cleaning the house.

13 Connecting Words; Interjections

This section on the parts of speech will conclude with a look at connecting words (prepositions and conjunctions) and emotive words (interjections).

13a Prepositions

Prepositions are structure words or function words; they do not change their form. A preposition is part of a prepositional phrase, and it usually precedes the rest of the phrase, which includes a noun or pronoun as the object of the preposition:

> She sent an email <u>to her friend</u>.

Make a question of the preposition and ask *what* or *whom* and the answer will always be the object: *To* whom? Her friend.

1. Functions of prepositions and prepositional phrases

A preposition *links* its object to some other word in the sentence; the prepositional phrase then functions as either an *adjectival* or an *adverbial* modifier:

He laid the camera <u>on the table</u>.

Here, *on* links *table* to the verb *laid*; the phrase *on the table* therefore functions as an adverb describing *where* the camera was laid.

It was a time <u>for celebration</u>.

Here, *for* links *celebration* to the noun *time*; the phrase therefore functions as an adjective indicating *what kind of* time.

13a

2. Placement of prepositions

Usually, like articles, prepositions signal that a noun or pronoun soon follows. But prepositions can also come at the ends of clauses or sentences, for example in a question, for emphasis, or to avoid stiffness:

Which backpack do you want to look <u>at</u>?

They had several issues to contend <u>with</u>.

It isn't wrong to end a sentence or clause with a preposition, in spite of what many people have been taught; just don't do it so often that it calls attention to itself.

3. Common prepositions

Most prepositions indicate a spatial or temporal relation, or such things as purpose, concession, comparison, manner, and agency. Here is a list of common prepositions; note that several consist of more than one word:

about	across	against	alongside
above	across from	ahead of	among
according to	after	along	apart from

around	considering	in spite of	regardless of
as	contrary to	into	round
as for	despite	like	since
at	down	near	such as
away from	during	next to	through
because of	except	notwithstanding	throughout
before	except for	of	till
behind	excepting	off	to
below	for	on	toward(s)
beneath	from	on account of	under
beside	in	onto	underneath
besides	in addition to	on top of	unlike
between	including	opposite	until
beyond	in front of	out	up
but	in order to	outside	upon
by	in place of	over	with
by way of	in relation to	past	within
concerning	inside	regarding	without

A dictionary will be extremely helpful in guiding you in the use of prepositions.

13b Conjunctions: Coordinate, Correlative, Subordinate

Conjunctions are another kind of structure word or function word. As their name indicates, conjunctions are words that "join together." There are three kinds of conjunctions: *coordinating*, *correlative*, and *subordinating*.

1. Coordinating conjunctions

There are only seven **coordinating conjunctions**, so they are easy to remember:

and   but   for   nor   or   so   yet

When you use a coordinating conjunction, choose the appropriate one. *And* indicates addition, *nor* indicates negative addition (equivalent to *also not*), *but* and *yet* indicate contrast or opposition, *or* indicates choice, *for* indicates cause or reason, and *so* indicates effect or result.

Coordinating conjunctions have three main functions, which are discussed below.

Joining words, phrases, and subordinate clauses

And, *but*, *or*, and *yet* join coordinate elements within sentences. The elements joined are usually of equal importance and of similar grammatical structure and function. When joined, they are sometimes called compounds. Here are examples of how various kinds of sentence elements may be compounded:

I saw <u>Jaylen</u> and <u>Ralph</u>. (two direct objects)

<u>Jaylen</u> or <u>Ralph</u> saw me. (two subjects)

They <u>danced</u> and <u>sang</u>. (two verbs)

The gnome was <u>short</u>, <u>fat</u>, and <u>melancholic</u>. (three predicate adjectives)

He drove <u>quickly</u> yet <u>carefully</u>. (two adverbs)

The bird flew <u>in the door</u> and <u>out the window</u>. (two adverbial prepositional phrases)

<u>Tired</u> but <u>determined</u>, the hiker plodded on. (two past participles)

People <u>who invest wisely</u> and <u>who spend carefully</u> often have boring lives. (two adjective clauses)

Obviously the elements being joined won't always have identical structures, but don't disappoint readers' natural expectations that compound elements will be parallel.

When three or more elements are compounded, the conjunction usually appears only between the last two, though *and* and *or* can appear throughout for purposes of rhythm or emphasis:

13b

There was a tug-of-war <u>and</u> a potato sack race <u>and</u> an egg race <u>and</u> a three-legged race <u>and</u> . . . well, there was just about any kind of game anyone could want at a picnic.

Joining independent clauses

All seven coordinating conjunctions can join independent clauses to make compound (or compound-complex) sentences. The clauses will be grammatically equivalent, since they are independent; but they needn't be grammatically parallel or even of similar length, though they often are both, for parallelism is a strong stylistic force. Here are some examples:

The players fought, the umpires shouted, <u>and</u> the fans booed.

Jaylen saw me, <u>but</u> Ralph didn't.

I won't do it, <u>nor</u> will she. (With *nor* there must be some sort of negative in the first clause. Note that after *nor* the normal subject–verb order is reversed.)

There was no way to avoid it, <u>so</u> I decided to get as much out of the experience as I could.

13b

Joining sentences

In spite of what many of us have been taught, it isn't wrong to begin a sentence with *And* or *But*, or for that matter any of the other coordinating conjunctions. Be advised, however, that *For*, since it is so similar in meaning to *because*, often sounds strange at the start of a sentence, as if introducing a fragmentary subordinate clause. *And* and *But* make good openers—as long as you don't overuse them. An opening *But* or *Yet* can nicely emphasize a contrast or other turn of thought. An opening *And* can also be emphatic:

He told the employees of the company he was sorry. <u>And</u> he meant it.

For punctuation with coordinating conjunctions, see Part IV.

2. Correlative conjunctions

ELL **Correlative conjunctions** come in pairs. They *correlate* ("relate together") two parallel parts of a sentence. The following are the principal ones:

either . . . or	neither . . . nor
whether . . . or	both . . . and
not . . . but	not only . . . but also

Correlative conjunctions enable you to write sentences containing forcefully balanced elements, but don't overdo them. They are also more at home in formal than in informal writing. Some examples:

<u>Either</u> Rodney <u>or</u> Elliott is going to drive.

She accepted <u>neither</u> the first <u>nor</u> the second job offer.

<u>Whether</u> by accident <u>or</u> by design, the number turned out to be exactly right.

<u>Both</u> the administration <u>and</u> the student body are pleased with the new plan.

She <u>not only</u> plays well <u>but also</u> sings well.

<u>Not only</u> does she play well, <u>but</u> she <u>also</u> sings well.

Notice, in the last example, how *also* (or its equivalent) can be moved away from the *but*. And in the last example, note how *does* is needed as an auxiliary because the clause is in the present tense. Except for these variations, make what follows one term exactly parallel to what follows the other: *the first* || *the second*; *by accident* || *by design*; *plays well* || *sings well*.

Further, with the *not only . . . but also* pair, you should usually make the *also* (or some equivalent) explicit. Its omission results in a feeling of incompleteness:

incomplete: He was not only smart, but charming.

complete: He was not only smart, but also charming.

complete: He was not only smart, but charming as well.

To ensure that you use this correlative pairing effectively, keep in mind the following:

a. For clauses containing *compound verbs* (one or more auxiliary verbs attached to a main verb), place *not only* at the beginning of the clause and then place the first auxiliary verb *before* the subject. Then, place *but* before the subject of the second clause and *also* after the auxiliary verb.

> He has been a great star and he has served his fans well.

> <u>Not only</u> has he been a great star, <u>but</u> he has <u>also</u> served his fans well.

b. For sentences in the *simple present* or *simple past* tenses (other than those in which the main verb is *to be*), you must add the appropriate form of *do/does/did* before the subject of the *not only* clause when *not only* appears at the beginning of the clause.

> She looks rested and she looks happy.

> <u>Not only</u> *does* she look rested, <u>but</u> she <u>also</u> looks happy.

> She looked rested and she looked happy.

> <u>Not only</u> *did* she look rested, <u>but</u> she <u>also</u> looked happy.

> She is rested and she is happy.

> <u>Not only</u> *is* she rested, <u>but</u> she is <u>also</u> happy.

c. When *not only* appears inside the clause, you do not have to reverse the order of the auxiliary verb and subject, nor do you have to add *do/does/did*.

> She has worked hard at her job and at her hobbies.

> She has worked hard <u>not only</u> at her job <u>but also</u> at her hobbies.

13b

3. Subordinating conjunctions

A **subordinating conjunction** introduces a *subordinate* (or *dependent*) clause and links it to the *independent* (or *main* or *principal*) clause to which it is grammatically related:

> She writes <u>because</u> she has something to say.

The subordinating conjunction *because* introduces the adverbial clause *because she has something to say* and links it to the independent clause whose verb it modifies. The *because*-clause is *subordinate* because it cannot stand by itself: by itself it would be a *fragment*. Note that a subordinate clause can also come first:

> <u>Because</u> she has something to say, she writes articles for magazines.

13b

> <u>That</u> Raj will win the prize is a foregone conclusion.

Here *That* introduces the noun clause *That Raj will win the prize*, which functions as the subject of the sentence. Note that whereas a coordinating conjunction is like a spot of glue between two structures and not a part of either, a subordinating conjunction is an integral part of its clause. In the following sentence, for example, the subordinating conjunction *whenever* is a part of the adverbial clause that modifies the imperative verb *Leave*:

> Leave <u>whenever you feel tired</u>.

Here is a list of the principal subordinating conjunctions:

after	even though	once	till
although	ever since	rather than	unless
as	if	since	until
as though	if only	than	what
because	in case	that	whatever
before	lest	though	when(ever)

where(ever)	whether	while	why
whereas	which	who	

There are also many terms consisting of two or more words ending in *as*, *if*, and *that* that serve as subordinating conjunctions, including *as long as*, *as soon as*, *as far as*, *as if*, *even if*, *only if*, *but that*, *except that*, *now that*, *in that*, *provided that*, and *in order that*.

13c Interjections

An **interjection** is a word or group of words *interjected* or dropped into a sentence in order to express emotion. Strictly speaking, interjections have no grammatical function; they are simply thrust into sentences and play no part in their syntax, though sometimes they act like sentence modifiers. They are often used in dialogue and are not that common in academic writing.

> But——really!——what did you expect?
>
> Oh, what fun!
>
> It was, well, a bit of a disappointment.

A mild interjection is usually set off with commas. A strong interjection is sometimes set off with dashes and is often accompanied by an exclamation point. An interjection may also be a minor sentence by itself:

> Ouch! That hurt!

14 Diction

The style of a piece of writing is largely determined by diction: by choice and use of words. Diction, then, is near the heart of effective writing and style. This section isolates the principal challenges writers encounter in choosing and using words and offers some suggestions for meeting them.

14a Level

In any piece of writing, use words that are appropriate to you, to your topic, and to the circumstances in which you are writing. Consider the *occasion*, the *purpose*, and the *audience*. Avoid words and phrases that call attention to themselves rather than to the meaning you want to convey. In writing a formal academic essay, adopt diction appropriate to the discipline and the audience. Avoid slang and colloquial or informal terms at one extreme, and pretentious language at the other. These principles also apply in other writing for your courses and the workplace, where it is usually preferable to adopt a straightforward, moderate style—a level of diction that both respects the intelligence of the reader and strives to communicate with the reader as effectively as possible.

1. Slang

Since **slang** is the exact opposite of **formal diction**, it is seldom appropriate in a formal context.

If you are considering using slang in your writing, consult not only one or more good dictionaries but also members of your audience: trust your ear, your common sense, and your good taste. If you do use a slang term, do not use quotation marks to call attention to it.

2. Informal, colloquial

Even dictionaries can't agree on what constitutes slang versus **informal** or **colloquial** usage. There are many words and phrases that may be labeled *inf* or *colloq* in a dictionary, and although not slang, they do not ordinarily belong in formal writing. For example, unless you are aiming for a somewhat informal level, you should avoid such abbreviations as *esp.*, *etc.*, *no.*, *orig.*, and *OK*; and you may wish to avoid contractions (*can't, don't,* etc.), though they are common in our own discourse in this book and in everyday speech.

3. Pretentious language

Efforts to impress with unnecessarily formal or pretentious diction often backfire. Imagine yourself trying to take seriously someone who wrote "It was felicitous that the canine in question was demonstrably more exuberant in emitting threatening sounds than in attempting to implement said threats by engaging in actual physical assault," instead of simply saying "Luckily, despite having a vicious bark, the dog was quite gentle." This is an exaggerated example, but it illustrates how important it is to be straightforward.

14b Concrete and Abstract Diction

1. Concreteness and specificity

Concrete words denote things that are tangible, capable of being apprehended by our physical senses (*child*, *sky*, *flowers*). **Abstract** words denote intangibles, like ideas or qualities (*postmodernism*, *agriculture*, *nature*). Much of the writing you do is a blend of the abstract and the concrete. The more concrete your writing, the more readily your readers will grasp it, for the concreteness will provide images for their imaginations to respond to. If you write

> Transportation is becoming a major problem in our city.

and leave it at that, readers will understand you. But if you write, or add,

> In the downtown section of this city, too many cars and too few buses travel the streets.

you know that your readers will see exactly what you mean: in their minds they will see the traffic jams and the overloaded buses.

As your writing moves from generalizations to specifics, it will move from the abstract to the concrete. *General* and *specific* are relative terms: a general word designates a *class* (e.g., *modes of transportation*); a more specific word designates members of that class (*vehicles*, *ships*, *airplanes*); a still more specific word designates members of a still smaller class (*cars*, *trucks*, *bicycles*, *buses*); and so on, getting narrower, the classes and sub-classes getting smaller, until—if one needs to go that far—one arrives at a single, unique item, a class of one (e.g., *the car sitting in your own parking spot*).

Of course it is appropriate to write about "plant life," and then to narrow it, say, to "flowers"; and if you can write about "marigolds," "roses," "daffodils," and so on, you'll be more specific. Don't vaguely write "We experienced a warm day" when you could write more clearly, "We stayed outdoors all afternoon in the 78-degree weather," or "We basked in the warm spring sunshine all afternoon."

Of course, abstract and general terms are legitimate and often necessary, for one can scarcely present all ideas concretely. Try, though, to be as concrete and specific as your subject and the context will allow.

2. Weak generalizations

14b

A common weakness of student writing is an overdependence on unsupported generalizations. Consider: "Children today are reluctant readers." Few readers would or should accept such a general assertion, for the statement calls for considerably more illustration, evidence, and qualification. It evokes all kinds of questions: All children? Of all ages? In all countries? What are they reluctant to read? What is the connotation of *reluctant* here? Is such reluctance really something new? Merely stating a generalization or assumption is not enough; to be clear and effective it must be illustrated and supported by specifics.

14c Euphemisms

Euphemisms are substitutes for words whose meanings many find to be unpleasant and therefore, in certain circumstances, undesirable. In social settings we tend to ask for the location not of the toilet, which is what we want, but of the restroom, the bathroom, the washroom, or the powder room.

But in other situations, the euphemism is sometimes abused. Euphemisms used to gloss over some supposed unpleasantness may deceive. Innocent civilians killed in bombing raids are referred to as "collateral damage," and assassination squads are termed "special forces." What was once an economic depression is now, in an attempt to miti-gate its negative implications, termed a "recession," or an "economic downturn," or even a mere "growth cycle slow-down." Government officials who have patently lied admit only that they "misspoke."

Such euphemisms commonly imply a degree of virtue not justified by the facts. Calling genocide "ethnic cleans-ing" seriously distorts the meanings of both "ethnic" and "cleansing." Some euphemisms cloud or attempt to hide the facts in other ways. Workers are "laid off" or "declared redundant" or even "downsized" rather than "fired." An escalation in warfare is described as a "troop surge"; a civil war is referred to as "factional unrest" or "an insurgency." In your own writing, you should avoid using such terms unless you have a strong reason for doing so.

Other euphemisms help people avoid the unpleasant reality of death, which is often called "passing away" or "loss"; the lifeless body, the cadaver or corpse, is deemed "the remains." Such usages may be acceptable, even desir-able, in certain circumstances, since they may enable one to avoid aggravating the pain and grief of the bereaved. But in other circumstances, direct, more precise diction is preferable.

14d Wrong Words

Any error in diction is a "wrong word," but a par-ticular kind of incorrect word choice is customar-ily marked **wrong word (ww)** in essays or tests. The use of *infer* where the correct word is *imply* is an example. Don't write *effect* when you mean *affect*. Other kinds of wrong word choices occur as well; here are a few examples:

> *ww:* Late in the summer I met my best friend, <u>which</u> I hadn't seen since graduation.

> *ww:* Certain areas of the beach were <u>absent</u> of rocks.

Whom, not *which,* is the correct pronoun for a person. The wrong phrase came to the second writer's mind; *devoid of* was the one wanted.

Idiom

ELL A particular kind of word choice has to do with using **idioms**. An idiom is an expression peculiar to a given language, one that may not make logical or grammatical sense but that is understood because it is customary. Here are some examples: *to shake it off, to draw the line, to step up, to take a stab at*. These idioms have a colloquial flavor about them and may even sound like clichés or euphemisms. But other idioms are a part of our everyday language and occur in formal writing as well; for example: to "do justice to" something, to "take after" someone, to "get along with" someone.

Most mistakes in idiom result from using a wrong preposition in combination with certain other words. For example, we get *in* or *into* a car, but *on* or *onto* a bus; one is usually angry *with* a person, but *at* a thing. In some parts of the country, people stand *in* line; in others, they stand *on* line. Here are some examples of errors in idiom:

> **incorrect:** She was absorbed <u>by</u> the novel. (*correct*: absorbed in)

> **incorrect:** She took the liberty <u>to introduce</u> herself to the group. (*correct*: liberty of introducing)

> **incorrect:** He plans to get married <u>with</u> my youngest sister. (*correct*: get married to)

Idiomatic expressions sometimes involve choosing between an infinitive and a prepositional gerund phrase. After some expressions either is acceptable; for example:

> He is afraid <u>to lose</u>. He is afraid <u>of losing</u>.

> They are hesitant <u>to attend</u>. They are hesitant <u>about attending</u>.

But some terms call for one or the other:

> They propose <u>to go</u>. They are prepared <u>to go</u>.

> They insist <u>on going</u>. They are insistent <u>on going</u>.

Idiom is a matter of usage. But a good online or print dictionary can often help; ask your professor for recommendations. If your home or native language is not English, you could benefit from the online, searchable Oxford Advanced American Dictionary, a learner's dictionary; find out if you can access this resource through your college's library subscription.

14f Wordiness, Clichés, Jargon, and Associated Problems

Avoid diction that decreases precision and clarity. Using too many words, or tired words, or fuzzy words weakens communication. Edit out of your own writing wordy and pretentious phrases like *make a determination* (instead use *determine*), *at this point in time* (instead use *now*), *due to the fact that* (instead use *because*), and *be of assistance to* (instead use *help*).

1. Wordiness (w)

Generally, the fewer words you use to make a point, the better. Useless words clutter up a sentence; they dissipate its force, cloud its meaning, blunt its effectiveness.

> *w:* What a person should try to do when communicating by writing is to make sure the meaning of what he or she is trying to say is clear.

> *revised:* A writer should strive to be clear.

Expletives

When used to excess, expletive constructions can be a source of weakness and wordiness. There is nothing inherently wrong with them, and they are invaluable in enabling us to form certain kinds of sentences the way we want to. But if you can get rid of an expletive without creating awkwardness or losing desired emphasis, do it. Don't write

> *w:* There are several reasons why it is important to revise carefully.

when you can so easily get rid of the excess caused by the *there are* and *it is* structure:

> ***revised:*** Careful revision is important for several reasons.

> ***revised:*** For several reasons, careful revision is important.

2. Repetition

Repetition can be useful for coherence and emphasis. But unnecessary repetition usually produces wordiness, and often awkwardness as well. Consider this example:

> ***rep:*** Looking at the general appearance of the buildings, you can see that special consideration was given to the choice of colors for these buildings.

> ***revised:*** Looking at the buildings, you can see that special consideration was given to the choice of colors.

3. Redundancy

Redundancy, another cause of wordiness, is repetition of an idea rather than a word. Something is redundant if it has already been expressed earlier in a sentence. To begin a sentence with "In my opinion, I think . . . " is redundant. To speak of a "new innovation" is to be redundant. Here are some other phrases that are redundant:

advance planning	erode away
added bonus	general consensus
basic fundamentals	mental attitude
but nevertheless	more preferable
character trait	necessary prerequisite
climb up	past history
close scrutiny	proceed ahead
completely eliminate	protest against
consensus of opinion	reduce down
continue on	refer back
enter into	revert back

One common kind of redundancy is sometimes called "doubling"—adding an unnecessary second word (usually an adjective) as if to make sure the meaning of the first is clear:

> *red:* The report was brief and concise.

Either *brief* or *concise* alone would convey the meaning.

4. Ready-made phrases

Prefabricated or formulaic phrases that leap to our minds whole are almost always wordy. They are a kind of cliché, and many also sound like jargon. You can often edit them out of a draft altogether, or at least use shorter equivalents:

at that time, at that point in time (use *then*)

at the present time, at this time, at this point in time (use *now*)

at the same time (use *while*)

by means of (use *by*)

due to the fact that, because of the fact that, on account of the fact that, in view of the fact that, owing to the fact that (use *because*)

during the course of, in the course of (use *during*)

for the purpose of (use *for, to*)

for the reason that, for the simple reason that (use *because*)

in all likelihood, in all probability (use *probably*)

in height (use *high*)

in length (use *long*)

in order to (use *to*)

in spite of the fact that (use *although*)

in the event that (use *if*)

in this day and age (use *now, today*)

period of time (use *period, time*)

previous to, prior to (use *before*)

5. Triteness, clichés

Trite or hackneyed expressions, clichés are another form of wordiness: they are tired, worn out, all too familiar, and therefore contribute little to a sentence. Since they are prefabricated phrases, they are another kind of deadwood that can be edited out of a draft.

Here are a few examples to suggest the kinds of expressions to edit from your work:

a matter of course	many and diverse
all things being equal	moment of truth
as a last resort	needless to say
as a matter of fact	nipped in the bud
as the crow flies	no way, shape, or form
beat a hasty retreat	off the beaten path (or track)
busy as a bee	on the right track
by leaps and bounds	one and the same
by no manner of means	par for the course
by no means	pretty as a picture
clear as crystal (or mud)	pride and joy
cool as a cucumber	raining cats and dogs
doomed to disappointment	read between the lines
easier said than done	rears its ugly head
from dawn till dusk	rude awakening
gentle as a lamb	sadder but wiser
good as gold	seeing is believing
head over heels	sharp as a tack
if and when	silver lining
in a manner of speaking	slowly but surely
in one ear and out the other	smart as a whip
in the long run	strike while the iron is hot
it goes without saying	strong as an ox
it stands to reason	the wrong side of the tracks

14f

last but not least	think outside the box
lock, stock, and barrel	what goes around comes around
love at first sight	when all is said and done

Edit for the almost automatic couplings that occur between some adjectives and nouns:

acid test	devastating effect	proud possessor
ardent admirers	drastic action	sacred duty
budding genius	festive occasion	severe stress
bulging biceps	hearty breakfast	tangible proof
blushing bride	heated opposition	vital role
consummate artistry	knee-jerk reaction	

6. Jargon

The word **jargon**, in a narrow sense, refers to terms peculiar to a specific discipline, such as psychology, chemistry, literary theory, or computer science, terms unlikely to be fully understood by an outsider. Here we use it in a different sense, to refer to all the incoherent, unintelligible phraseology that clutters contemporary expression. The private languages of particular disciplines or special groups are quite legitimately used in writing for members of those communities. Much less legitimate is the confusing, incomprehensible language that so easily finds its way into the speech and writing of most of us.

The following list is a sampling of words and phrases that are virtually guaranteed to decrease the quality of expression, whether spoken or written:

along the lines of, along that line, in the line of

angle

aspect

background (as a verb)

basis, on the basis of, on a . . . basis

bottom line

case

concept, conception

concerning, concerned

connection, in connection with, in this (that) connection

considering, consideration, in consideration of

definitely

dialogue (especially as a verb)

escalate

evidenced by

expertise

14f

facet

factor

implemented, implementation

importantly

indicated to (for *told*)

input, output

in regard to, with regard to, regarding, as regards

in relation to

in respect to, with respect to, respecting

in terms of

in the final analysis

meaningful

mega-

motivation

ongoing

parameters

phase

picture, in the picture

posture

realm

relate to

relevant

replicate

scenario, worst-case scenario

sector

self-identity

situation

standpoint, vantage point, viewpoint

type, -type

viable

-wise

worthwhile

Writers addicted to wordiness and jargon will prefer long words to short ones, and pretentious-sounding words to relatively simple ones. Generally, choose the shorter and simpler form. For example, the shorter word in each of the following pairs is preferable:

analysis, analyzation	(re)orient, (re)orientate
connote, connotate	preventive, preventative
courage, courageousness	remedy (vb.), remediate
disoriented, disorientated	symbolic, symbolical
existential, existentialistic	use (n. & vb.), utilize, utilization

14g Usage: A Checklist of Troublesome Words and Phrases

ELL This section features words and phrases that have a history of being especially confusing or otherwise troublesome. This list is selective rather than exhaustive; we have tried to keep it short enough to be manageable.

advice, advise

Advice is a noun, usually used in non-count form. *Advise* is a verb that is usually transitive.

> My faculty advisor has given me good <u>advice</u> on planning my major. (noun)

> He <u>advised</u> his brother to consider studying abroad for a year. (transitive verb in past-tense form; its direct object is *his brother*)

affect, effect

Affect is a transitive verb meaning "to act upon" or "to influence"; *effect* is a noun meaning "result, consequence":

> He tried to <u>affect</u> the outcome, but his efforts had no <u>effect</u>.

amount, number

Use *number* only with count nouns (i.e., with nouns that have both singular and plural forms), and use *amount* only with non-count nouns: a *number* of coins, an *amount* of change; a large *number* of cars, a large *amount* of traffic. *Number* usually takes a singular verb after the definite article and a plural verb after the indefinite article.

> <u>The number</u> of students taking the workshop <u>is</u> encouraging.

> <u>A number</u> of students <u>are</u> planning to take the workshop.

between, among

Generally, use *between* when there are two persons or things, and *among* when there are more than two:

> There is growing distrust <u>between</u> the two national leaders.

> They divided the cost equally <u>among</u> the three of them.

complementary, complimentary

Complementary is the adjective describing something that adds to or completes something else. *Complimentary* is the adjective describing something free (*complimentary* tickets or passes) or comments intended to praise or flatter someone.

> Complementary exercises reinforcing the principles covered in this chapter are available on the course website.
> (the exercises will complete the module)

> Her comments on his new haircut were complimentary.
> (her comments were positive)

comprise, compose

Distinguish carefully between these words. Strictly, *comprise* means "consist of, contain, take in, include":

> The municipal region comprises several cities and towns.

14g

Compose means "constitute, form, make up":

> The seven cities and towns compose the municipal region.

continual, continuous

These words are sometimes considered interchangeable, but *continual* more often refers to something that happens frequently or even regularly but with interruptions, and *continuous* to something that occurs constantly, without interruptions:

> The speaker's voice went on in a continuous drone, in spite of the heckler's continual attempts to interrupt.

farther, further

Use *farther* and *farthest* to refer to physical distance and *further* and *furthest* everywhere else, such as when referring to time and degree or when the meaning is something like "more" or "in addition":

> To go any farther down the road is the furthest thing from my mind.

> Rather than delay any further, he began his research, starting with the book farthest from him.

Without <u>further</u> delay, she began her speech.

feel(s)

Don't loosely use the word *feel* when what you really mean is *think* or *believe*. *Feel* is more appropriate to emotional or physical attitudes and responses, *think* and *believe* to those dependent on reasoning:

> The defendant <u>felt</u> cheated by the decision; she <u>believed</u> that her case had not been judged impartially.

good, bad, badly, well

To avoid confusion and error with these words, remember that *good* and *bad* are adjectives, *badly* and *well* adverbs (except when *well* is an adjective meaning "healthy").

> The model looks <u>good</u> in that business suit. (He is attractive.)
>
> That suit looks <u>bad</u> on that person only because it fits <u>badly</u>.
>
> Nathan was <u>bad</u>. (He misbehaved.)
>
> Nathan acted <u>badly</u>. (His performance as Hamlet was terrible.)

happen, occur

These verbs sometimes pose a problem for students with English as an additional language. Both verbs are intransitive and cannot take the passive-voice form in any tense.

> *wrong:* The revolution <u>was happened</u> in 1917.
>
> *right:* The revolution <u>happened</u> in 1917.
>
> *wrong:* My parents' wedding <u>was occurred</u> in September 1970.
>
> *right:* My parents' wedding <u>occurred</u> in September 1970.

infer, imply

Use *imply* to mean "suggest, hint at, indicate indirectly" and *infer* to mean "conclude by reasoning, deduce." A listener or reader can *infer* from a statement something that its speaker or writer *implies* in it:

Her speech strongly <u>implied</u> that we could trust her.

I <u>inferred</u> from her speech that she was trustworthy.

its, it's
Its—without the apostrophe—is the possessive form of *it*; *it's*—with the apostrophe—is the contracted form of *it is*, or occasionally of *it has* (as in "*It's* been a long day").

lack, lack of, lacking, lacking in
Note the following standard usages:

This paper <u>lacks</u> a clear argument. (*lack* as a transitive verb)

A major weakness of his argument was its <u>lack</u> of evidence. (*lack* as a noun followed by the preposition *of*)

<u>Lacking</u> confidence, she gave up on her research. (*lacking* as a present participle followed by a direct object)

<u>Lacking</u> in experience, they had difficulty in job interviews. (*lacking* as a present participle in combination with the preposition *in*)

less, fewer
Use *fewer* to refer to things that are countable (i.e., nouns that have both singular and plural forms), and use *less* to refer to things that are measured rather than counted or that are considered as units (i.e., non-count nouns):

<u>fewer</u> dollars, <u>less</u> money

<u>fewer</u> hours, <u>less</u> time

<u>fewer</u> cars, <u>less</u> traffic

let, make
The verbs *let* and *make* are parts of an idiom that causes problems, especially for those whose home or native language is not English. When *let* or *make* is followed by a direct object and an infinitive, the infinitive does not include the customary *to*:

id: They <u>let</u> me <u>to borrow</u> their new car.

revised: They <u>let</u> me <u>borrow</u> their new car.

id: Our professor <u>made</u> us <u>to participate</u> in the experiment.

revised: Our professor <u>made</u> us <u>participate</u> in the experiment.

lie, lay

Since *lay* is both the past tense of *lie* and the present tense of the verb *lay*, some writers habitually confuse these two verbs. If necessary, memorize their principal parts: *lie, lay, lain*; *lay, laid, laid*. The verb *lie* means "recline" or "be situated"; *lay* means "put" or "place." *Lie* is intransitive; *lay* is transitive:

I <u>lie</u> down now; I <u>lay</u> down yesterday; I have <u>lain</u> down several times today.

I <u>lay</u> the book on the desk now; I <u>laid</u> the book on the desk yesterday; I have <u>laid</u> the book on the desk every morning for a week.

like, as, as if, as though

Like is a preposition:

Roger is dressed exactly <u>like</u> Kazu.

But if a verb is placed after *Kazu*, then what follows *like* becomes a full clause, forcing *like* to serve incorrectly as a conjunction; use the conjunction *as* when a clause follows:

us: Roger is dressed exactly <u>like</u> Ray is.

revised: Roger is dressed exactly <u>as</u> Ray is.

In similar constructions that express an imagined comparison or possibility, use *as if* or *as though* to introduce clauses:

It looks <u>like</u> rain.

It looks <u>as if</u> [or *as though*] it will rain.

loan, lend

Although some people restrict *loan* to being a noun, it is generally acceptable as a verb equivalent to *lend*—except in such figurative uses as "*lend* a hand."

14g

may, might

Don't confuse your reader by using *may* where *might* is required:

a. after another verb in the past tense:

> **us:** She thought she <u>may</u> get a raise. (use *might*)

In the present tense, either *may* or *might* would be possible:

> She thinks she <u>may</u> get a raise. (It's quite likely that she will.)

> She thinks she <u>might</u> get a raise. (It's less likely, but possible.)

b. for something hypothetical rather than factual:

> **us:** This imaginative software program <u>may</u> have helped Beethoven, but it wouldn't have changed the way Mozart composed. (use *might*)

14g

of

Avoid incorrect use of *of* as a result of mispronunciation:

> **ww:** We would <u>of</u> stayed for dinner if not for the weather. (use *have*)

> **ww:** The prime minister should <u>of</u> apologized for his remarks. (use *have*)

Because of the way we sometimes speak, such verb phrases as "would have," "could have," "should have," and "might have" are pronounced as contractions (*would've, could've, should've, might've*). Because of the way we hear these words, the *'ve* mistakenly becomes *of*.

presently

Presently can mean either "in a short while, soon" or "at present, currently, now"; as a result, its use can lead to ambiguity. Use the alternative terms (*soon, now,* etc.) and your meaning will be clear.

raise, rise

The verb *raise* is transitive, requiring an object: "I *raised* my hand; he *raises* horses." *Rise* is intransitive: "The temperature *rose* sharply; I *rise* each morning at dawn." If necessary, memorize their principal parts: *raise, raised, raised; rise, rose, risen.*

recommend

When this transitive verb appears in a clause with an indirect object, that object must be expressed as a prepositional phrase with *to* or *for*, and it must follow the direct object:

> *id:* She recommended <u>me</u> this restaurant.
>
> *id:* She recommended <u>to me</u> this restaurant.
>
> *revised:* She recommended this restaurant <u>to me</u>.

A number of other verbs fit the same idiomatic pattern as *recommend*. Among the most common are *admit, contribute, dedicate, demonstrate, describe, distribute, explain, introduce, mention, propose, reveal, speak, state,* and *suggest.* Note, however, that with several of these verbs, if the direct object is itself a noun clause, it usually follows the prepositional phrase:

> He admitted to me <u>that he had been lying</u>.

> She explained to me <u>what she intended to do</u>.

set, sit

Set (principal parts *set, set, set*) means "put, place, cause to sit"; it is transitive, requiring an object: "He *set* the glass on the counter." *Sit* (principal parts *sit, sat, sat*) means "rest, occupy a seat, assume a sitting position"; it is intransitive: "The glass *sits* on the counter." "May I *sit* in the easy chair?"—though it can be used transitively in expressions like "I sat myself down to listen" or "She sat him down at the desk." (See also **lie, lay.**)

simple, simplistic

Don't use *simplistic* when all you want is *simple. Simplistic* means "oversimplified, unrealistically simple":

> We admire the book for its <u>simple</u> explanations and straightforward advice.

> The author's assessment of the war's causes was narrow and <u>simplistic</u>.

Similarly, *fatalistic* does not mean the same as *fatal.*

14g

since

Since can refer both to time ("*Since* April we haven't had any rain") and to cause ("*Since* she wouldn't tell him, he had to figure it out for himself"). Therefore, don't use *since* in a sentence where it could refer either to time or to cause:

> **ambig:** Since you went away, I've been sad and lonely.

till, until, 'til

Till and *until* are both standard and have the same meaning. *Until* is somewhat more formal, and (like the two-syllable *although*) is usually preferable at the beginning of a sentence. The contraction *'til* is little used nowadays, except in informal contexts, such as personal emails or letters.

too

Used as an intensifier, *too* is sometimes illogical; if an intensifier is necessary in such sentences as these, use *very*:

> **ww:** I don't like my cocoa <u>too</u> hot.
> **revised:** I don't like my cocoa <u>very</u> hot.

> **ww:** She didn't care for the brown suit <u>too</u> much.
> **revised:** She didn't care for the brown suit <u>very</u> much.

But often you can omit the intensifier as unnecessary:

> She didn't care much for the brown suit.

14g

toward, towards

These are interchangeable, but in American (as opposed to British) English, the preposition *toward* is usually preferred to *towards,* just as the adverbs *afterward, forward* (meaning *frontward*), and *backward* are to their counterparts ending in *s.*

unique, absolute, necessary, essential, complete, perfect, fatal, equal, (im)possible, infinite, empty, full, straight, round, square, etc.

In writing, especially formal writing, treat these and other such adjectives as absolutes that cannot logically be compared or modified by such adverbs as *very* and *rather*. Since by definition something *unique* is the *only one of its kind* or *without equal*, clearly one thing cannot be "more unique" than another, or even "very unique"; in other words, *unique* is not a synonym for *unusual* or *rare*. Similarly with the others: one thing cannot be "more necessary" than another. Since *perfect* means "without flaw," there cannot be degrees of perfection.

usage, use, utilize, utilization

The noun *usage* is appropriate when you mean customary or habitual use, whether verbal or otherwise (e.g., "English usage"), or a particular verbal expression being characterized in a particular way ("an ironic usage," "an elegant usage"). Otherwise, the shorter noun *use* is preferable. As a verb, *use* should nearly always suffice; *utilize,* often pretentiously employed instead, should carry the specific meaning "put to use, make use of, turn to practical or profitable account." Similarly, the noun *use* will almost always be more appropriate than *utilization*. Phrases like *use of, the use of, by the use of,* and *through the use of* tend toward jargon and are almost always wordy.

14g

while

As a subordinating conjunction, *while* is best restricted to meanings having to do with time:

> While Vijay mowed the lawn, Honoree raked up the grass clippings.

When it means "although (though)" or "whereas," it can be imprecise, even ambiguous:

> While I agree with some of his reasons, I still think my proposal is better. (*Although* would be clearer.)

> While he polishes the furniture, she cooks the meals. (Fuzzy or ambiguous; *whereas* would make the meaning clear.)

PART IV
Essentials of Punctuation

INTRODUCTION

Good punctuation is essential to clear and effective writing. It helps writers clarify meaning and tone and, therefore, helps readers understand what writers communicate: try removing the punctuation marks from a piece of prose, and then see how difficult it is to read it. Punctuation points to meaning that in spoken language would be indicated by pauses, pitch, tone, and emphasis. In effect, punctuation helps readers *hear* a sentence the way a writer intends. Commas, semicolons, colons, and dashes help to clarify the internal structure of sentences; often the very meaning of a sentence depends on how it is punctuated.

The conventions of punctuation have come to be agreed upon by writers and readers of English for the purpose of clear and effective communication. Although good writers do sometimes stray from these conventions, they usually do so because they have a sufficient command of them to break a rule in order to achieve a desired effect.

Hyphens and *apostrophes* are dealt with in the discussion of mechanics and spelling in Part V: see #32k for discussion of hyphens, and see #32-l.8, #32m, and #32n for discussion of apostrophes.

15 The Comma ,

The **comma** indicates a slight pause, lightly separating elements within a sentence. It is the most neutral and the most used punctuation mark. Use commas to separate words, phrases, and clauses from each other when no heavier or more expressive mark is required or desired.

Main functions of commas

Basically, commas are used in three ways; if you know these conventions, you should have little trouble with commas:

1. Generally, use a comma between independent clauses joined by a coordinating conjunction (*and, but, or, nor, for, yet, so*; see #13b.1):

    > We went to the National Gallery, and then we walked to the Vietnam Memorial.

2. Generally, use commas to separate items in a series:

    > Robert Bateman, Emily Carr, and Mary Pratt are three Canadian painters.

    > Painting landscapes can be a relaxing, rewarding, enjoyable experience.

3. Generally, use commas to set off parenthetical elements, such as introductory words, phrases, and clauses; non-restrictive elements; or sentence interrupters:

    > Grasping the remote control firmly, she walked away.

    > Caffe latte, which has always been a popular drink in Europe, is now popular in North America.

    > There are, however, some exceptions.

Other conventional uses of the comma

1. Use a comma between elements of an emphatic contrast:

    > This is a practical lesson, not a theoretical one.

2. Use a comma to indicate a pause where a word has been acceptably omitted:

> Ron is a conservative; Syed, a liberal.

3. Use commas to set off a noun of address:

> Ava, please write a thank-you note to your grandparents.

4. Generally, use commas with a verb of speaking before or after a quotation:

> Then Dora remarked, "That book gave me nightmares."

> "It doesn't matter to me," said Felipe laughingly.

5. Use commas after the salutation of informal letters (*Dear Jackson,*) and after the sign-off of all letters (*Yours truly,*). In formal letters, a colon is conventional after the salutation.

6. Use commas with dates:

> She left on January 11, 2019, and was gone a month. (Note the comma *after* the year.)

When referring only to month and year, you may use a comma or not, but be consistent:

> The book was published in March, 2018, in Boston.

> It was published here in March 2018.

7. Use commas to set off geographical names and addresses:

> She left Topeka, Kansas, and moved to Columbus, Ohio, in hopes of finding a better-paying job. (Note the commas *after* the names of the states.)

> Their new address will be 1242 North High Street, Columbus, Ohio 43201.

15

The Comma with Coordinating Conjunctions

Generally, use a comma between independent clauses joined by one of the coordinating conjunctions (*and*, *but*, *for*, *nor*, *or*, *so*, and *yet*):

> The revision of the paper proved difficult, and she found herself working late into the night.

> It was a serious speech, but the audience loved it.

> Naieli could go into debt for the new car, or she could go on driving her old jalopy.

> Don knew he shouldn't do it, yet he couldn't stop himself.

In some cases, the clauses are short and the information in both necessary to form a complete idea, the comma or commas may be omitted:

> We studied all night so we could pass.

When the clauses are parallel in structure, the comma may often be omitted:

> Art is long and life is short.

When two clauses have the same subject, a comma is often unnecessary.

> It was windy and it was wet.

> The play was well produced and it impressed everyone who saw it.

When the subject is omitted from the second clause, a comma should not be used:

> It was windy and wet.

Independent clauses joined by *but* and *yet*, which explicitly mark a contrast, will almost always need a comma, even if they are short or parallel or have the same subject:

> It was windy, yet it was warm.

And when you join two clauses with the coordinating conjunction *for*, always put a comma in front of it to prevent its being misread as a preposition:

> Amanda was eager to leave early, for the restaurant was sure to be crowded.

The conjunction *so* almost always needs a comma.

15b The Comma with Items in a Series

1. Generally, use commas between words, phrases, or clauses in a series of three or more:

    > He sells books, magazines, candy, and life insurance.

    > She promised the voters to cut taxes, to limit government spending, and to improve transportation.

    > Carmen explained that first she had visited the art gallery, then she had walked in the park, and finally she had gone to a movie.

2. Different style sheets have different rules about using (or not using) the final comma in a series (known as the Oxford comma or the "serial comma") before the conjunction, but most instructors recommend or require that writers use it. This is because omitting this comma can be misleading. That final pause will give your sentences a better rhythm, and you will avoid the kind of possible confusion shown in the following examples:

    > I would like to thank my parents, Taylor Swift and Donald Glover. (Are your parents really Taylor Swift and Donald Glover? If they aren't, use a comma to separate them.)

    > The speech covered imposing tariffs, investing in roads, slowing down inflation and recruiting. (Did it really mention slowing down recruiting? No; recruiting is a topic covered in the speech.)

15b

3. Use commas between two or more adjectives preceding a noun if they are parallel, each modifying the noun itself; do not put commas between adjectives that are not parallel:

> He is an intelligent, efficient, ambitious officer.

> She is a tall young woman.

> She wore a new black felt hat, a long red coat, and a woolen scarf with red, white, and black stripes.

In the first sentence, each adjective modifies *officer*. In the second, *tall* modifies *young woman*; it is a *young woman* who is *tall*, not a *woman* who is *tall* and *young*. In the third, *new* modifies *black felt hat*, *black* modifies *felt hat*, and *long* modifies *red coat*; *red*, *white*, and *black* all separately modify *stripes*.

But it isn't always easy to tell whether or not such adjectives are parallel. It often helps to think of each comma as substituting for *and*: try putting *and* between the adjectives. If *and* sounds logical there, the adjectives are probably parallel and should be separated by a comma; if *and* doesn't seem to work, a comma won't either. Another test is to change the order of the adjectives. If it sounds odd to say *a felt black hat* instead of *a black felt hat*, then the adjectives probably aren't parallel. A final aid to remember: usually no comma is needed after a number (*three blind mice*) or after common adjectives for size or age (*tall young woman*; *long red coat*; *old brick house*).

15b

15c The Comma with an Introductory Word, Phrase, or Subordinate Clause

Set off an introductory word or short phrase if you want a distinct pause for emphasis or qualification or to prevent misreading:

> Generally, follow my advice about punctuation.

> Usually, immature people are difficult to work with.

Conjunctive adverbs are frequently set off by commas to prevent potential misreadings. In particular, the word *however* is usually set off by a comma when used in this way.

> However, we did not expect her to arrive on a unicycle.

Set off a long introductory adverbial phrase with a comma:

> After many years as leader of the union, Jean retired gracefully.

> To get the best results from your ice cream maker, you must follow the instruction manual carefully.

Also use a comma between an introductory subordinate clause and an independent (main) clause:

> After I had selected all the items I wanted, I discovered that I had left my wallet at home.

> When the party was over, I went straight home.

However, when the introductory clause is short and when there would be no pause if the sentence were spoken aloud, you may omit the comma. But if omitting the comma could cause misreading, retain it:

> Whenever I wanted, someone would bring me something to eat.

15c

> After the sun had set, high above the mountains came the fighter jets.

Whenever you're not sure the meaning will be clear without it, use a comma.

Always set off an introductory participle or participial phrase with a comma:

> Puzzled, Petra turned back to the beginning of the chapter.

> Finding organic chemistry unexpectedly difficult, Kevin sought extra help.

Always set off introductory absolute phrases with commas:

> The doors locked and bolted, they went to bed feeling secure.

Note: Absolute phrases need to be set off with commas no matter where they appear in a sentence:

> Faris went on stage, head held high, a grin spreading across his face.

Also, participles and participial phrases that appear at the end of a sentence almost always need to be set off. Read the sentence aloud; if you feel a distinct pause, use a comma:

> Kevin sought extra help, finding organic chemistry unexpectedly difficult.

Occasionally such a sentence will flow clearly and smoothly without a comma, especially if the modifier is essential to the meaning:

> Shirin left the room feeling victorious.

> She sat there looking puzzled.

15d The Comma with Nonrestrictive Elements

Words, phrases, and clauses are nonrestrictive (or nonessential) when they are not essential to the principal meaning of a sentence. A nonrestrictive element should be set off from the rest of the sentence, usually with commas, though dashes and parentheses can also be used. A restrictive (or essential) modifier is essential to the meaning and should not be set off:

> *restrictive:* Anyone wanting a refund should see the manager.

> *nonrestrictive:* Alex, wanting a refund, asked to see the manager.

The participial phrase explains why Alex asked to see the manager, but the sentence is clear without it: "Alex asked to see the manager"; the phrase *wanting a refund* is therefore not essential and is set off with commas. But without the phrase the first sentence wouldn't make sense: "Anyone should see the manager"; the phrase *wanting a refund* is essential and is not set off. The comma-or-no-comma question most often arises with *relative clauses* (see #3f and #7a.4); *appositives*, though usually nonrestrictive, can also be restrictive, and some other elements can also be either restrictive or nonrestrictive.

1. Restrictive and nonrestrictive relative clauses

Always set off a nonrestrictive relative clause; do not set off restrictive relative clauses:

> She is a woman *who likes to travel.* (The relative clause is essential; therefore, use no commas.)

> Rosario, *who likes to travel,* is going to Greece this summer. (The relative clause is not essential; therefore, add commas.)

Consider the following pair of sentences:

> *incorrect:* Students, who are hard-working, should expect much from their education.

> *correct:* Students who are hard-working should expect much from their education.

Set off as nonrestrictive, the relative clause applies to all students, which makes the sentence untrue. Left unpunctuated, the relative clause is restrictive, making the sentence correctly apply only to students who are in fact hard-working.

15d

Note: To determine whether a clause is restrictive or nonrestrictive, try the following test: If you can use the relative pronoun *that*, you know the clause is restrictive; *that* cannot begin a nonrestrictive clause:

> The book <u>that</u> I wanted to read was not in the library.

Further, if the pronoun can be omitted altogether, the clause is restrictive, as with *that* in the preceding example and *whom* in the following:

> The person [whom] I most admire is the one who works hard and plays hard.

2. Restrictive and nonrestrictive appositives

Always set off a nonrestrictive appositive:

> Jan, <u>our youngest daughter</u>, keeps the lawn mowed all summer.

> *King Lear* is a noble work of literature, <u>one that will live in human minds for all time</u>.

> Virginia is going to bring her sister, <u>Vanessa</u>.

In the last example, the comma indicates that Virginia has only the one sister. Left unpunctuated, the appositive would be restrictive, meaning that Virginia has more than one sister and that the particular one she is going to bring is the one named Vanessa.

15e The Comma with Sentence Interrupters

Sentence interrupters are parenthetical elements—words, phrases, or clauses—that interrupt the syntax of a sentence. Set off light, ordinary interrupters with a pair of commas:

> This document, <u>the lawyer says</u>, will complete the contract. (explanatory clause)

> Thank you, <u>David</u>, for this much needed advice and the sundae. (noun of address)

16 The Semicolon ;

The **semicolon** is a heavy separator, often almost equivalent to a period or full stop. It indicates a longer pause than a comma does. Basically, semicolons have two functions:

1. To both connect and separate closely related independent clauses that are not joined by one of the coordinating conjunctions (see #13b.1):

> So-called spring water tastes like plastic to me; tap water does not.

> The lab had 20 new computers; however, there were 25 students in the class.

2. Use a semicolon instead of a comma if a comma would not be heavy enough, for example, if the clauses or the elements in a series have internal commas of their own:

> The invitees included Aria, who liked to tell jokes; Karim, who liked to hear jokes; and Austin, who didn't like jokes at all.

> The drawer was full of writing supplies, including blue, black, and red pens; pencils of varying lengths, and a colorful array of highlighters.

16a The Semicolon with Independent Clauses

To avoid a *comma splice* (see #25a), generally use a semicolon between independent clauses that are not joined with one of the coordinating conjunctions (*and*, *but*, *or*, *nor*, *for*, *yet*, *so*):

> The actual prize is not important; it is the honor connected with it that matters.

> Leanna was exhausted and obviously not going to win; nevertheless, she persevered and finished the race.

16b The Semicolon with Conjunctive Adverbs and Transitions

Be sure to use a semicolon and not just a comma between independent clauses that you join with a conjunctive adverb, including *however* and *therefore*. Here is a list of most of the common ones:

accordingly	finally	likewise	similarly
afterward	further	meanwhile	still
also	furthermore	moreover	subsequently
anyway	hence	namely	then
besides	however	nevertheless	thereafter
certainly	indeed	next	therefore
consequently	instead	nonetheless	thus
conversely	later	otherwise	undoubtedly

The same practice applies to common transitional phrases such as these:

after this	if not	in the meantime
as a result	in addition	on the contrary
for example	in fact	on the other hand
for this reason	in short	that is

 The Semicolon with Items in a Series

If the phrases or clauses in a series are unusually long or contain other internal punctuation, you may separate them with semicolons rather than commas:

> How wonderful it is to awaken in the morning when the birds are clamoring in the trees; to see the bright light of a summer morning streaming into the room; to realize, with a sudden flash of joy, that it is Sunday and that this perfect morning is completely yours; and then to lounge in a deckchair without a thought of tomorrow.

> Topeka, Kansas; Harrisburg, Pennsylvania; and Juno, Alaska, are all capital cities.

17 The Colon :

16b

Colons are commonly used to introduce lists, examples, and long or formal quotations, but their possibilities in more everyday sentences are often overlooked. A colon is useful because it looks forward or anticipates: it gives readers a push toward the next part of the sentence. In the preceding sentence, for example, the colon sets up a sense of expectation about what is coming. It points out, even emphasizes, the relation between the two parts of the sentence—that is, the second part clarifies what the first part says. A semicolon in the same spot would bring readers to an abrupt halt, leaving it up to them to make the necessary connection between the two parts.

> Vita's garden contained only white flowers: roses, primulas, and primroses.

Let me add just this: anyone who expects to lose weight must be prepared to exercise.

It was an unexpectedly lovely time of year: trees were in blossom, garden flowers bloomed all around, the sky was clear and bright, and the temperature was just right.

Don't get carried away and overuse the colon: its effectiveness would wear off if it appeared more than once or twice a page.

Note: One space after a colon is the norm. And only one space follows colons setting off subtitles or in footnotes or bibliographical entries.

17a The Colon with Items in a Series

When used between items in a series, colons can add emphasis because they are unusual, but mainly their anticipatory nature produces a cumulative effect suitable when successive items in a series build to a climax:

She held on: she persevered: she fought back: and eventually she won out, regardless of the punishing obstacles.

It blew: it rained: it hailed: it sleeted: it even snowed——it was a most unusual June.

17b

(Note how the dash in the last example prepares for the final clause.)

17b The Colon Between a Title and a Subtitle

Use a colon between the title and the subtitle of a book, an article, an essay, or any other document:

Home Words: Discourses of Children's Literature (a book)

"A Residential School Memoir: Basil Johnston's *Indian School Days*" (an article)

"The State in Question: Hobbes, Rousseau, and Hegel" (an essay)

161

The Colon in the Salutation of a Business Letter

In a formal business letter, the salutation line ends with a colon:

> Dear Professor Chow:

> Dear Mayor Black:

17d The Colon Introducing a Block Quotation

Colons are conventionally used to introduce "block" quotations:

> Jane Austen begins her novel *Pride and Prejudice* with the observation:
>
> > It is a truth universally acknowledged, that a single man in possession of a good fortune must be in want of a wife. However little known the feelings or views of such a man may be on his first entering a neighbourhood, this truth is so well fixed in the minds of the surrounding families, that he is considered as the rightful property of some one or other of their daughters.

18 The Dash —

The **dash** is a popular punctuation mark, especially in email and other more informal communications. Use a dash only when you have a definite reason for doing so. Like the colon, the dash sets up expectations in a reader's mind. But whereas the colon sets up an expectation that what follows will somehow explain, summarize, define, or otherwise comment on what has gone before, a dash suggests that what follows will be somehow surprising, involving some sort of twist, or at least a contrary idea. Consider the following sentence:

> The teacher praised my wit, my intelligence, my organization, and my research——and penalized the paper for its poor spelling and punctuation.

Here, the dash adds to the punch of what follows it. A comma there would deprive the sentence of much of its force; it would even sound odd, since the resulting matter-of-fact tone would not be in harmony with what the sentence was saying.

The dash is also handy in some long and involved sentences, for example after a long series before a summarizing clause:

> Our longing for the past, our hopes for the future, and our neglect of the present moment——all these and more go to shape our everyday lives, often in ways unseen or little understood.

Even here, the emphatic quality of the dash serves the meaning, though its principal function is to mark the abrupt break.

As with colons, don't overuse dashes. They are even stronger marks, but they lose effectiveness if used often.

18a The Dash with Items in a Series

You can emphasize items in a series by putting dashes between them—but don't do it often. The sharpness of the breaks greatly heightens the effect of a series:

> Rising taxes——rising insurance rates——rising gas costs——skyrocketing food prices: it is becoming more and more difficult to live decently and still keep within a budget.

Dashes can also be effective in a quieter context:

> Upon rounding the bend, we were confronted with a breathtaking panorama of lush valleys with meandering streams——flower-covered slopes——great rocks and trees——and, overtopping all, the mighty peaks with their hoods of snow.

18b The Dash with Sentence Interrupters

Use a pair of dashes to set off abrupt interrupters or other interrupters that you wish to emphasize. An interrupter that sharply breaks the syntax of a sentence will often be emphatic for that very reason, and dashes will be appropriate to set it off:

> The increase in enrollment——over 50 percent——demonstrates the success of our program.

> He told me——believe this or not!——that he would never visit the city again.

Wherever you want emphasis or a different tone, you can use dashes where commas would ordinarily serve:

> The modern age——as we all know——is a noisy age.

Dashes are also useful to set off an interrupter consisting of a series with its own internal commas; set off with commas, such a structure can be confusing:

> *confusing:* Sentence interrupters are parenthetical elements, words, phrases, or clauses, that interrupt the syntax of a sentence.

> *clear:* Sentence interrupters are parenthetical elements——words, phrases, or clauses——that interrupt the syntax of a sentence.

18b

19 Parentheses ( )

Use **parentheses** to set off abrupt interrupters or other interrupters that you wish to de-emphasize; often interrupters that could be emphatic can be played down to emphasize the other parts of a sentence:

> The stockholders who voted for him (quite a sizable group) were obviously dissatisfied with our recent conduct of the business.

> Some extreme sports (hang-gliding for example) involve unusually high insurance claims.

By de-emphasizing something striking, parentheses can also achieve an effect similar to that of dashes, though by an ironic tone rather than an insistent one.

Parentheses have three principal functions in non-technical writing: (1) to set off certain kinds of interrupters (see the preceding paragraph), (2) to enclose cross-referenced information within a sentence (as we do throughout this book), and (3) to enclose numerals or letters setting up a list or series, as we do in this sentence. Note that if a complete sentence is enclosed in parentheses within another sentence (here is an example of such an insertion), it needs neither an opening capital letter nor a closing period. Note also that if a comma or other mark is called for by the sentence (as in the preceding sentence, and in this one), it comes *after* the closing parenthesis, not before the opening one. Exclamation points and question marks go inside the closing parenthesis only if they are a part of what is enclosed. (When an entire sentence or more is enclosed, the terminal mark of course comes inside the closing parenthesis—as does this period.)

20 Quotation Marks " "

There are two kinds of quotation:

1. Dialogue or direct speech, as you might find in a story, novel, or essay

2. Verbatim quotation from a published work or other source, as in a research paper

For the use of **quotation marks** around titles of shorter works, see #29a and c.

Quotation Marks with Direct Speech

Enclose all direct speech in quotation marks:

> I remember hearing my mother say to my absentminded father, "Henry, why is the newspaper in the fridge?"

In written dialogue, it is conventional to begin a new paragraph each time the speaker changes:

> "Henry," she said, a note of exasperation in her voice, "why is the newspaper in the fridge?"

> "Oh, yes," he replied. "The fish is wrapped in it."
> She examined it. "Well, there may have been a fish in it once, but there is no fish in it now."

Even when passages of direct speech are incomplete, the part that is verbatim should be enclosed in quotation marks:

> After only two weeks, he said he was "fed up" and that he was "going to look for a more interesting job."

20b Quotation Marks with Direct Quotation from a Source

Enclose in quotation marks any direct quotation from another source that you run into your own text:

> According to Anthony Powell, "Books do furnish a room."

1. Prose

Prose quotations of four or fewer lines are normally run into the text and enclosed in quotation marks. However, quotations of more than four lines should be treated as block quotations:

> When asked why she writes about food, M.F.K. Fisher answers directly:
>
> > It seems to me that our three basic needs, for food and security and love, are so mixed and mingled and entwined that we cannot straightly think of one without the others. So it happens that when I write of hunger, I am really writing about love and the hunger for it, and warmth and the love of it and the hunger for it . . . and then the warmth and richness and fine reality of hunger satisfied . . . and it is all one.

Indent a block quotation, but do not place quotation marks around it. However, do reproduce any quotation marks that appear within the original.

If you're quoting only a single paragraph or part of a paragraph, do not include the paragraph indentation. If you are quoting a passage that is longer than one paragraph, include the indentations for the second and subsequent paragraphs.

Note: When you write an essay for class, you should indent and double space all block quotations.

2. Poetry

Similarly, set off quotations of more than three lines of poetry as a block quotation. A quotation of one, two, or three lines of poetry may also be set off as a block quotation if you want to give it special emphasis.

However, otherwise, run a quotation of three or fewer lines into your text. When you run in more than one line of poetry, indicate each line break with a slash, with a space on each side:

> Dante's spiritual journey begins in the woods: "Midway this way of life, we're bound upon / I woke to find myself in a dark wood / Where the right road was wholly lost and gone."

20c Single Quotation Marks for a Quotation Within a Quotation ' '

Put single quotation marks around a quotation that occurs within another quotation; this is the only standard use for single quotation marks:

> In Joseph Conrad's *Heart of Darkness*, after a leisurely setting of the scene by the unnamed narrator, the drama begins when the character who is to be the principal narrator first speaks: "'And this also,' said Marlow suddenly, 'has been one of the dark places of the earth.'"

20d Quotation Marks Around Words Used in a Special Sense

Put quotation marks around words used in a special sense or words for which you wish to indicate some qualification:

> What she calls a "ramble," I would call an exhausting hike.

Note: Some writers put quotation marks around words referred to as words, but it is often better practice to italicize them:

> The word *toboggan* comes from a Mi'kmaq word for sled.

Don't put quotation marks around slang terms, clichés, or similar words. If a word or phrase is so unfamiliar, informal, or overused that you have to apologize for it, you shouldn't be using it in formal writing. And avoid using quotation marks for emphasis; this is not correct Standard English usage.

20e Other Marks with Quotation Marks

As a rule, periods and commas go inside closing quotation marks; semicolons and colons go outside them:

> "Knowing how to write well," he said, "can be a source of great pleasure"; and then he added that it had "one other important quality": he identified it simply as "hard work."

Question marks and exclamation points can go either outside or inside, depending on whether they apply to the quotation or to the whole sentence:

> "What smells so good?" she asked.

> Who said, "Change is inevitable except from a vending machine"?

20d 20f Ellipses for Omissions . . .

If when quoting from a written source you omit one or more words from the middle of the passage you are quoting, indicate the omission with the three *spaced* periods of an **ellipsis**. For example, if you wanted to quote only part of the passage from Austen quoted at length earlier (#17d), you could format it like this:

> As Jane Austen wryly observes, "a single man in possession of a . . . fortune must be in want of a wife."

Note that you need not indicate an ellipsis at the beginning of an excerpted quotation.

When the ellipsis is preceded by a complete sentence, include the period (or other end punctuation) of the original before the ellipsis points. Similarly, if when you omit something from the end of a sentence what remains is grammatically complete, a period (or question mark or exclamation point, if appropriate) goes before the ellipsis. In either case, the end punctuation marking the end of the sentence is closed up:

> As Jane Austen wryly observes, "a single man in possession of a good fortune must be in want of a wife. . . . [T]his truth is so well fixed in the minds of the surrounding families, that he is considered as the rightful property of some one or other. . . ."

Three periods can also indicate the omission of one or more entire sentences, or even whole paragraphs. Again, if the sentence preceding the omitted material is grammatically complete, it should end with a period preceding the ellipsis.

An ellipsis should also be used to indicate that material from a quoted line of poetry has been omitted. When quoting four or more lines of poetry, use a row of spaced dots to indicate that one or more entire lines have been omitted:

> E.J. Pratt's epic "Towards the Last Spike" begins:
> It was the same world then as now——the same,
> Except for little differences of speed
> And power, and means to treat myopia.
>
> . . . .
> The same, but for new particles of speech. . . .

Note: Don't omit material from a quotation in such a way that you distort what the author is saying or destroy the integrity of the syntax. Similarly, don't quote unfairly "out of context"; for example, if an author qualifies a statement in some way, don't quote the statement as if it were unqualified.

21 Brackets [ ]

Brackets are used primarily to enclose something inserted in a direct quotation:

> She noted that "he [the lead actor] was difficult to work with."

And if you have to put parentheses inside parentheses—as in a footnote or a bibliographical entry—change the inner ones to brackets.

Keep such changes to a minimum, but enclose in square brackets any editorial addition or change you find it necessary to make within a quotation—for example, a clarifying fact or a change in tense to make the quoted material fit the syntax of your sentence:

> The author states that "the following year [2017] marked a turning point in [his] life."

> One of my friends wrote me that her "feelings about the subject [were] similar to" mine.

If you want to indicate that an error in the quotation occurs in the original, use the word *sic* (Latin for *thus*) italicized and in brackets:

> One of my friends wrote me: "My feelings about the subject are similiar [*sic*] to yours."

22 The Period .

Use a **period** to mark the end of statements and neutral commands:

> Most Americans own a smartphone.

> Don't let yourself be fooled by cheap imitations.

Use a period after most abbreviations:

Esq.	Mr.	Ms.	Dr.	Jr.
Ph.D.	B.A.	St.	Mt.	etc.

Usage of periods with place names varies by style sheet. USA and U.S.A. are both correct in different contexts. Some place names, such as L.A. for Los Angeles and D.C. for District of Columbia, are always abbreviated using periods. However, standard postal two-letter state or country abbreviations never use periods:

KY	CA	NZ	NY	UK

Periods are not used after measurements and other symbols (unless they occur at the end of a sentence):

mi	in	lb	mc^2	oz
kw	F	Hz	Au	Zr

Periods are often omitted with initials, especially of groups or organizations, and especially if the initials are acronyms—that is, words or names made up of initials (AIDS, NATO):

UN	UNICEF	WHO	DOE	USMC
NPR	TV	APA	MLA	CEO

When in doubt, consult a good dictionary.

Note: A period after an abbreviation at the end of a sentence also serves as the sentence's period.

23 The Question Mark ?

Use a **question mark** at the end of direct questions:

> When will the lease expire?

Do not use a question mark at the end of an indirect question:

> He asked when the lease would expire.

Note that a question mark is necessary after questions that aren't phrased in the usual interrogative way (as might occur if you were writing dialogue):

> You're leaving so early? (i.e., "Are you leaving so early?")

> You want him to accompany you? (i.e., "Do you want him to accompany you?")

A question appearing as a sentence interrupter still needs a question mark at its end:

> I went back to the beginning——what else could I do?—— and tried to get it right the second time.

> The man in the scuba outfit (what was his name again?) took a rear seat.

Since such interrupters are necessarily abrupt, use dashes or parentheses to set them off.

24 The Exclamation Point !

Use an **exclamation point** after an emphatic statement or after an expression of emphatic surprise or strong emotion:

> He came in first, yet it was only his second time in professional competition!

> Not again!

Occasionally an exclamation point may be doubled or tripled for emphasis. It may even follow a question mark, to emphasize the writer's or speaker's disbelief:

> She said what?!

> You bought what?! A giraffe?! What were you thinking?!

This device, which is called an interrobang, should not be used in formal and academic writing.

25 Avoiding Common Errors in Punctuation

25a Unwanted Comma Splice

Using only a comma between independent clauses not joined with a coordinating conjunction results in a **comma splice (cs)**:

> *cs:* The actual prize is not important, it is the honor connected with it that matters.

> *corrected:* The actual prize is not important; it is the honor connected with it that matters.

> *cs:* He desperately wanted to eat, nevertheless, he was too weak to get out of bed.

corrected: He desperately wanted to eat; nevertheless, he
was too weak to get out of bed.

As shown in these examples, the easiest way to fix a comma splice is to replace the comma with a semicolon (see #16a). See also #5b.

25b Unwanted Comma Between Subject and Verb

Generally, do not put a comma between a subject and its verb unless some intervening element calls for punctuation:

draft: His enthusiasm for the project and his desire to
be of help, led him to add his name to the list
of volunteers.

Don't be misled by the length of a compound subject. The comma after *help* in the last example is just as wrong, as the comma in the following sentence:

draft: Kiera, addressed the class.

But if some intervening element, for example an appositive or a participial phrase, requires setting off, use a *pair* of marks:

revision: His enthusiasm for the project and his desire to
be of help, both strongly felt, led him to add his
name to the list of volunteers.

revision: Kiera——the exchange student——addressed the
class.

25c Unwanted Comma Between Verb and Object or Complement

Although in Jane Austen's time it was conventional to place a comma before a clause beginning with *that*, today this practice is considered an error. Do not put a comma between a verb and its object or complement unless some intervening element calls for punctuation. Especially, don't mistakenly assume that a clause opening with *that* needs a comma before it:

> *draft:* Hafiz realized, that he could no longer keep his eyes open.

The noun clause beginning with *that* is the direct object of the verb *realized* and should not be separated from it. Only if an interrupter requires setting off should there be any punctuation:

> *revision:* Hafiz realized, moreover, that he could no longer keep his eyes open.

> *revision:* Hafiz realized, as he tried once again to read the paragraph, that he could no longer keep his eyes open.

25d Unwanted Comma After Last Adjective of a Series

Do not put a comma between the last adjective of a series and the noun it modifies:

> *draft:* How could anyone fail to be impressed by such an intelligent, outspoken, resourceful, fellow as Jonathan is?

The comma after *resourceful* is incorrect; to correct the sentence, the writer should remove it.

25e Unwanted Comma Between Coordinated Words and Phrases

Generally, don't put a comma between words and phrases joined by a coordinating conjunction; use a comma only when the coordinate elements are clauses (see #15a):

> *draft:* The dog and cat circled each other warily, and then went off in opposite directions.

> *draft:* She was not only intelligent, but also very kind.

Sometimes a writer uses such a comma for a mild emphasis, but if you want an emphatic pause a dash will probably work better:

revision: The dog and cat circled each other warily——and then went off in opposite directions.

Or the sentence can be slightly revised in order to gain the emphasis:

revision: She was not only intelligent; she was also very kind.

 Commas with Emphatic Repetition

If the two elements joined by a conjunction constitute an emphatic repetition, a comma is sometimes optional:

I wanted not only to win, but to win overwhelmingly.

This sentence would be equally correct and effective without the comma. But in the following sentence the comma is necessary:

It was an object of beauty, and of beauty most spectacular.

 Unwanted Comma with Short Introductory or Parenthetical Element

Generally, do not set off introductory elements or interrupters that are very short, not really parenthetical, or so slightly parenthetical that you feel no pause when reading them:

draft: Perhaps, she was trying to tell us something.

draft: But, it was not a case of mistaken identity.

draft: We asked if we could try it out, for a week, to see if we really liked it.

When the pause is strong, however, be sure to set it off:

It was only then, after the very formal dinner, that we were all able to relax.

Often such commas are optional, depending on the pattern of intonation the writer wants:

In Canada(,) the change of the seasons is sharply evident.

Last year(,) we went to Quebec City.

As she walked(,) she thought of her childhood in Cabbagetown.

Sometimes such a comma is necessary to prevent misreading:

> *incorrect:* After eating the cat Irene gave me jumped out the window.

> *revised:* After eating, the cat Irene gave me jumped out the window.

See also #15c.

25h Unwanted Comma with Restrictive Appositive

Don't incorrectly set off proper nouns and titles of literary works as nonrestrictive appositives (see #15d.2). For instance, it's "Dickens's novel *Great Expectations*," not "Dickens's novel, *Great Expectations*." Dickens, after all, wrote more than one novel.

> *incorrect:* In her poem, "Daddy," Sylvia Plath explores her complicated relationship with her father.

> *incorrect:* The home port of the Canadian Coast Guard icebreaker, the *Terry Fox*, is St. John's, Newfoundland.

25g

The punctuation makes it sound as though Plath wrote only this one poem and that the *Terry Fox* is the only icebreaker in the Canadian Coast Guard's fleet. The titles are restrictive: if they were removed, the sentences would not be clear. If the context is clear, the explanatory words often aren't needed at all:

> In "Daddy" Plath explores . . .

> The home port of the *Terry Fox* is . . .

The urge to punctuate before titles of literary works sometimes leads to the error of putting a comma between a possessive and the title.

> *incorrect:* I remember enjoying Adrienne Rich's, "Diving into the Wreck."

Unwanted Comma with Indirect Quotation

Do not set off indirect quotations as if they were direct quotations:

> *incorrect:* The author says, that civilization as we have come to know it is in jeopardy.

In an indirect quotation, what was said is being reported, not quoted. If the author is quoted directly, a comma is correct:

> If you ask the author she's sure to say, "Civilization as we have come to know it is in jeopardy."

See also #20a.

 ## Unwanted Question Mark After Indirect Question

Don't put a question mark at the end of indirect questions—questions that are only being reported, not asked directly:

> *incorrect:* I asked what we were doing here?

> *incorrect:* What he asked himself then was how he was going to explain it to the shareholders?

25k

 ## Unwanted Semicolon with Subordinate Element

Do not put a semicolon in front of a mere phrase or subordinate clause. Use a semicolon only where you could put a period instead:

> *incorrect:* They canceled the meeting; being disappointed at the low turnout.

> *incorrect:* Only about a dozen people showed up; partly because there had been too little publicity and no free muffins.

Those semicolons should be commas. Similarly, don't put a semicolon between a subordinate clause and an independent clause:

incorrect: When they got home, tired and with their eardrums ringing; Sheila said she was never going to another noisy show again.

revised: When they got home, tired and with their eardrums ringing, Sheila said she was never going to another noisy show again.

25-l Unwanted Colon After Incomplete Construction

Do not use a colon after an incomplete construction; a colon is appropriate only after an independent clause:

incorrect: She preferred comfort foods such as: potatoes, bread, and pasta.

The prepositional *such as* needs an object to be complete. Had the phrase been extended to "She preferred such foods as these" or ". . . as the following," it would have been complete, an independent clause, and a colon would have been correct.

revised: She preferred comfort foods such as the following: potatoes, bread, and pasta.

25k

25m Unwanted Double Punctuation: Comma or Semicolon with a Dash

Avoid putting a comma or a semicolon together with a dash. Use whichever mark is appropriate.

25n Run-on (Fused) Sentences

Failure to put any punctuation between independent clauses where there is also no coordinating conjunction results in a **run-on** or **fused sentence**:

> *run-on:* Philosophers' views did not always meet with the approval of the authorities therefore there was constant conflict between writers and the church or state.

A semicolon after *authorities* corrects this serious error. See #5c.

> *revised:* Philosophers' views did not always meet with the approval of the authorities; therefore, there was constant conflict between writers and the church or state.

PART V
Essentials of Mechanics and Spelling

CONTENTS

INTRODUCTION

Part V offers some practical advice on how to follow standard conventions of mechanics and spelling. By following these conventions, you will add consistency, clarity, and a sense of professionalism to your writing. If you have trouble with spelling, you will find the advice on spelling rules—in section #32—particularly valuable.

26 Formatting an Essay

26a Format

Unless directed otherwise, follow these conventions when you are preparing an essay for submission:

1. Use a plain, readable typeface (12-point Times New Roman or 10-point Arial).

2. Double-space your essay throughout and leave margins of about 1 inch on all four sides of the page. Justify the text flush left with a ragged (i.e., unjustified) right-hand margin.

3. Include your last name and a page number in the top right-hand corner of each page (except for the title page, if you use one). Most word-processing software, such as Google Docs or Microsoft Word, will enable you to generate these headers automatically.

4. On the first page of a long essay, begin about 1 inch from the top, at the left margin, and on separate double-spaced lines put your name, your instructor's name, the course number, and the date of submission; then using the same spacing as between all previous lines, put the title, centered. In some cases, this information will appear on a title page. If you are using a separate title page, center the title about 1 inch from the top of the first page following the title page.

5. Set the title in standard font size and in upper- and lowercase roman letters, making sure to capitalize the title correctly (see #28k). Do not put the whole title in capital letters or in boldface type, and do not underline it or put a period after it. Do not put your title in quotation marks (unless part of it is in fact a quotation); if it includes the title of a poem, story, book, etc., or a ship's name, use italics or quotation marks appropriately (see #29). Do not use the title of a published work by itself as your own title. Here are two examples of effective titles:

> Of Pigoons and Wolvogs: Wildlife in Margaret Atwood's
> *Oryx and Crake*
>
> The Structure of "Just Walk on By"

6. Indent the first line of each paragraph one inch (approximately five spaces). Do not leave extra space between paragraphs. Also indent long block quotations one inch. Be sure to double-space your entire essay, including block quotations, and make sure there is the same spacing before, within, and after a block quotation.

7. Leave only one space after any end punctuation. Use two hyphens, with no space before or after either one, to make a dash; most word-processing software will automatically convert two hyphens to a dash.

8. Never begin a line with a comma, semicolon, period, question mark, exclamation point, or hyphen. On rare occasions, a dash or the dots of an ellipsis may have to come at the beginning of a line, but if possible, place them at the end of the preceding line.

9. Print your document on plain white recycled paper of good quality, 8.5 by 11 inches in size. Use only one side of each page. Make sure there is plenty of ink or toner in your printer's cartridge before you print your essay.

10. If after proofreading your printed essay you decide that you have to make additional changes, make the changes and reprint the page or pages you have revised.

11. Staple the pages of your essay together. Unless requested by your instructor, do not submit your essay in a folder or electronically.

If you are preparing a handwritten document, as may be the case for an in-class essay or examination, use a format similar to what you would create using software. Write on every other line, using blue or black ink, and write as legibly as possible. Use lined paper with clean edges. To change or delete a word or short phrase if you are using a pen, draw a single horizontal line through it and write the new word or phrase, if any, above it. If you wish to insert a word or short phrase, place a caret (^) below the line at the point of insertion and write the addition above the line.

26a

If you wish to start a new paragraph where you haven't indented, put the symbol ¶ in the left margin and insert a caret where you want the paragraph to begin.

26b Syllables and Word Division

Generally, do not divide words at the end of a line. One circumstance in which you may need to insert a word break is in a reference to an electronic source identified by its URL (uniform resource locator). Often, the best place to break a URL is immediately after a punctuation mark. Introducing a hyphen or other punctuation into a URL is not recommended, for it will introduce ambiguity and make the website difficult for your reader to locate and access:

> To learn more about NBC's *This Is Us*, visit the show's main website (www.nbc.com/this-is-us).

On the *rare* occasions when you need to divide a word at the end of a line, either use the automatic word-break function in your word-processing software or break the words manually. To break a word manually, insert a hyphen between two of its syllables. (Check a good dictionary if you are uncertain of a word's syllable divisions.) Note that the hyphen should appear at the end of the line, after the first part of the word, and the next line should begin with the second part of the word. Never begin a new line with a hyphen.

27 Abbreviations

Abbreviations are expected in technical and scientific writing, legal writing, business writing, memos, reports, reference works, bibliographies and works cited lists, footnotes, tables, and charts, and sometimes in journalism. The following relatively few kinds are in common use.

27a Titles Before Proper Names

The following abbreviations can be used with or without initials or given names:

Mr.   (Mr. Eng; Mr. Marc Ramsay)

Mrs.	(Mrs. L.W. Smith; Mrs. Tazim Khan)
Ms.	(Ms. Joubert; Ms. Lakhiri)
Dr.	(Dr. Paula Yang; Dr. P. Francis Jackson)
St.	(St. John; St. Beatrice)

27b Titles and Degrees After Proper Names

David Adams, M.D. (*but not* Dr. David Adams, M.D.)

Claire T. McFadden, D.D.S.

Martin Luther King, Jr.

Academic degrees not following a name may also be abbreviated:

Amir is working on his M.A. thesis.

27c Standard Words Used with Dates and Numerals

720 B.C.E. (*or* 720 B.C., *or* 720 B.P.)

231 C.E. (*or* A.D. 231), the second century C.E. (*or* the second century A.D.)

7 a.m. (*or* 7 A.M.), 8:30 p.m. (*or* 8:30 P.M.)

no. 17

27d Agencies and Organizations Known by Their Initials (see also #22)

Capitalize names of agencies and organizations commonly known by their initials:

UNICEF   MLA   CBS   NAFTA   NATO   WHO

27e

27e Scientific and Technical Terms Known by Their Initials (see also #22)

Some scientific, technical, or other terms (usually of considerable length) are commonly known by their initials:

LED	URL	SMO	DNA	FM
ISBN	HTML	CFO	IRS	IEP

27f Latin Expressions Commonly Used in English

i.e. (that is)   etc. (and so forth)

e.g. (for example)   vs. (versus)

cf. (compare)   et al. (and others)

In formal writing, it is better to spell out the English equivalent.

Note: If you use *e.g.*, use it only to introduce the example or list of examples; following the example or list, write out *for example*:

Deciduous trees—e.g., oaks, maples, and birches—lose their leaves in the fall.

Deciduous trees—oaks, maples, and birches, for example—lose their leaves in the fall.

If you introduce a list with *e.g.* or *for example* or even *such as*, it is illogical to follow it with *etc.* or *and so forth*.

27g Terms in Official Titles

Capitalize abbreviated terms used in official titles being copied exactly:

Johnson Bros., Ltd.   Kansas City Life Insurance Co.

Smith & Sons, Inc.   Chrysler LLC

28 Capitalization

Generally, capitalize proper nouns, abbreviations of proper nouns, and words derived from proper nouns.

28a Names and Nicknames

Capitalize names and nicknames of real and fictional people and individual animals:

David Suzuki	Serena Williams	Sting
Harry Potter	Sherlock Holmes	Cinderella
Big Bird	King Kong	Spot

28b Professional and Honorific Titles

Capitalize professional and honorific titles when they directly precede and thus are parts of names:

Professor Tamara Jones (*but* Tamara Jones, professor at the University of Pittsburgh)

Rabbi Samuel Singer (*but* Mr. Singer was rabbi of our synagogue.)

Normally titles that follow names aren't capitalized unless they have become part of the name:

Bill de Blasio, mayor of New York City

Kamala Harris, the senator

> *but*

Catherine the Great

Smokey the Bear

Some titles of particular distinction are customarily capitalized even if the person isn't named:

The Queen vacationed in Scotland.

On Easter Sunday, the Pope will address the crowd gathered in St. Peter's Square.

The university was honored with a visit by the Dalai Lama.

28c Place Names

Capitalize place names—including common nouns (*river, street, park,* etc.) when they are parts of proper nouns:

Saratoga Springs	Nevada	the Amazon
Central Park	Newport	Chinatown
Gulf of Mexico	Japan	Lake Erie
Niagara Falls	the Andes	Mississippi River
the Gobi Desert	Asia	Trafalgar Square
the Rocky Mountains	Mount Etna	Main Street

As a rule, don't capitalize *north, south, east,* and *west* unless they are part of specific place names (North Dakota, West Fourth Street, the South Shore) or designate specific geographical areas (the frozen North, the East Coast, the Deep South, the Pacific Northwest, the Wild West, the Far East).

28d Months, Days, and Holidays

Capitalize the names of the months (January, February, etc.) and the days of the week (Monday, Tuesday, etc.), but not the seasons (spring, summer, autumn, fall, winter). Also capitalize holidays, holy days, and festivals (Christmas, Yom Kippur, Memorial Day, Halloween, Ramadan).

28e Religious Names

Capitalize names of deities and other religious names and terms:

the Holy Ghost	God	the Virgin Mary
the Bible	the Torah	the Talmud
the Dead Sea Scrolls	Islam	Allah
the Prophet	the Qur'an	Apollo
Jupiter	Vishnu	Taoism

Note: Some people capitalize pronouns referring to a deity; others prefer not to. Either practice is acceptable as long as you are consistent.

28c

28f Names of Nationalities and Organizations

Capitalize names of nationalities and other groups and organizations and of their members:

Canadian, American, Australian, Malaysian, Scandinavian

Democrats, Republicans

Roman Catholics, the Roman Catholic Church

Teamsters

the San Francisco Giants, the Cincinnati Bengals

28g Names of Institutions and Sections of Government, Historical Events, and Buildings

Capitalize names of institutions; sections of government; historical events, periods, and documents; and specific buildings:

Whitman College, the Kennedy School of Government

the Department of Education, Congress, the Senate, the House of Representatives

the French Revolution, World War I, the Iraq War, the Cretaceous Period, the Renaissance, the Magna Carta, the Treaty of Versailles, the U.S. Constitution, the Ming Dynasty

the British Museum, the Museum of Popular Culture, Trinity Church

28h Academic Courses and Languages

Capitalize specific academic courses, but not the subjects themselves, except for languages:

Philosophy 101, Gender Studies 300, Statistics 204, English 112, Food Writing, Introduction to the Humanities

an English course, a major in French (*but* a history course, an economics major, a degree in psychology)

28h

28i Derivatives of Proper Nouns

Capitalize derivatives of proper nouns:

African American, Latina, Celtic, Iroquois

Confucianism, Christian

Shakespearean, Keynesian, Edwardian, Miltonic, the Bechdel Test

28j Abbreviations of Proper Nouns

Capitalize abbreviations of proper nouns:

| HMO | EPA | GNP | OSHA |
| NYC | D.C. | DMV | HPD |

Note that abbreviations of agencies and organizations commonly known by their initials do not need periods (see #27d). When in doubt about whether to use periods with abbreviations, consult your dictionary. See also #22.

28k Titles of Written and Other Works

In the titles of written and other works, including student essays, use a capital letter to begin the first word, the last word, and all other important words; leave uncapitalized only articles (*a, an, the*) and any conjunctions and prepositions less than five letters long (unless one of these is the first or last word):

The Blind Assassin	*Little Fires Everywhere*
"The Dead"	*Educated*
"America the Beautiful"	"A Dream Within a Dream"
After the Gold Rush	*The Invisible Man*

But there can be exceptions; for example the conjunctions *Nor* and *So* are usually capitalized, and the relative pronoun *that* is sometimes not capitalized (*All's Well that Ends Well*).

If a title includes a hyphenated word, capitalize the part after the hyphen only if it is a noun or an adjective or is otherwise an important word:

Self-Portrait

The Scorched-Wood People

Murder Among the Well-to-do

Capitalize the first word of a subtitle, even if it is an article:

Beyond Remembering: The Collected Poems of Al Purdy

See #29b for the use of italics in titles.

 First Words

1. Capitalize the first word of a quotation that is intended as a sentence or that is capitalized in the source, but not fragments from other than the beginning of such a sentence:

    When he said "Let me take the wheel for a while," I shuddered at the memory of what had happened the last time I had let him "take the wheel."

    If something interrupts a single quoted sentence, do not begin its second part with a capital letter:

    "It was all I could do," she said, "to keep from laughing out loud."

2. Capitalize the first word of an independent sentence in parentheses only if it stands by itself, apart from other sentences. If it is incorporated within another sentence, it is neither capitalized nor ended with a period.

    She did as she was told (there was really nothing else for her to do), and the tension was relieved. (But of course she would never admit to herself that she had been manipulated.)

3. An incorporated sentence following a colon may be capitalized if it seems to stand as a separate statement,

28-1

for example if it is itself long or requires emphasis; the current trend is away from capitalization.

> There was one thing, she said, which we must never forget: No one has the right to the kind of happiness that deprives someone else of deserved happiness.

> It was a splendid night: the sky was clear except for a few picturesque clouds, the moon was full, and even a few stars shone through. (The first *The* could be capitalized if the writer wanted particular emphasis on the details.)

28m Personification or Emphasis

Occasionally, writers who have good control of tone may choose to capitalize a personified abstraction or a word or phrase to which they want to impart a special importance of some kind:

> In his quest to succeed, Greed and Power came to dominate his every waking thought.

Sometimes the slight emphasis of capitalization can be used for a humorous or ironic effect:

> He insisted on driving His Beautiful Car: everyone else preferred to walk the two blocks without enjoying its jerks and jolts and carbon monoxide fumes.

And occasionally, but rarely, you can capitalize whole words and phrases or even sentences for a special sort of graphic emphasis:

> When we reached the excavation site, we were confronted by a sign warning us in no uncertain terms to
> KEEP OUT——TRESPASSERS WILL BE PROSECUTED.

28-l

29 Titles (see also #28k)

29a Quotation Marks for Short Works and Parts of Longer Works

Put quotation marks around the titles of short works and of parts of longer works, such as short stories, articles, essays, short poems, chapters of books, songs, individual episodes of television programs, and sections of websites:

> Leonard Cohen's "Joan of Arc" and "Democracy" are songs featured in this documentary about art songs and politics.

> "A Wilderness Station" is a story by Alice Munro that begins in the 1850s.

> Of the ten episodes in the STARZ documentary *America to Me*, I was the most moved by the fourth one, "There's Nothing Funny About Race."

> "The History of English," posted on the website *Oxford Dictionaries*, provides a very brief overview of historical influences on the English language.

29b Italics for Whole or Major Works

Use italics (see #30) for titles of written works published as units, such as books, magazines, journals, newspapers, and plays; films and television programs; entire websites; paintings and sculptures; and musical compositions (other than single songs), such as operas and ballets:

> *Paradise Lost* is Milton's greatest work.

> *The New Yorker* is a weekly magazine.

> The literary journal *Tin House* is published quarterly.

> I prefer *The Washington Post* to *USA Today*.

> *Stranger Things* is a Netflix original program that both viewers and critics love.

> I was tired of hearing Ravel's *Boléro* played so often.

> Picasso's *Guernica* is a disturbing representation of the Spanish Civil War.

29b

Note that instrumental compositions may be known by name or by technical detail, or both. A formal title is italicized (Beethoven's *Pastoral Symphony*); technical identification is usually not (Beethoven's Sixth Symphony, or Symphony no. 6, op. 68, in F major).

29c Titles Within Titles

If an essay title includes a book title, the book title is italicized:

> "Things Botanical in *The Lost Garden* and *A Student of Weather*"

If a book title includes something requiring quotation marks, retain the quotation marks and italicize the whole thing:

> *From Fiction to Film: James Joyce's "The Dead"*

If a book title includes something that itself would be italicized, such as the name of a ship or the title of another book, either put the secondary item in quotation marks or leave it in roman type (i.e., not italicized):

> *The Aftermath of the "Titanic"*

> *D.H. Lawrence and* Sons and Lovers: *Sources and Criticism*

Note: Double-check in the titles you cite for the role of the definite article, *the*: italicize and capitalize *the* only when it is actually a part of the title: Toni Morrison's *Beloved*; Yann Martel's the *Life of Pi*; *The North American Encyclopedia*; the *Atlas of Ancient Archaeology*. Refer to a newspaper the way it refers to itself on its front page or masthead: *The New York Times*; the *Los Angeles Times*.

30 Italics

Italics are a special kind of slanting type that contrasts with the surrounding type to draw attention to a word or phrase, such as a title (see #29). The other main uses of italics are discussed below. In handwritten work, such as an exam, represent italic type by underlining.

30a Names of Ships and Planes

Italicize names of individual ships, planes, and the like:

the *Starship Enterprise*   *Spirit of St. Louis*

the *Santa Maria*   the *Discovery*

30b Non-English Words and Phrases

Italicize non-English words and phrases not yet sufficiently common to be entirely at home in English. English
contains many terms that have come from other languages
but that are no longer thought of as non-English and are
therefore not italicized, for example:

moccasin	prairie	genre	tableau
bamboo	arroyo	corral	sushi
chutzpah	spaghetti	paprika	eureka

There are also words that are sufficiently Anglicized not
to require italicizing but that usually retain their original
accents and diacritical marks, for example:

cliché   résumé   fête   façade

But English also makes use of many terms still felt by
many writers to be sufficiently non-English to need italicizing, for example:

bildungsroman   *coup d'état*   *jihad*

chez   *joie de vivre*

raison d'être   *savoir faire*

30c Words Referred to as Words

Italicize words, letters, numerals, and the like when you
refer to them as such:

The word *helicopter* is formed from Greek roots.

There are two *r*'s in *embarrass*. (Note that only the *r* is
    italicized; the *s* making it plural stays roman.)

The number *13* is considered unlucky by many people.

Don't use *&* as a substitute for *and*.

See also #20d. To learn more about using apostrophes for plurals of such elements, see #32-l.8.

30d For Emphasis

On rare occasions, italicize words or phrases—or even whole sentences—that you want to emphasize, for example, as they might be stressed if spoken aloud:

> One thing he was now sure of: *that* was a bad idea.

> If people try to tell you otherwise, *don't listen to them.*

Like other typographical devices for achieving emphasis (boldface, capitalization), this method should be avoided in academic and other formal writing.

31 Numerals

Numerals are appropriate in technical and scientific writing, and newspapers sometimes use them to save space. But in ordinary writing certain conventions, limit their use.

31a Time of Day

Use numerals for the time of day with *a.m.* or *p.m.* and *midnight* or *noon*, or when minutes are included:

> 3 p.m. (*but* three o'clock, three in the afternoon)

> 12 noon, 12 midnight (these are often better than the equivalents, *12 p.m.* and *12 a.m.*, which may not be understood)

> 4:15, 4:30 (*but* a quarter past four; half past four)

31b Dates

Use numerals for dates:

> September 12, 2017, *or* 12 September 2017

The year is almost always represented by numerals, and centuries are usually spelled out:

Was 2000 the last year of the twentieth century or the first
year of the twenty-first century?

Note: The suffixes *st*, *nd*, *rd*, and *th* go with numerals in
dates only if the year is not given; or the number may be
written out:

May 12, 1955	May 12th
the twelfth of May	May twelfth

 ## Addresses

Use numerals for addresses:

2132 Fourth Avenue	P.O. Box 91
4771 128th Street	Apartment 8

 ## Technical and Mathematical Numbers

Use numerals for technical and mathematical numbers,
such as percentages and decimals:

31 percent	31%
37 degrees Celsius	37°C
2.54 inches	2.54 in

Parts of a Written Work

Use numerals for page numbers and other divisions of a
written work, especially in documentation (see #37):

page 27, p. 27, pp. 33–38	Chapter 4, Ch. 4
Part 2, parts 1 and 2	Section 3, sec. 3
act 4, scene 2	2 Samuel 22: 3
line 13, lines 3 and 5, ll. 7–9	

Note that in some contexts it may be conventional to use
Roman numerals or a mix of Roman and Arabic numerals:

Act IV, Scene ii	Chapter IV
Book IX, canto 120	II Samuel 19: 1

31f Fractions

Spell out numbers when they are expressed as compound fractions:

> one-third; one-half; five thirty-seconds

31g Numbers of More Than Two Words

Generally, spell out numbers that can be expressed in one or two words; use numerals for numbers that would take more than two words:

> four; thirty; eighty-three; two hundred; seven thousand; 115; 385; 2120

> three dollars; five hundred dollars; $3.48; $517

Note: If you are writing about more than one number, say for purposes of comparison or giving statistics, numerals are usually preferable:

> Enrollment dropped from 250 two years ago, to 200 last year, to only 90 this year.

Following this convention will help you to avoid mixing numerals and words in the same context.

31h Commas with Numerals

Commas have long been conventional to separate groups of three figures in long numbers:

> 3,172,450   17,920

Street addresses of four or more figures are usually not separated by commas or spaces, though they may use hyphens:

> 1888 Bay Mills Avenue

> 76-66 Austin Street

32 Spelling Rules and Common Causes of Error

Some writers have little trouble with spelling: others have a lot —but hopefully not "alot"! The good news is that good spelling comes with practice; taking the time to look up a word now will help you remember its proper spelling the next time you need to use it. And learning how to spell words properly will benefit you not only in your college or university classes but also in your future career. Accurate spelling is essential to good communication. It also signals professionalism, care for your work, and attention to detail—all qualities that employers value highly.

English spelling isn't as bizarre as some people think, but there are oddities. Sometimes the same sound can be spelled in several ways (*fine*, *offer*, *phone*, *cough*; or *so*, *soap*, *sow*, *sew*, *beau*, *dough*), or a single element can be pronounced in several ways (*cough*, *tough*, *dough*, *through*, *bough*, *fought*). When such inconsistencies occur in longer and less familiar words, sometimes only a dictionary can help us.

Many spelling errors fall into clear categories. Familiarizing yourself with the main rules and the main sources of confusion will help you avoid these errors.

ie or *ei*

The old jingle should help: use *i* before *e* except after *c*, or when sounded like *a* as in *neighbor* or *weigh*.

ie: achieve, believe, chief, field, fiend, piece, shriek, wield

***ei* after *c*:** ceiling, conceive, deceive, perceive, receive

***ei* when sounded like *a*:** eight, neighbor, sleigh, veil, weigh

However, there are a number of common exceptions to this "rule," including the following:

ancient	caffeine	counterfeit	deficient
either	efficient	foreign	forfeit
glacier	height	heir	leisure
neither	their	science	society
seize	sovereign	weird	species

When in doubt, consult your dictionary.

32b Final *e* Before a Suffix

When a suffix is added to a root word that ends in a silent *e,* certain rules generally apply. If the suffix begins with a *vowel* (*a, e, i, o, u*), the *e* is usually dropped:

desire + able = desirable	forgive + able = forgivable
sphere + ical = spherical	argue + ing = arguing
come + ing = coming	allure + ing = alluring
continue + ous = continuous	desire + ous = desirous

(*Dyeing* retains the *e* to distinguish it from *dying*. If a word ends with two *e*'s, both are pronounced and therefore not dropped: *agreeing, fleeing*.)

If the suffix begins with *a* or *o*, most words ending in *ce* or *ge* retain the *e* in order to preserve the soft sound of the *c* (like *s* rather than *k*) or the *g* (like *j* rather than hard as in *gum*):

notice + able = noticeable	outrage + ous = outrageous

(Note that *vengeance* and *gorgeous* also have such a silent *e*.) Similarly, words like *picnic* and *frolic* require an added *k* to preserve the hard sound before suffixes beginning with *e* or *i*: *picnicked, picnicking*; *frolicked, frolicking*. (An exception to this rule is *arc*: *arced, arcing*.) When the suffix does not begin with *e* or *i*, these words do not require an added *k*: *tactical, frolicsome*.

If the suffix begins with a *consonant*, the silent *e* of the root word is usually not dropped:

awe + some = awesome

effective + ness = effectiveness

definite + ly = definitely

hoarse + ly = hoarsely

immediate + ly = immediately

mere + ly = merely

(But note a common exception: *awe + ful = awful*.)

And there is a subgroup of words whose final *e*'s are sometimes wrongly omitted. The *e*, though silent, is essential to keep the sound of the preceding vowel long:

completely	extremely	hopelessness	livelihood
loneliness	remoteness	severely	tasteless

But such an *e* is sometimes dropped when no consonant intervenes between it and the long vowel:

due + ly = duly   true + ly = truly

argue + ment = argument

32c Final *y* After a Consonant and Before a Suffix

When the suffix begins with *i*, keep the *y*:

baby + ish = babyish   carry + ing = carrying

try + ing = trying   worry + ing = worrying

(**Note:** Words ending in *ie* change to *y* before adding *ing*: *die + ing = dying*; *lie + ing = lying*.)

When the suffix begins with something other than *i*, change *y* to *i*:

happy + er = happier   duty + ful = dutiful

happy + ness = happiness   silly + est = silliest

harmony + ous = harmonious   angry + ly = angrily

But here are some exceptions: *shyly, shyness*; *slyer, slyly*; *flyer* (though *flier* is sometimes used); *dryer* (as a noun—for the comparative adjective use *drier*).

32d Doubling of a Final Consonant Before a Suffix

When adding a suffix, *double* the final consonant of the root if all three of the following apply:

1. that consonant is preceded by a single vowel,
2. the root is a one-syllable word or a word accented on its last syllable, and
3. the suffix begins with a vowel.

Words with one-syllable roots:

bar + ed = barred   bar + ing = barring

fit + ed = fitted   fit + ing = fitting   fit + er = fitter

hot + er = hotter   hot + est = hottest

Words accented on last syllable:

allot + ed = allotted   allot + ing = allotting

commit + ed = committed   commit + ing = committing

occur + ed = occurred   occur + ing = occurring

occur + ence = occurrence

But when the addition of the suffix shifts the accent of the root word away from the last syllable, do not double the final consonant:

infer + ed = inferred   infer + ing = inferring
                          but inference

prefer + ed = preferred   prefer + ing = preferring
                          but preference

refer + ed = referred   refer + ing = referring
                          but reference

Do not double the final consonant if it is preceded by a single consonant (*sharp + er = sharper*) or if the final consonant is preceded by two vowels (*fail + ed = failed, stoop + ing = stooping*) or if the root word is more than one syllable and *not* accented on its last syllable (*benefit + ed = benefited, parallel + ing = paralleling*) or if the suffix begins with a consonant (*commit + ment = commitment*).

32e The Suffix *ly*

32d

When *ly* is added to an adjective already ending in a single *l*, that final *l* is retained, resulting in an adverb ending in *lly*. If you pronounce such words carefully you will be less likely to misspell them:

accidental + ly = accidentally   cool + ly = coolly

incidental + ly = incidentally   mental + ly = mentally

natural + ly = naturally   political + ly = politically

If the root ends in a double *ll*, one *l* is dropped: *full + ly = fully*, *chill + ly = chilly*, *droll + ly = drolly*.

Note: Many adjectives ending in *ic* have alternative forms ending in *ical*. But even if they don't, nearly all add *ally*, not just *ly*, to become adverbs—as do nouns like *music* and *stoic*. Again, careful pronunciation will help you avoid error:

> alphabetic, alphabetical, alphabetically
>
> basic, basically
>
> cyclic, cyclical, cyclically
>
> drastic, drastically
>
> scientific, scientifically
>
> symbolic, symbolical, symbolically

An exception: *publicly*.

Troublesome Word Endings

Several groups of suffixes, or word endings, plague many spellers. There are no rules governing these suffixes, and pronunciation is seldom any help; one either knows them or does not. The following examples will at least alert you to the potential trouble spots:

able, ably, ability; ible, ibly, ibility

It should be helpful to remember that many more words end in *able* than in *ible*; yet it is the *ible* endings that cause the most trouble:

-able		**-ible**	
advisable	inevitable	audible	inexpressible
comparable	laudable	contemptible	irresistible
debatable	noticeable	deductible	negligible
desirable	quotable	eligible	plausible
immeasurable	respectable	flexible	responsible
indubitable	veritable	incredible	visible

ent, ently, ence, ency; ant, antly, ance, ancy

	-en-		**-an-**
apparent	independent	appearance	flamboyant
coherent	permanent	blatant	irrelevant
consistent	persistence	brilliant	maintenance
excellent	resilient	concomitant	resistance
existence	tendency	extravagant	warrant

tial, tian; cial, cian

	-tia-		**-cia-**
confidential	influential	beneficial	mathematician
dietitian	martial	crucial	mortician
existential	spatial	commercial	physician

ce; se

	-ce		**-se**
choice	fence	course	expense
defence	presence	dense	phrase
evidence	voice	dispense	sparse

ative; itive

	-ative		**-itive**
affirmative	informative	additive	positive
comparative	negative	competitive	repetitive
imaginative	restorative	genitive	sensitive

cede, ceed, or sede

Memorize if necessary: the *sede* ending occurs only in *supersede*. The *ceed* ending occurs only in *exceed*, *proceed*, and *succeed*. All other words ending in this sound use *cede*: *accede*, *concede*, *intercede*, *precede*, *recede*, *secede*.

32f

32g Changes in Spelling of Roots

Be careful with words whose roots change spelling, often because of a change in stress, when they are inflected for a different part of speech, for example:

clear, clarity	maintain, maintenance
curious, curiosity	prevail, prevalent
despair, desperate	pronounce, pronunciation
exclaim, exclamatory	repair, reparable
generous, generosity	repeat, repetition
inherit, heritage, *but* heredity, hereditary	

 Faulty Pronunciation

Here is a list of words some of whose common misspellings could be prevented by careful pronunciation:

academic	detrimental	government	nuclear
accelerate	dilapidated	governor	optimism
accidentally	disgruntled	gravitation	original
amphitheatre	disgust	hereditary	particular
analogy	disillusioned	hurriedly	peculiar
approximately	elaborate	immersing	permanently
architectural	emperor	insurgence	phenomenon
athlete	environment	interpretation	philosophical
authoritative	epitomize	intimacy	predilection
biathlon	escape	inviting	prevalent
camaraderie	especially	irrelevant	pronunciation
candidate	etcetera	itinerary	quantity
celebration	evident	larynx	repetitive
conference	excerpt	lightning	reservoir
congratulate	February	limpidly	sacrilegious
controversial	film	lustrous	separate
definitely	foliage	mathematics	significant
deteriorating	further	negative	similar

strength	surprise	ultimatum	visible
subsidiary	temporarily	village	vulnerable
suffocate	triathlon	villain	wondrous

Note: Don't omit the *d* or *ed* from such words as *used* and *supposed*, *old-fashioned* and *prejudiced*, which are often pronounced without the *d* sound. And be careful not to omit whole syllables that are near duplications in sound. Write carefully, run a spell-check when possible, and proofread, sounding the words to yourself. Here are some examples of such "telescoped" words that occur frequently:

Right	*Wrong*	*Right*	*Wrong*
convenience	~~convience~~	institution	~~instution~~
criticize	~~critize~~	politician	~~politian~~
examining	~~examing~~	remembrance	~~rembrance~~
inappropriate	~~inappriate~~	repetition	~~repition~~

32i Confusion with Other Words

Don't let false analogies and similarities of sound lead you astray.

A writer who thinks of a word like:	*May spell another word* **wrong***, like this:*	*Instead of* **right***, like this:*
air	~~ordinairy~~	ordinary
breeze	~~cheeze~~	cheese
comrade	~~comraderie~~	camaraderie
democracy	~~hypocracy~~	hypocrisy
desolate	~~desolute~~	dissolute
diet	~~diety~~	deity
exalt	~~exaltant~~	exultant
familiar	~~similiar~~	similar
ideal	~~idealic~~	idyllic
knowledge	~~priviledge~~	privilege
prize	~~surprize~~	surprise

32h

religious	~~sacreligious~~	sacrilegious
restaurant	~~restauranteur~~	restaurateur
sink	~~zink~~	zinc
size	~~rize~~	rise
solid	~~solider~~	soldier
summer	~~grammer~~	grammar
young	~~amoung~~	among

32j Homophones and Other Words Sometimes Confused

1. Be careful to distinguish between **homophones** that are pronounced alike but spelled differently. Below is a list of some that can be troublesome. Consult a dictionary for any whose meanings you aren't sure of; this is a matter of meaning as well as of spelling (and see #14d):

aisle, isle	forth, fourth
alter, altar	hear, here
assent, ascent	heard, herd
bear, bare	hole, whole
birth, berth	its, it's
board, bored	led, lead
boarder, border	manner, manor
born, borne	meat, meet
break, brake	past, passed
by, buy, bye	patience, patients
capital, capitol	piece, peace
complement, compliment	plain, plane
council, counsel	pore, pour
course, coarse	pray, prey
desert, dessert	presence, presents
die, dye; dying, dyeing	principle, principal
discreet, discrete	rain, rein, reign

32j

right, rite, write	there, their, they're
road, rode, rowed	to, too, two
sight, site, cite	whose, who's
stationary, stationery	your, you're

2. There are also words that are not pronounced exactly alike but that are similar enough to be confused. Again, look up any whose meanings you aren't sure of:

accept, except	emigrate, immigrate
access, excess	eminent, imminent, immanent
acquire	enquire, inquire, acquire
adopt, adapt, adept	ensure, insure, assure
adverse, averse	envelop, envelope
advice, advise	evoke, invoke
affect, effect	illusion, allusion
afflicted, inflicted	incident, incidence
allude, elude	incredulous, incredible
angle, angel	ingenious, ingenuous
appraise, apprise	insight, incite
assume, presume	instant, instance
bizarre, bazaar	later, latter
breath, breathe	loose, lose
choose, chose	moral, morale
cloth, clothe	practice, practise
conscious, conscience	quite, quiet
custom, costume	tack, tact
decent, descent, dissent	than, then
decimate, disseminate	were, we're, where
device, devise	whether, weather
diary, dairy	while, wile

32j

3. Be careful also to distinguish between such terms as the following, for although they sound the same, they function differently depending on whether they are spelled as one word or two:

already, all ready	awhile, a while
altogether, all together	everybody, every body
anybody, any body	everyday, every day
anymore, any more	everyone, every one
anyone, any one	maybe, may be
anytime, any time	someday, some day
anyway, any way	sometime, some time

32k Hyphenation

To hyphenate or not to hyphenate? Since the conventions are constantly changing, sometimes rapidly, make a habit of checking your dictionary for current usage. (For hyphens to divide a word at the end of a line, see #26b.) Here are the main points to remember:

1. Use hyphens in compound numbers from *twenty-one* to *ninety-nine*.

2. Use hyphens with fractions used as adjectives:

    > A two-thirds majority is required to defeat the amendment.

    When a fraction is used as a noun, you may use a hyphen, though many writers do not:

    > One quarter of the audience was asleep.

3. Use hyphens with compounds indicating time, when these are written out: *seven-thirty, nine-fifteen.*

4. Use an en-dash as opposed to a hyphen between a pair of numbers (including hours and dates) indicating a range: pages 73-78, June 20-26. The en-dash is slightly longer than the hyphen and means *to*. If you introduce the range with *from,* write out the word *to*: *from June 20 to June 26.* If you use *between,* write out the word *and*: *between June 20 and June 26.*

5. Use hyphens with prefixes before proper nouns:

all-American	pan-Asian	pseudo-Modern
anti-British	pre-Babylonian	trans-Siberian

32k

But there are well-established exceptions, for example:

antichrist	postmodern	postcolonial
transatlantic	transpacific	transnational

6. Use hyphens with compounds beginning with the prefix *self*: *self-assured, self-confidence, self-deluded, self-esteem, self-made, self-pity*, etc. (The words *selfhood, selfish, selfless*, and *selfsame* are not hyphenated, because in these words *self* is the root, not a prefix.) Hyphens are conventionally used with certain other prefixes: *all-important, ex-premier, quasi-religious*. Hyphens are conventionally used with most, but not all, compounds beginning with *vice* and *by*: *vice-chancellor, vice-consul, vice-president, vice-regent*, etc., BUT *viceregal, viceroy; by-election, by-product*, etc., BUT *bygone, bylaw, byroad, bystander, byword*. Check your dictionary.

7. Use hyphens with the suffixes *elect* and *designate*: *mayor -elect, ambassador-designate*.

8. Use hyphens with *great* and *in-law* in compounds designating family relationships: *great-grandfather, great-aunt, mother-in-law, son-in-law*.

9. Use hyphens to prevent a word's being mistaken for an entirely different word:

   > He <u>recounted</u> what had happened after the ballots had been <u>re-counted</u>.

   > If you're going to <u>re-strain</u> the juice, I'll <u>restrain</u> myself from drinking it now, seeds and all.

10. Use hyphens to prevent awkward or confusing combinations of letters and sounds: *anti-intellectual, doll-like, e-book, e-learning, photo-offset, re-echo*.

11. Hyphens are sometimes necessary to prevent ambiguity:

    ambig: The ad offered six week old kittens for sale.

    clear: The ad offered six week-old kittens for sale.

    clear: The ad offered six-week-old kittens for sale.

Note the difference a hyphen makes to the meaning of the last two examples.

12. Some nouns composed of two or more words are conventionally hyphenated, for example:

free-for-all	half-and-half	jack-o'-lantern
runner-up	merry-go-round	rabble-rouser
shut-in	trade-in	two-timer

13. When two or more words occur together in such a way that they act as a single adjective before a noun, they are usually hyphenated to prevent misreading:

a <u>well-dressed</u> man   <u>greenish-grey</u> eyes

a <u>once-in-a-lifetime</u> chance   a <u>three-day-old</u> strike

When they occur after a noun, misreading is unlikely and no hyphen is needed:

The man was <u>well dressed</u>.

Her eyes are <u>greenish grey</u>.

But many compound modifiers are already listed as hyphenated words; for example, the *Oxford Dictionaries* lists these, among others:

first-class	fly-by-night	good-looking
habit-forming	open-minded	right-hand
short-lived	tongue-tied	wide-eyed

Such modifiers retain their hyphens even when they follow the nouns they modify:

The tone of the speech was quite <u>matter-of-fact</u>.

Note: Since one cannot mistake the first part of a compound modifier when it is an adverb ending in *ly*, even in front of a noun, do not use a hyphen:

He is a <u>happily married</u> man.

14. Verbs, too, are sometimes hyphenated. A dictionary will list most of the ones you might want to use, for example:

32k

double-click	pan-broil	pole-vault
re-educate	second-guess	sight-read
soft-pedal	spot-check	two-time

Note: Some expressions can be spelled either as two separate words or as compounds (either hyphenated or unhyphenated), depending on what part of speech they are functioning as, for example:

He works <u>full time</u>. *but* He has a <u>full-time</u> job.

Be sure to <u>back up</u> your files, and store the <u>backup</u> in a safe place.

 Plurals

1. Regular nouns

For most nouns, add *s* or *es* to the singular form to indicate plural number:

one building, two buildings   one box, two boxes

2. Nouns ending in *o*

Some nouns ending in *o* preceded by a consonant form their plurals with *s*, while some use *es*. For some either form is correct—but use the one listed first in your dictionary. Here are a few examples:

altos	echoes
pianos	heroes
solos	potatoes

3. Nouns ending in *f* or *fe*

For some nouns ending in a single *f* or an *fe*, change the ending to *ve* before adding *s*, for example:

knife, knives	life, lives	shelf, shelves
leaf, leaves	loaf, loaves	thief, thieves

But for some simply add *s*:

32k

beliefs	gulfs	safes
griefs	proofs	still lifes

Some words ending in *f* have alternative plurals:

dwarfs *or* dwarves	scarves *or* scarfs
hoofs *or* hooves	wharves *or* wharfs

The hockey team the *Maple Leafs* is a special case, a proper noun that doesn't follow the rules governing common nouns.

4. Nouns ending in *y*

For nouns ending in *y* preceded by a vowel, add *s*:

keys	toys	valleys

For nouns ending in *y* preceded by a consonant, change the *y* to *i* and add *es*:

city, cities	cry, cries
country, countries	family, families

Exception: Most proper nouns ending in *y* simply take *s*:

From 1949 to 1990 there were two <u>Germanys</u>.

But note that we refer to the Rocky Mountains as the *Rockies* and to the Canary Islands as the *Canaries*.

5. Compounds

Generally, form the plurals of compounds simply by adding *s*:

major generals	lieutenant-governors
webmasters	merry-go-rounds
prizewinners	great-grandmothers

32-1

But if the first part is a noun and the rest is not, or if the first part is the more important of two nouns, that one is made plural:

governors general	daughters-in-law
passersby	townspeople

6. Irregular plurals

Some nouns are irregular in the way they form their plurals, but these are common and generally well known, for example:

child, children	foot, feet
mouse, mice	woman, women

Some plural forms are the same as the singular, for example:

one deer, two deer	one series, two series
one moose, two moose	one sheep, two sheep

7. Borrowed words

The plurals of words borrowed from other languages (mostly Latin and Greek) can pose a problem. Words used formally or technically tend to retain their original plurals; words used more commonly tend to form their plurals according to English rules. Since many such words are in transition, you will probably encounter both plural forms. When in doubt, use the preferred form listed in your dictionary. Here are some examples of words that have tended to retain their original plurals:

alumna, alumnae	larva, larvae
alumnus, alumni	madame, mesdames
analysis, analyses	medium, media
basis, bases	nucleus, nuclei
crisis, crises	parenthesis, parentheses
criterion, criteria	phenomenon, phenomena
datum, data	stimulus, stimuli
hypothesis, hypotheses	synthesis, syntheses
kibbutz, kibbutzim	thesis, theses

32-I

But note that it has become acceptable in informal and non-scientific contexts to treat *data* and *media* as if they were singular.

Here are some with both forms, the choice often depending on the formality or technicality of the context:

antenna, antennae (insects) *or* antennas (radios, etc.)

apparatus, apparatus *or* apparatuses

appendix, appendices *or* appendixes

beau, beaux *or* beaus

cactus, cacti *or* cactuses

château, châteaux *or* châteaus

curriculum, curricula *or* curriculums

focus, foci *or* focuses (focusses)

formula, formulae *or* formulas

index, indices *or* indexes

lacuna, lacunae *or* lacunas

matrix, matrices *or* matrixes

memorandum, memoranda *or* memorandums

referendum, referenda *or* referendums

stratum, strata *or* stratums

syllabus, syllabi *or* syllabuses

symposium, symposia *or* symposiums

terminus, termini *or* terminuses

ultimatum, ultimata *or* ultimatums

And here are a few that now tend to follow regular English patterns:

bureau, bureaus   sanctum, sanctums

campus, campuses   stadium, stadiums

genius, geniuses (*genii* for mythological creatures)

32-1

8. Numerals, symbols, letters, and words used as words

An apostrophe and an *s* may be used to form the plural of numerals, symbols, letters, and words referred to as words:

the 1870's

the three *R*'s   two *and*'s

215

Note that when a word, letter, or figure is italicized, the apostrophe and the *s* are not.

Many people prefer to form such plurals without the apostrophe: *1870s, ¶s, Rs, and*s. But this practice can be confusing, especially with lowercase letters and words, which may be misread:

> ***confusing:*** How many *ss* are there in Nipissing?

> ***confusing:*** Too many *this*s can spoil a good paragraph.

In cases such as these, it is clearer and easier to use the apostrophe. Keep in mind that it is sometimes better to rephrase instances that are potentially awkward:

> *Accommodate* is spelled with a double-*c* and a double-*m*.

 Apostrophes to Indicate Omission

Use apostrophes to indicate omitted letters in contractions and omitted (though obvious) numerals:

aren't (are not)	they're (they are)
can't (cannot)	won't (will not)
doesn't (does not)	wouldn't (would not)
don't (do not)	you're (you are)
isn't (is not)	back in '03
it's (it is)	the crash of '29
she's (she is)	the summer of '96

If an apostrophe is already present to indicate a plural, you may omit the apostrophe that indicates omission: the *20*'s, the *90*'s.

 Possessives

1. To form the possessive case of a singular or a plural noun that does not end in *s*, add an apostrophe and *s*:

the car's color	deer's hide	children's books
the girl's teacher	Jehan's briefcase	the women's jobs

2. To form the possessive of compound nouns, use *'s* after the last noun:

    > The Solicitor General's report is due tomorrow.

    > Hebba and Mike's dinner party was a huge success.

    If the nouns don't actually form a compound, each will need the *'s*:

    > Hebba's and Mike's versions of the dinner party were markedly different.

3. You may correctly add an apostrophe and an *s* to form the possessive of singular nouns ending in *s* or an *s*-sound:

the class's achievement	an index's usefulness
a platypus's bill	Keats's poems

    However, some writers prefer to add only an apostrophe if the pronunciation of an extra syllable would sound awkward:

Achilles' heel	Moses' sons
for convenience' sake	Bill Gates' foundation

    But the *'s* is usually acceptable or even preferred, depending on the style sheet: *Achilles's heel; for convenience's sake; Moses's sons; Bill Gates's foundation*.

4. To indicate the possessive case of plural nouns ending in *s*, add only an apostrophe:

the cannons' roar	the girls' sweaters
the Joneses' garden	the Chans' cottage

    Note: When forming possessive pronouns, do not use apostrophes:

hers (NOT her's)	its (NOT it's)
ours (NOT our's)	theirs (NOT their's)
yours (NOT your's)	whose (NOT who's)

5. Possessive with *'s* or with *of*: Especially in formal writing, the *'s* form is more common with the names of

32n

living creatures, the *of* form with the names of inani-
mate things:

the cat's tail	the leg of the chair
the girl's coat	the contents of the report
Sheldon's home town	the surface of the desk

But both are acceptable with either category. The *'s*
form, for example, is common with nouns that refer
to things thought of as made up of people or animals
or as extensions of them:

the team's strategy	the committee's decision
the company's employee	the government's policy
the city's bylaws	Mexico's climate
the factory's output	the heart's affections

or things that are "animate" in the sense that they are
part of nature:

the dawn's early light	the wind's velocity
the comet's tail	the sea's surface
the plant's roots	the sky's color

or periods of time:

today's paper	a day's work
a month's wages	winter's storms

Even beyond such uses the *'s* may be appropriate;
sometimes there is a sense of personification, but not
always:

beauty's friend	at death's door
freedom's light	*Love's Labour's Lost*
time's fool	the razor's edge

32n

For the sake of emphasis or rhythm you will occasionally want to use an *of*-phrase where *'s* would be
normal; for example, *the jury's verdict* lacks the punch
of *the verdict of the jury*. You can also use an *of*-phrase to
avoid awkward pronunciations (see above: those who
don't like the sound of *Dickens's novels*, for example,

can refer to *the novels of Dickens*) and unwieldy or ambiguous constructions (*the opinion of the deputy commissioner of development* is clearer than *deputy commissioner of development's opinion*).

6. Double possessives: There is nothing wrong with double possessive, showing possession with both an *of*-phrase and a possessive inflection. They are standard with possessive pronouns and can be used similarly with common and proper nouns:

a favorite <u>of</u> mine	a friend <u>of</u> the family *or* <u>of</u> the family's
a friend <u>of</u> hers	a contemporary <u>of</u> Shakespeare *or* <u>of</u> Shakespeare's

And a sentence like "*The story was based on an idea of Shakespeare*" is at least potentially ambiguous, whereas "*The story was based on an idea of Shakespeare's*" is clear. But if you feel that this sort of construction is unpleasant to the ear, you can usually manage to revise it to something like "*on one of Shakespeare's ideas.*" And avoid such double possessives with a *that* construction: "*His hat was just like that of Arthur's.*"

32n

PART VI

Essentials of Research: Planning, Writing, and Documenting Sources

CONTENTS

INTRODUCTION

A paper based on research should follow the principles governing any good essay. It should represent you as a thinker, and it should contribute your distinctive perspectives on a question of interest to you. Research essays also call upon you to seek out the findings and the views of others who have investigated a topic and to give full credit to those sources. Part VI discusses and illustrates the stages of writing a research essay and the details to keep in mind to do a good job.

33 The Research Plan

Begin by preparing a **research plan**, a strategy to focus your research and especially to budget the right amount of time to spend on the stages of the assignment. Draft this plan early—that is, no more than a day or two after you first receive the assignment—and then be prepared, if necessary, to revise it as circumstances change.

33a Formulating Research Questions

Your plan should consist first of a **researchable question**. This question should be of sufficient interest and importance to sustain you through the research and writing process. As you move on and gain more insight into the topic, be confident enough to modify the original question.

33b Designing a Timeline

As important as determining the researchable question is establishing a **realistic timeline** for the stages of your project. Consider how your assignment will fit in with other projects and commitments you have. Then ask yourself how much time you will give to each of the following tasks:

- Searching for sources
- Evaluating and reading sources
- Notetaking and synthesizing sources
- Organizing and planning the first draft
- Writing and revising second and subsequent drafts
- Editing and polishing the final draft

Try as much as possible to set a firm date for the end of your research and the beginning of your writing, and try to give yourself at least a week for writing and polishing the drafts of your assignment.

33c Identifying and Evaluating Sources

Most of the research you do for an academic research paper will involve finding and consulting library resources.

Therefore, you will need to learn your way around your library and its website. Most libraries offer remote access to some or all of their electronic resources, so you may be able to do much of your research from home. However, there will likely still be times when you need to visit your library in person to find a specific resource. If you have any questions, you can always contact a librarian.

Often, one focus of your research should be academic and peer-reviewed articles. These articles are written by academics for an audience of scholars and other experts in their particular area of study. They are particularly trustworthy resources because they have been read and critiqued by experts to ensure their accuracy. Peer-reviewed articles are usually found in specialty publications that may not be readily available or free to the public. To find such articles, you will typically search through databases. If you are looking for books, audio or video recordings, or similar media, you will typically search your library's catalog.

1. Searching databases

Databases provide information on articles published in magazines, newspapers, and academic journals. Your library likely subscribes to many databases, each of which is tailored to a specific topic or discipline, so it is worthwhile to take some time to get to know the options your library offers for searching different databases. You can often find guidelines and advice for using databases on your library's website; if you have any additional questions, remember that you can always consult a librarian.

Once you have determined the kinds of databases you want to explore, you can begin by searching for a key word or phrase identifying your topic or subtopic. If your search turns up too many articles that are not directly related to your topic, you may need to use more specific key words. When you do find an article of interest, you will likely be able to access it online. If the article is not available online, as might be the case if it is older and has not yet been digitized, you may need to do a simple search of your library's catalog to determine the call number and location of the print-based periodical on the library shelf.

33c

2. Searching library catalogs

A library's catalog contains brief descriptions of all resources available through the library. Some listings may provide a link to the full text of the resource, but in other cases you will need to use the call number provided in the listing to find the resource on the library shelves.

Most catalogs allow you to perform a simple search or an advanced search. In a simple search, you can look for a resource by typing a specific title, an author's name, or key words related to the topic into the catalog's main search field. Simple searches work best when you already know the exact resource that you want to find. In contrast, advanced searches—in which you can specify key words as well as additional information such as the format, language, year of publication, and even genre of the resource—work best when you have a more general idea of the *sort* of material you want to find.

3. Evaluating Internet sources

The Internet is a largely unregulated source of information. Thus, you need to evaluate carefully and critically all information you find online. As you search for online resources, keep the following in mind:

a. Look for authoritative information on websites maintained by recognized researchers or scholars, or by reputable public or private institutions. Anonymous and personal websites and sites such as *Wikipedia* are not considered authoritative sources for scholarly research.

b. Look for the credentials (the accomplishments and publications) of the identified authors of the website and consider these when weighing the research value of the site.

c. Consider using online databases and search engines that target peer-reviewed articles. Examples include Academic Search Complete and Google Scholar.

d. Check that the websites you plan to use contain current information and have been updated recently.

e. Ensure that claims are supported by evidence, and that the sources of all statistics, research findings,

33c

and other secondary information have been fully documented.

f. Avoid using a website whose links to other sites are broken, as it may not be well maintained or particularly reliable in its content.

g. Look for evidence of bias. Broad generalizations, poorly reasoned assumptions, inaccurate or overly negative representations of opposing views, lack of support from credible sources, and strong appeals to emotion rather than logic are all signs of a biased article. If you detect bias, investigate the author's reputation; you may find that the author is known for being unreliable or for representing a special interest group.

h. Watch for plagiarism. Writers and website managers sometimes copy sections of other people's works— or even republish entire articles—without citing the original source. If you suspect that some content has been plagiarized, copy a distinct phrase from it and perform a Google search for those words enclosed in quotation marks. The search results will help you verify the true source of the material.

33d Producing a Preliminary Bibliography

Once you have decided on a researchable question, designed a timeline, and established criteria for identifying and evaluating sources, the first major step in gathering information is to compile a **preliminary bibliography**. As you consult various sources (for example, periodical indexes, essay indexes, general and particular bibliographies, encyclopedias and dictionaries, your library's catalogues, and the Internet), make a list of books, articles, websites, and so on that may be useful sources of information about your topic. Next, look in the appropriate part of your library's catalogue or databases to find out which books and articles are available through your library. Record the call numbers of non-electronic resources as well as the URLs (uniform resource locators) or DOIs (digital object identifiers) of electronic resources.

33d ○

When you begin looking at the actual books, articles, websites, and other sources on your preliminary list, study and evaluate each book or article to see how useful it looks, and note its likely value as a source. Decide whether the source is scholarly and credible, whether it is promising or appears to be of little or no use, whether it looks good for a particular part of your project, or whether only part of it looks useful.

33e Notetaking

Once you have compiled your working bibliography and begun consulting the items it lists, reading and taking notes will become a priority for you. Initially, your notes will likely focus on brief descriptions of sources and of their relevance.

Taking notes about what you read is by far preferable to cutting and pasting together materials you have duplicated or downloaded from the Internet because it involves you actively—from the beginning of the research process—in filtering source material and then recording it as much as possible in your own terms. In fact, copying, cutting, and pasting at this stage delays your synthesis of sources and increases the risk of recording someone else's thoughts without any note of the original source. Whether inadvertent or not, the inclusion of such unfiltered material in finished essays without proper acknowledgment constitutes **plagiarism** (learn more in Chapter 36) and breaches academic integrity.

Your preliminary research should explore your subject, investigating and weighing its possibilities, and attempting to limit it as much as necessary to meet the demands of time and especially the length stipulated for the project. At some point during this early stage you should be able to construct a **preliminary outline or plan**, subject to change as you go along.

Following are some tips for good notetaking:

1. **Label each note carefully with information about the source.**
2. **Be as brief as possible.**

33d

3. **Distinguish carefully between direct quotation and paraphrase or summary.** Generally, quote only when you feel strongly that the author's own way of putting something will be especially effective in your essay. When you do quote directly, be careful: your quotation must accurately reproduce the original, including its punctuation, spelling, and even any peculiarities that you think might be incorrect. Set quotes apart from your own words by enclosing them in quotation marks.

4. **Enclose your own ideas in square brackets and label them with the phrase "MY OWN IDEA."**

5. **Use your own words as much as possible.**

6. **Quote from the original source.** When you quote, or even paraphrase or summarize, do so from the original source if possible. Second-hand quotations may be not only inaccurate but misleading as well.

7. **Distinguish between facts and opinions.** If you are quoting or paraphrasing a supposed authority on a subject, be careful not to let yourself be unduly swayed. Rather than note that "aspirin is good for heart and stroke patients," say that "Dr. Jones claims that aspirin is good for heart and stroke patients." In research-based writing, the credibility of your own presentation depends on such matters of attribution. A research paper missing such attributions is ineffective.

8. **Be careful to record the correct page numbers.**

9. **Enclose explanatory material in square brackets.** Whenever you insert explanatory material (for example, a noun or noun phrase to explain a pronoun) in a quotation, use square brackets.

10. **Use [*sic*].** When there is something in a quotation that is obviously wrong (for example, a factual mistake or a spelling error), insert [*sic*] after it.

11. **Indicate ellipses.** Whenever you omit a word or words from a quotation, use three spaced periods to indicate the ellipsis.

12. **Record the dates on which you accessed web-based sources.** Materials posted online are often updated, so recording your date of access will help to explain

33e

any discrepancies between your notes and the original source at a later date.

34 Writing the Essay

When your research is complete and you've organized the notes you intend to use to fit into your working outline, you are ready to begin writing the essay. As you write your first draft, include in your text the information that will eventually become part of your documentation. That is, at the end of each quotation, paraphrase, summary, statistic, or direct reference, enclose in parentheses the last name of the author and the relevant page number(s). If you are using more than one work by the same author, also include the titles of the sources. If you are using works by multiple authors who have the same surname, also include surnames or first initials for those authors. Once you have finished your first draft, you can adjust the citations as necessary to meet the requirements of the citation style you are using (see #37).

35 Acknowledging Sources

The purpose of acknowledging sources through documentation is fourfold:

1. It demonstrates that you, the writer, are a genuine researcher who has done the considerable work of investigating authorities and experts in the field(s) assumed in your researchable question.
2. It acknowledges your indebtedness to particular sources.
3. It lends weight to your statements and arguments by citing experts and authorities to support them.
4. It enables an interested reader to pursue the subject further by consulting cited sources, or possibly to evaluate a particular source or to check the accuracy of a reference or quotation.

It is not necessary to provide documentation for facts or ideas or quotations that are well known or "common knowledge"—such as the fact that Shakespeare wrote

33e

Hamlet, or that Hamlet said "To be or not to be," or that Sir Isaac Newton formulated the law of gravity, or that the story of Adam and Eve appears in the book of Genesis in the Bible, or that the moon is not made of green cheese. But if you are at all uncertain whether or not something is "common knowledge," play it safe: it is far better to over-document and appear a little naive than to under-document and engage in the unethical practice of plagiarism.

If a piece of information appears in three or more different sources, it qualifies as "common knowledge" and need not be documented. For example, such facts as the elevation of Mt. St. Helens, the current population of the world, or the date of the execution of Ted Bundy can be found in dozens of reference books. But it can be risky for a student, or any non-professional, to trust such a guideline when dealing with other kinds of material. For example, there may be dozens of articles, websites, and books referring to or attempting to explain something like a neutrino, or red shift, or black holes, or discoveries at the Olduvai Gorge, or Jungian readings of fairy tales, or the importance of the Human Genome Project, or deep structure in linguistic theory, or warnings about bioterrorism, or neoplatonic ideas in Renaissance poetry, or the nature and consequences of the great potato famine, or the origin of the name *America;* nevertheless, it is unlikely that a relatively non-expert writer will be sufficiently conversant with such material to recognize and accept it as "common knowledge." If something is new to you, and if you have not thoroughly explored the available literature on the subject, it is best to acknowledge a source. When in doubt, check with your instructor.

36 Quotation, Paraphrase, Summary, and Academic Integrity

A direct **quotation** preserves the exact wording of the original source. A well-documented **paraphrase**, on the other hand, reproduces the content of the original, but in different words. Paraphrase is a useful technique in research-based writing because it enables writers to refer to source material while still using their own words and thus to avoid too much direct quotation. But a paraphrase, to be legitimate, should give clear credit *at its beginning* to the source and should not use significant words and phrases from an original without enclosing them in quotation marks. In other words, begin your paraphrase by identifying your source in an attribution (for example, "Biographer John English suggests . . ." or "John English, Pierre Trudeau's biographer, argues . . ."). Be sure to provide the relevant page number(s) in your citation, as you would for a direct quotation (see #37). A paraphrase is usually about the same length as the material it paraphrases, though it may be slightly shorter. A **summary**, however, is by definition a condensation, a boiled-down version in one's own words expressing the principal points of an original source. It is often the best evidence of a writer's effective synthesis of secondary-source material.

Some writers make the serious mistake of thinking that only direct quotations need to be documented; on the contrary, it is important to know and remember that *paraphrase and summary must also be fully documented*. Failure to document a paraphrase or summary is a breach of **academic integrity** known as **plagiarism**, a form of intellectual dishonesty and theft for which there are serious academic penalties. To familiarize yourself with your institution's policies on academic integrity and on plagiarism, consult your institution's most recent academic calendar.

To illustrate the differences between a legitimate and an illegitimate use of source material, here is a paragraph reproduced from Rupert Brooke's *Letters from America*, followed by

a. legitimate paraphrase,
b. illegitimate paraphrase,
c. combination paraphrase and quotation,
d. summary, and
e. a comment on plagiarism.

> Such is Toronto. A brisk city of getting on for half a
> million inhabitants, the largest British city in Canada
> (in spite of the cheery Italian faces that pop up
> at you out of excavations in the street), liberally

36

endowed with millionaires, not lacking its due share
of destitution, misery, and slums. It is no mushroom
city of the West, it has its history; but at the same time
it has grown immensely of recent years. It is situated
on the shores of a lovely lake; but you never see that,
because the railways have occupied the entire lake
front. So if, at evening, you try to find your way to the
edge of the water, you are checked by a region of
smoke, sheds, trucks, wharves, storehouses, "depôts,"
railway-lines, signals, and locomotives and trains
that wander on the tracks up and down and across
streets, pushing their way through the pedestrians,
and tolling, as they go, in the American fashion, an
immense melancholy bell, intent, apparently, on some
private and incommunicable grief. Higher up are the
business quarters, a few sky-scrapers in the American
style without the modern American beauty, but one
of which advertises itself as the highest in the British
Empire; streets that seem less narrow than Montreal
[sic], but not unrespectably wide; "the buildings are
generally substantial and often handsome" (the too
kindly Herr Baedeker). Beyond that the residential
part, with quiet streets, gardens open to the road,
shady verandahs, and homes, generally of wood, that
are a deal more pleasant to see than the houses in a
modern English town. (Brooke 80–81)

The parenthetical reference for this block quotation,
which is given in MLA style, begins one space after the
final punctuation mark. It includes the author's last name
and the page numbers on which the original appeared. The
complete bibliographical entry for Brooke's work would
appear in the list of works cited as follows:

Brooke, Rupert. *Letters from America*. Sidgwick and
Jackson, 1916.

 36a Legitimate Paraphrase

During his 1913 tour of the United States and Canada,
Rupert Brooke sent back to England articles about

his travels. In one of them, published in the 1916 book *Letters from America*, he describes Toronto as a large city, predominantly British, containing both wealth and poverty. He says that it is relatively old, compared to the upstart new cities farther west, but that nevertheless it has expanded a great deal in the last little while. He implies that its beautiful setting is spoiled for its citizens by the railways, which have taken over all the land near the lake, filling it with buildings and tracks and smell and noise. He also writes of the commercial part of the city, with its buildings which are tall (like American ones) but not very attractive (unlike American ones); one of them, he says, claims to be the tallest in the British Empire. (He pokes fun at Baedeker for being over-generous with his comments about the city's downtown architecture.) The streets he finds wider than those of Montreal, but not too wide. Finally, he compares Toronto's attractive residential areas favorably with those of English towns (80–81).

This is legitimate paraphrase. Even though it uses several individual words from the original (*British, railways, tracks, American, British Empire, streets, residential, English town[s]*), they are a small part of the whole; more important, they are common words that would be difficult to replace with reasonable substitutes without distorting the sense. And, even more important, they are used in a way that is natural to the paraphraser's own style and context. Paraphrase, however, does not consist in merely substituting one word for another, but rather in assimilating something and restating it in your own words and your own syntax.

Note that the writer has carefully kept Brooke's point of view apparent throughout by including him in each independent clause (a technique that also establishes good coherence): *Rupert Brooke, he describes, He says, He implies, He also writes, he says, He pokes fun, he finds, he compares.*

36b Illegitimate Paraphrase

An illegitimate paraphrase of Brooke's paragraph might begin like this:

36a

> Brooke describes Toronto as a <u>brisk</u> kind of city with
> nearly <u>half a million inhabitants</u>, with some <u>Italian faces</u>
> <u>popping up</u> among the British, and with both <u>millionaires</u>
> <u>and slums</u>. He deplores the fact that the <u>lake front</u> on which
> <u>it is situated</u> has been <u>entirely occupied by the railways</u>,
> who have turned it into <u>a region of smoke and storehouses</u>
> and the like, and <u>trains that wander back and forth, ringing</u>
> <u>their huge bells</u> (80–81).

The parenthetical reference at paragraph's end does *not*
protect the writer from the charge of plagiarism, for too
many of the words and phrases and too much of the syntax are Brooke's own. The words and phrases underlined
are all "illegitimate": they still have the diction, syntax,
and stylistic flavor of Brooke's original, and therefore they
constitute plagiarism.

Had the writer put quotation marks around the underlined words, the passage would no longer be plagiarism—but it would still be illegitimate, or at least very
poor, paraphrase, for if so substantial a part is to be left in
Brooke's own words and syntax, the whole might as well
have been quoted directly.

Paraphrase and Quotation Mixed

A writer who felt that a pure paraphrase was too flat and
abstract, who felt that some of Brooke's more striking
words and phrases should be retained, might choose to
mix some direct quotation into a paraphrase:

> In *Letters from America*, Rupert Brooke characterizes
> Toronto as a "brisk," largely British city having the
> usual urban mixture of wealth and poverty. Unlike
> the "mushroom" cities farther west, he says, Toronto
> has a history, though he points out that much of its
> growth has been recent. He notes, somewhat cynically,
> that the people are cut off from the beauty of the lake
> by the railways and all their "smoke, sheds, trucks,
> wharves, storehouses, 'depôts,' railway-lines, signals,
> and locomotives and trains" going ding-ding all over the
> place (80–81).

36c

This time the context is very much the writer's own, but some of the flavor of Brooke's original has been retained through the direct quotation of a couple of judiciously chosen words and the cumulative list quoted at the end. The writer is clearly in control of the material.

36d Summary

The purpose of a summary is to substantially reduce the original, conveying its essential meaning in a sentence or two. A summary of Brooke's passage might go something like this:

> Rupert Brooke describes Toronto as large and
> mainly wealthy, aesthetically marred by the railway
> yards along the lake, with wide-enough streets,
> tall but (in spite of Baedeker's half-hearted approval)
> generally unprepossessing buildings, and a residential
> area more attractive than comparable English ones
> (80–81).

In general, try to refer to an author by name in your text—and the first time by full name. If for some reason you do not want to bring the author's name into your text (for example, if you were surveying a variety of opinions about a particular city and did not want to clutter your text with all their authors' names), then you would still need to make the source clear, according to whichever citation style you are using (#37).

36e Maintaining Academic Integrity and Avoiding Plagiarism

Had one of the foregoing versions of the passage not mentioned Brooke, nor included quotation marks around words taken directly from the original, nor included documentation, it would have been plagiarism. A student doing research is part of a community of scholars (professors, investigators, instructors, other students, and researchers), all of whom are governed by the codes of academic honesty that define effective research and identify plagiarism—whether intentional or accidental—as a serious offense. (Note that you can greatly reduce the likelihood of "accidental" plagiarism by taking notes in your own words and by clearly recording the sources of material you quote or summarize when you are researching your topic. See #33e.)

Your college or university calendar will no doubt include a detailed definition of plagiarism and a statement of policy on the academic discipline (failing marks, suspension, a note on one's academic transcript) arising from a finding of plagiarism. You should review this information and discuss any questions or concerns with your instructors and academic advisors.

When you are working on a research project, keep in mind that you are ethically bound to give credit twice—*in the text* of the written document and *in the works cited list*—to all sources of information you have used. All of the following kinds of material require acknowledgment:

- Direct quotations—whether short or long
- Your summaries and paraphrases of sources
- Ideas, theories, and inspirations drawn from a source and expressed in your own words
- Statistical data compiled by institutions (for example, think tanks and governmental or non-governmental organizations) and other researchers
- Original ideas and original findings drawn from course lectures and seminars
- Graphic materials (diagrams, charts, photographs, illustrations, film and television clips, audio and video recordings, and so on)
- Materials drawn from authored or unauthored websites

Remember that giving credit for this kind of material does not diminish your own work: it enhances the credibility of your claims and demonstrates just how much genuine research you have done on your project. It shows you adding your voice and your views to those of the community of scholars and researchers of which you are a part.

36e

One final note. It is possible to commit self-plagiarism. This happens when a writer submits the same work—in whole or in part—for two different courses or assignments. If you are working in the same subject or topic area for two different courses or assignments, it is essential to discuss the ethical issues involved with both instructors to whom the work will be submitted.

36f Integrating and Contextualizing Quotations

When you use direct quotations, you must integrate them into your writing as seamlessly as possible, and you must ensure that their meaning remains clear in their new context. A good way to start is by asking yourself what the original author was doing with the words. For example, was the author *analyzing, arguing, challenging, defending, demonstrating, illustrating, examining, observing, noting, hypothesizing, introducing,* or *suggesting* something important? Once you've selected the most appropriate verb, you can use it to anchor the quotation to your discussion:

> As Rupert Brooke <u>observes</u> about Toronto in the early 1900's, "It is no mushroom city of the West, it has its history" (80).

Finding the right verb to contextualize a quotation will help you convey to the reader—and clarify to yourself—your reason for including the quoted material in your paper.

In some cases, you may need to alter the grammar, syntax, or punctuation of a quotation to make it conform to your own grammar and syntax. The examples given below demonstrate how you might do this in a variety of situations. These examples use quotations taken from the following passage, which comes from Mary Shelley's *Frankenstein; or, The Modern Prometheus*:

> I am by birth a Genevese; and my family is one of the most distinguished of that republic. My ancestors had been for many years counsellors and syndics; and my father had filled several public situations with honor

36e

and reputation. He was respected by all who knew him for his integrity and indefatigable attention to public business. He passed his younger days perpetually occupied by the affairs of his country; a variety of circumstances had prevented his marrying early, nor was it until the decline of life that he became a husband and the father of a family.

a. altered for pronoun reference:

Victor Frankenstein begins his story by stating that "[he is] by birth a Genevese; and [his] family is one of the most distinguished of that republic" (Shelley 31).

The first-person pronouns have been changed to third person in order to fit the third-person point of view in the sentence as a whole. The changed pronouns and the accompanying verb (*is* for *am*) appear in square brackets.

b. altered for consistent verb tense:

As we first encounter him in the description at the beginning of his son's narrative, Victor's father is a man "respected by all who [know] him for his integrity and indefatigable attention to public business" (Shelley 31).

The verb in square brackets has been changed from past to present tense to conform with the tense established by the *is* of the student's sentence.

c. altered for punctuation:

The first words of Victor Frankenstein's narrative——"I am by birth a Genevese" (Shelley 31)——reveal a narrator preoccupied with himself, his birth, and his nationality.

The semicolon of the original has been dropped to avoid its clashing with the enclosing dashes of the student's own sentence.

d. selective quotation:

Victor describes his father as a man of "honor and reputation ... respected by all who knew him for his

> integrity and indefatigable attention to public business"
> and "perpetually occupied by the affairs of his country"
> (Shelley 31).

Here the student writer has incorporated select words and phrases. The ellipsis indicates that material has been omitted in the interests of the student's own sentence structure.

37 Documentation

To be effective, documentation must be complete, accurate, and clear. Completeness and accuracy depend on careful recording of necessary information as you do your research and take notes. Clarity depends on the way you present that information to your reader. You will be clear only if your audience can follow your method of documentation. Before you begin any research project, investigate the method of documentation you need to use. This section presents three frequently used styles:

1. Modern Language Association (**MLA**), which is in wide use in the humanities
2. American Psychological Association (**APA**), which is used in some of the social and other sciences as well as in education studies
3. The *note* method recommended by *The Chicago Manual of Style*, which is used in various disciplines

Which method you choose will depend on what discipline (field of study) you are writing in and on the wishes of your audience.

Note: Each example on the following pages has color coding to help you recognize the common elements among the in-text and reference citations, so that you can construct them more easily. The color key is found at the bottom of each page.

37a MLA Style

As detailed in the eighth edition of the *MLA Handbook* (2016), MLA style uses internal citations within a paper

36f

to attribute quotations, paraphrases, or summaries. In MLA, internal citations consist of the author's last name and where relevant, a page reference. Using this method, you provide a short parenthetical reference in the text, and you list all sources in a list titled Works Cited at the end of your paper. The entries in the list of works cited contain full bibliographic information, and they are alphabetized by the last names of authors, editors, or other creators (or by title, when no author, editor, or other creator is named).

The pages that follow illustrate examples of the most common patterns of MLA documentation: each in-text parenthetical reference is accompanied by its works-cited entry. Note that parenthetical references are usually placed at the end of the sentence in which the citation occurs. Note also that in an actual paper, the examples that follow would be double-spaced.

A note on number ranges: When you give a number range (e.g., a range of page numbers) in MLA style, provide the first and second numbers in full for numbers up to 99 (e.g., 5–88, 97–99). For larger numbers, give the first number in full but only the last two digits of the second number, unless additional digits are required for clarity (e.g., 122–28 for a range from 122 to 128, but 385–460 for a range from 385 to 460).

A Book by One Author (or Editor)
In-Text Citation

> **A survey revealed that many North American cities "did not provide pedestrian amenities at all, and only half, in any way, encouraged their citizens to reach their destinations by foot" (Friedman 136).**

When you don't mention the author by name in your sentence, the parenthetical reference includes the author's last name and a page reference, with *no intervening punctuation*. If you can include the author's name and credentials in your text, however, the parenthetical reference will be

Author *Title* Publication information **Electronic source**

shorter, the context of the quotation clearer, and the credibility of the point stronger:

> **Avi Friedman, winner of the United Nations World Habitat award, notes that "most North American cities did not provide pedestrian amenities at all, and only half, in any way, encouraged their citizens to reach their destinations by foot" (136).**

Works-Cited Entry

> Friedman, Avi. *A Place in Mind: The Search for Authenticity.* Vehicle Press, 2010.

The works-cited reference for a book includes

- the author's name (last name, followed by a comma, and full first name, followed by a period);
- the full title of the book (italicized), followed by a period;
- the publisher's name, followed by a comma; and
- the year of publication, followed by a period.

In the publisher's name, omit an initial article (*A*, *An*, or *The*) and corporate words or abbreviations such as *Company*, *Inc.*, and *Ltd.*, but keep descriptive words like *Books or Press*. For a university press, substitute *U* for *University* and *P* for *Press*. Note that when a works-cited entry exceeds one line, the second and subsequent lines should be indented a half inch.

If you access a book online, include at the end the DOI (digital object identifier) or the URL (uniform resource locator) that will direct the reader to the book. If you access a book through a website or a database, include the name of the website or database immediately before the DOI or URL.

> Melville, Herman. *Moby-Dick, or the Whale.* 1922. *Barleby.com, 2013,* www.bartleby.com/91/.

37a
MLA

Author   *Title*   Publication information   **Electronic source**

A Book by Two Authors (or Editors)
In-Text Citation

> In the book's introduction, the writers note that "newcomers to the prairies were beset by a seemingly endless series of unforgiving challenges" (Calder and Wardhaugh 11).

Works-Cited Entry

> Calder, Alison, and Robert Wardhaugh, editors. *History, Literature, and the Writing of the Canadian Prairies.* U of Manitoba P, 2005.

A Book by Three or More Authors (or Editors)
In-Text Citation

> Students should draft a research plan "no more than a day or two" after receiving an essay assignment (Messenger et al. 224).

Give the last name of the author or editor listed first on the work's title page, followed by "et al." (an abbreviation for Latin *et alii*, "and others").

Works-Cited Entry

> Messenger, William E., et al. *The Oxford Handbook.* 2nd ed., Oxford UP, 2019.

Two or More Works by the Same Author (or Editor)
In-Text Citation

If you cite multiple works by the same author, the in-text citations must include short versions of the works' titles. In most cases, you can reduce a title to an initial noun or noun phrase (omit an opening *A*, *An*, or *The*). If the title begins with something other than a noun or a noun phrase (e.g., a verb, a conjunction, or a preposition), use the first word of the title.

Author   *Title*   Publication information   **Electronic source**

The most talented fiction writers devote "time and effort into exploring particular emotional issues" and learning "how to externalize" the expression of emotion (Oatley, *Passionate Muse* 187). When they are successful in their efforts, their fiction "enters the mind" and "prompts us towards emotions" (Oatley, *Such Stuff* 7).

Works-Cited Entry

The works are listed alphabetically by title, and the author's name is replaced by three consecutive hyphens in the second entry.

> Oatley, Keith. *Such Stuff as Dreams: The Psychology of Fiction.* Wiley-Blackwell, 2011.
>
> ---. *The Passionate Muse: Exploring Emotion in Stories.* Oxford UP, 2012.

More Than One Work in the Same Citation
In-Text Citation

> World War II left Americans shaken and grieving, but it also brought them together more than ever before through a growing sense of patriotism and national identity (Kennedy 615–68; Perret 300).

Works-Cited Entry

> Kennedy, David. *Freedom from Fear: The American People in Depression and War, 1929–1945.* Oxford UP, 1999, pp. 615–68.
>
> Perrett, Geoffrey. *Days of Sadness, Years of Triumph: The American People, 1939–1945.* Vol. 1, Penguin Press, 1973, p. 300.

A Work by a Government Agency or a Corporate Author

A government agency is one of the many branches or departments of government at the international, federal, state, county, or city level. A corporate author is a group, association, or institute of authors who are not named individually on the title page of a work.

In-Text Citation

> In the aftermath of a disaster, veterans can get assistance if they face challenges keeping up with mortgage or other payments (United States Department of Veterans Affairs 2).

Works-Cited Entry

> United States, Department of Veterans Affairs, Office of Operations, Security, and Preparedness/ Office of Emergency Management and Resilience. *Disaster Assistance for Veterans.* 9 Oct. 2018, www.osp.va.gov/VA_Disaster_ Assistance_to_Veterans_Brochure_2018.pdf.

Omit any article (*A*, *An*, or *The*) at the beginning of the group's name. If the group listed as the author is also listed as the publisher, begin with the title. And if you list a government agency in the author position, begin with the name of the country, province, territory, or state in which the agency operates, as in the example above.

A Work by an Anonymous Author

Begin with a short version of the title.

In-Text Citation

> The most expensive white diamond ever bought at auction is "the 118.28-carat oval-cut gem that sold . . . for $30.6 million in 2013" ("Colors" 34).

Here "Colors" is short for "The Colors of Money," the title of an unsigned magazine article.

Works-Cited Entry

> "The Colors of Money." *Forbes*, 23 Nov. 2015, p. 34.

Author   *Title*   Publication information   **Electronic source**

A Multivolume Work

In-Text Citation

Include the volume number, followed by a colon, after the author's name.

> **In an entry dated 3 August 1908, she described her second book as "not nearly so good as *Green Gables*" (Montgomery 1: 338).**

Works-Cited Entry

> Montgomery, Lucy Maud. *The Selected Journals of L. M. Montgomery.* Edited by Mary Rubio and Elizabeth Waterston. Oxford UP, 1985–2004. 5 vols.

The range "1985–2004" indicates that the first volume of the journals was published in 1985 and the last volume in 2004.

Quotation at Second Hand

Try as often as possible to quote from primary sources. If you quote from a secondary source, identify it and give a full context (date, name of the speaker or writer, circumstances) for the words you quote:

In-Text Citation

> **Lionel Trilling proposed, "A work of art is itself authentic by reason of its entire self-definition: it is understood to exist wholly by the laws of its own being" (qtd. in Erickson 124).**

Works-Cited Entry

> Erickson, Rebecca. "The Importance of Authenticity for Self and Society." *Symbolic Interaction*, vol. 18, no. 2, 1995, pp. 121–41.

A Literary Work Available in Many Editions

To enable readers to locate quotations in any edition they may have access to, include the page number for the edition you have consulted as well as any volume, chapter, section, or other division number(s) attached to the material.

Prose Works
In-Text Citation

> Jane Austen presents readers of *Pride and Prejudice* with the heroine's father, the likable Mr. Bennet, an "odd . . . mixture of quick parts, sarcastic humour, reserve, and caprice" (3; vol. 1, ch. 1).

Works-Cited Entry

> Austen, Jane. *Pride and Prejudice.* 1813. Oxford UP, 2008.

The year 1813 is the year of the work's first publication.

A Play in Prose
In-Text Citation

> In the first moments of the play, Constance asks herself this hypothetical question: "What if a Fool were to enter the worlds of both *Othello* and *Romeo and Juliet*?" (14; act 1, sc. 1).

Works-Cited Entry

> MacDonald, Ann-Marie. *Goodnight Desdemona (Good Morning Juliet).* 1990. Vintage, 1998.

A Play in Verse
In place of the page number, include act, scene, and line numbers, separated with periods:

In-Text Citation

> In *As You Like It*, Silvius describes what it means to love:
>> It is to be all made of fantasy,
>> All made of passion, and all made of wishes,
>> All adoration, duty, and observance,
>> All humbleness, all patience and impatience,
>> All purity, all trial, all obedience. (5.2.94–98)

Author   *Title*   Publication information   **Electronic source**

Works-Cited Entry

> Shakespeare, William. *As You Like It.* Edited by
> Roma Gill, Oxford UP, 2002.

A Short Poem

If the lines are numbered, give the line number(s) preceded by "line" (for one line) or "lines" (for multiple lines) the first time the poem is cited. In subsequent citations, give only the line number(s). Do not include page numbers.

In-Text Citation

> Robert Burns begins the poem by comparing his
> love to "a red, red rose / That's newly sprung in
> June" (lines 1–2) and to "the melodie / That's
> sweetly play'd in tune" (3–4).

If the lines are unnumbered, include neither line nor page numbers.

Works-Cited Entry

> Burns, Robert. "A Red, Red Rose." *Robert Burns in
> Your Pocket*, Waverley, 2009, p. 228.

A Long Poem with Divisions
In-Text Citation

Include part, stanza, book, canto, and/or line numbers—whichever are given in the original poem—separated with periods. If the lines are unnumbered, provide page numbers.

> Those who find Satan heroic are overlooking
> Milton's flat statements, for example that the
> Father of Lies is "in pain, / Vaunting aloud,
> but racked with deep despair," and that his
> "words . . . bore / Semblance of worth, not
> substance" (lines 125–26, 528–29).

Here, the second set of line numbers is separated from the first by a comma.

Author   *Title*   Publication information   **Electronic source**

Works-Cited Entry

> Milton, John. *Paradise Lost.* Edited by William
> Kerrigan et al., Random House, 2007.

An Essay in an Edited Collection
In-Text Citation

> In the conclusion to her essay, Julie Cruikshank
> observes that an important purpose of traditional
> oral narratives is "to resolve symbolically those
> areas that cannot easily be worked out in the
> sphere of human activity" (194).

Works-Cited Entry

> Cruikshank, Julie. "Oral History, Narrative
> Strategies, and Native American
> Historiography." *The Canadian Oral History
> Reader*, edited by Kristina R. Llewellyn et al.,
> McGill–Queen's UP, 2015, pp. 180–97.

An Article in a Journal
In-Text Citation

> E. Ray Dorsey encourages researchers to write
> clearly for their multidisciplinary audience, asking
> them to make complex concepts "simple" and to
> "give examples, draw analogies, and be visual" (2).

Works-Cited Entry

> Dorsey, E. Ray. "A Digital Journal for a Digital Era."
> *Digital Biomarkers*, vol. 1, no. 1, May 2017,
> pp. 1–3.

If the journal does not provide an issue number or a month of publication, omit these details.

If you retrieved the article online, include the DOI (digital object identifier) assigned to the article at the end. If the article has not been assigned a DOI, provide the URL (uniform resource locator) that will lead your reader

Author *Title* Publication information **Electronic source**

37a
MLA

to the article. If the online version is not paginated, do not include page numbers. And if you accessed the article through an online database, provide the name of the database (in italics) immediately before the DOI or the URL.

> Dorsey, E. Ray. "A Digital Journal for a Digital Era." *Digital Biomarkers*, vol. 1, no. 1, May 2017, pp. 1–3. *Karger*, doi:10.1159/000458512.

An Untitled Review
In-Text Citation

> The reviewer describes the collection as a "beautiful and nuanced work by a poet of considerable skill, intelligence and depth" (Kraus 443).

Works-Cited Entry

> Kraus, Brittany. Review of *Signed Wings*, by Lola Lemire Tostevin. *The Dalhousie Review*, vol. 94, no. 3, pp. 443–44.

An Article in a Newspaper or a Magazine
In-Text Citation

> Devyani Saltzman evokes a vivid image in her opening comments on the holy rivers of India: "Frigid and tumultuous, the white water of the Ganges sped past a rocky bank where family friends had set up a bonfire and chairs overlooking the river" (T1).

Works-Cited Entry

> Saltzman, Devyani. "At the Water's Edge." *The Globe and Mail*, 17 Feb. 2007, T1+.

In this example, "T1+" indicates that the article begins on page 1 of section T of the newspaper and then continues not on page 2 but later in the section.

If you have accessed the article online, follow the article's title with the name of the website (in italics), the date of publication, and the URL:

Author *Title* Publication information **Electronic source**

Saltzman, Devyani. "At the Water's Edge." *The Globe and Mail*, 17 Feb. 2007, www.theglobeandmail.com/life/at-the-waters-edge/article20393518/?page=all.

An Interview

In-Text Citation

In an interview with *Variety*, Martin Short notes that his partnership with Steve Martin works well because their mutual trust on stage allows them to "keep the kind of happy loose quality" that audiences love.

Note that no page number is given in this example because the original online source was unpaginated.

Works-Cited Entry

Short, Martin. "Steve Martin and Martin Short Talk State of Comedy, Refining Their Live Show for Netflix, and Thirty Years of Friendship." Interview by Scott Huver. *Variety,* 7 Aug. 2018, 9:00 a.m., variety.com/2018/tv/awards/emmys-martin-short-steve-martin-netflix-interview-1202895658/.

If the interview does not have a title, use the word *Interview* (followed by a period and not in italics or quotation marks) in place of the title, and include the name of the interviewer if possible.

An Online Document with No Page Numbers

In-Text Citation

If you are citing an online document that has no numbered divisions, include only the author's last name in the parenthetical citation.

Author   *Title*   Publication information   **Electronic source**

> **The National Ballet of Canada's recent production
> of *Swan Lake* was hailed as "a gorgeous,
> sumptuous feast for the eyes and ears" (Leung).**

However, if the document consists of numbered paragraphs or sections, include the paragraph or section number where you would normally include the page number, and add the abbreviation "par." (for "paragraph") or "sec." (for "section") before the number. Also add a comma to separate the author's name from the abbreviation: for example, "(Wallenstein, par. 3)."

Works-Cited Entry

For web-based material that does not fit into any other categories outlined in this section on MLA-style documentation, include as many of the following details as you can: the name of the author or creator of the material, the title of the material (enclose titles of web pages in quotation marks), the title of the website (in italics), the name of the website's publisher (only if the publisher has not already been named in the title of the website or as the author or creator), the date the material was posted, and the URL.

> Macaulay, Alastair. "Alvin Ailey Dancers Return
> Like Conquering Heroes." *The New York
> Times,* 4 Dec. 2017, www.nytimes.com/
> 2017/12/04/arts/dance/alvin-ailey-city-
> center.html.

If the author is not named, or if the author is a group whose name is also the name of the website, begin with the title. And if the material is not dated, or if you think your reader would benefit from knowing when you accessed the material, add the date of your access at the end, after the URL: for example, "Accessed 20 July 2016."

A Message on a Social Media Site
In-Text Citation

For a message posted to *Twitter*, *Facebook*, *Instagram*, or some other social media site, provide the name, username, or group name (whichever is used in the author position in the list of works cited) of the person or organization that posted the message.

> **Douglas Coupland offers the following advice on email etiquette: "If you find yourself bcc'ing an email, you probably shouldn't be sending it at all."**

> **A common definition of the word *bumfuzzle* is "to confuse; perplex; fluster" (Merriam-Webster).**

Works-Cited Entry

Begin with the name of the person or group that posted the message. If the author has not provided her or his real name, begin with author's screen name; if you know the author's real name, you can add it in parentheses (first name followed by last name) after the username. For short messages, provide the full text of the message in quotation marks, with spelling, punctuation, and capitalization that matches the original. For messages of more than 30 words or so, include a brief description in place of the title. Also provide the name of the site (in italics), the date and time (if provided) that the message was posted, and the URL.

> Coupland, Doug. "If you find yourself bcc'ing an email, you probably shouldn't be sending it at all." *Twitter*, 21 Apr. 2016, 12:16 p.m., twitter.com/DougCoupland/status/723228986512302081.

> Merriam-Webster. "'Bumfuzzle' means 'to confuse; perplex; fluster.'" *Twitter*, 29 Apr. 2016, 6:15 a.m., twitter.com/MerriamWebster/status/726037139931156484.

> Dalhousie University. Announcement of upcoming performance event "Different State of Mind." *Facebook*, 18 Feb. 2016, www.facebook.com/DalhousieUniversity/photos/a.113777601898. 107830.714248689 8/10153199944611899/ ?type=3&theater.

Author   *Title*   Publication information   **Electronic source**

> **Fullerton, Susannah.** Comment on Anne Shirley
> being a positive role model for young women.
> *Google+*, 1 Dec. 2013, **plus.google
> .com/+susannahfullerton.**

A Video or Sound Recording
In-Text Citation

Provide the last name of the recording's primary creator or the title of the recording (whichever comes first in the list of works cited), then include the time range (in hours, minutes, and seconds) for the content you are citing.

> ***YouTube* contributor Ideas at Play notes that
> "sitcoms have a rich history of teaching moral
> lessons," and posits that *The Good Place* goes a
> step further by engaging with moral complexities
> and teaching "nuanced lessons" (00:00:17-01:47).**

Works-Cited Entry

Begin with the name of the performer, speaker, director, writer, composer, or other creator most relevant to your paper, followed by a brief description of that person's role. (If the person's role will be obvious to your readers, you can omit the description.) Then include the title of the recording and any additional information that will help your reader identify the material. If the contributors aren't important to your discussion, you can begin with the title of the work and include the names of any significant contributors, along with a brief description of their roles, after the title.

For an **online video**, include the name of the video-hosting site (in italics), the name of the person or organization that posted the video, the date on which the video was posted, and the URL:

> **Ideas at Play.** "How *The Good Place* Redefines
> the Sitcom: Why You Should Watch (No
> Spoilers)." *YouTube*, 21 May 2018, **www
> .youtube.com/watch?v=URXF9CF3M-k.**

**37a
MLA**

Author *Title* Publication information **Electronic source**

If the video's description includes the date on which the events recorded in the video took place, you can add that date immediately after the video's title, followed by a period.

For a **motion picture**, include the name of the main production company or distributor and the year of release:

> Coogler, Ryan, director. *Black Panther.*
> Performances by Chadwick Boseman and
> Michael B. Jordan, Marvel Studios, 2018.

If you accessed the motion picture online, also include the name of the video-hosting site and the URL:

> Cooper Ryan, director. *Black Panther.* Marvel
> Studios, 2018. Netflix, **www.netflix.com/**
> **title/80201906.**

Treat a **television series** as you would treat a motion picture. For an individual **episode of a television series**, provide the name of the episode, the name of the series, the season number, and the episode number. If you watched the episode when it originally aired, replace the name of the production company or the distributor with the name of the network that aired the show, and give the date of broadcast:

> Price, Richard, and Steven Zaillian, writers. "The
> Call of the Wild." *The Night Of,* season 1,
> episode 8, HBO, 28 Aug. 2016.

For an **episode of a podcast**, include as many of the following details as you can find: the title of the episode, the title of the podcast, the season number, the episode number, the producer (if different from a named contributor), the release date, and the URL:

> "*The Outlander* by Gil Adamson." *Write Reads,*
> hosted by Kirt Callahan and Tania Gee,
> episode 36, 17 Feb. 2016, **writereads**
> **.wordpress.com/2016/02/17/write-reads-**
> **36-the-outlander-by-gil-adamson/.**

Author   *Title*   Publication information   **Electronic source**

For a **musical recording**, include the name of the recording company and the date. If the entry is for an individual **song**, provide the title of the song as well as the title of the album. And if you retrieved the recording online, include the URL:

> Cohen, Leonard. "Born in Chains." *Popular Problems*, Columbia, 2014, www
> .myplaydirect.com/leonard-cohen/
> features/31693444.

A Personal Email or Letter
In-Text Citation
If you need to cite an email, a letter, or some other form of personal communication, identify in the text the person who sent the message.

> Professional email messages should include a
> clear, concise subject line (Smith).

Works-Cited Entry
Begin with the name of the person who wrote the email or the letter. For an email, provide the subject line (enclosed in quotation marks) as the title; for an untitled letter, provide a brief description of the material. Conclude with the name of the person who received the message and the date on which it was sent.

> Smith, Henry. "Re: 5 Tips for Better Emails."
> Received by Chris Buonelli, 30 Nov. 2016.

> Kurtz, Andrew. Personal letter about writing
> effective summaries. Received by Dani
> Norris, 6 Jan. 2017.

Additional Examples
Following are some examples of works-cited entries for a few other kinds of print and non-print sources. Remember that in-text references to unpaginated electronic sources do not require page numbers.

**37a
MLA**

Author   *Title*   Publication information   **Electronic source**

A Book in Translation

Eco, Umberto, and Jean-Claude Carrière. *This Is Not the End of the Book*. Translated by Polly McLean, Harvill Secker, 2011.

A Lecture

Bluhm, Susanna. "Painting." Art Lecture Series, 31 Oct. 2018, 11:30 a.m., Lecture Hall Purce, Evergreen State College, Olympia.

A Thesis or a Dissertation

Haqqani, Shehnaz. *Islamic Tradition, Change, and Feminism: The Gendered Non-Negotiable*. U of Texas-Austin, 2018. *Texas ScholarWorks*, repositories.lib.utexas.edu/handle/2152/68731.

For a print version of a published thesis or dissertation, omit the name of the database and the URL.

A Blog Post

Fournier, Jess. "Incarcerated People are Going on a Nationwide Strike." *Feministing*, 21 Aug. 2018, feministing.com/2018/08/21/incarcerated-people-are-going-on-a-nationwide-strike/.

If the blog has a publisher who is not the author, and that publisher's name is not contained in the title of the blog, you can include the publisher's name after the title of the blog, followed by a comma.

A Work of Visual Art

Smith, Kiki. *Come Away from Her*. 2003. Brooklyn Museum.

If you are working from a published photograph of the work, include the necessary information to indicate where you found the photograph. Begin with the title of the book, website, or other resource in which the image appears.

Author   *Title*   Publication information   **Electronic source**

Smith, Kiki. *Come Away from Her.* 2003. Brooklyn Museum, 2005, **www.brooklynmuseum.org/ opencollection/objects/166799.**

Sample MLA Research Paper
Go to Appendix B to see a sample research paper that uses MLA style.

 ## APA Style

APA style is commonly used in psychology and the social sciences; the standard guide is the *Publication Manual of the American Psychological Association* (sixth edition, 2010). Like MLA style, this system also uses internal citations in the text, but for APA, the information provided is the name(s) of the author(s) and the date of publication. Page numbers are only required for direct quotations. Here is a sample internal citation in APA style:

> **National identity is deeply connected to a sense that there is a boundary between those who belong to a nation and those who do not (Winter, 2011).**

But if you refer to a particular part of the source, or if you quote from it, supply the relevant page number (preceded by "p." or numbers (preceded by "pp."):

> **As Elke Winter (2011) notes, "a pluralist 'national we' is bounded by opposition to a real or imagined 'Others' with a capital O" (p. 5).**

Note that if you name the author in the text, you don't need to repeat the name in the parenthetical reference.

If a work has *two authors*, list both names every time you refer to the source:

> **One study has found that progressive discipline in education "has the potential to enhance students' social and behaviour literacy" (Milne & Aurini, 2015, p. 51).**

37a MLA

Author   *Title*   Publication information   **Electronic source**

If a work has *three, four, or five authors*, list all of them the first time, but only the first and "et al." (not italicized or in quotation marks) thereafter. If it has *six or more authors*, list only the first and "et al." each time, including the first.

If you are citing an *online document with no page numbers*, count the paragraphs following the title or a heading and assign a number to the relevant paragraph:

> Law professor Michael Geist (2016) argues that "the emergence of new voices and the innovative approaches at older ones point to the likelihood that journalism is neither dead nor dying" (para. 12).

If you begin counting after a heading, include the first few words of the heading after the year:

> On its website, the agency affirms its commitment to "creating thriving public spaces for all New Yorkers," promising to "improve the quality, accessibility, efficiency, and sustainability" of the city's parks (NYC Parks, n.d., "Framework," para. 1).

In this example, "n.d." indicates that no date of publication was provided.

And if you are citing a specific portion of an *audio or video recording*, include the time at which the quotation begins in the original source:

> In a recent lecture, Jane Goodall offered the following inspirational words: "Each and every one of us makes a difference each and every day, and we have a choice what kind of difference we're going to make" (Concordia University, 2014, 53:28).

If you need to cite *more than one work in a single parenthetical citation*, order the entries alphabetically and separate them with a semicolon: for example, "(Meier et al., 2014; Pearce, Ford, Willox, & Smit, 2015)." If the works are by the same author, list the dates chronologically and separate them with commas: for example, "(Whitley, 2013, 2015, 2017)."

37b APA

Author *Title* Publication information **Electronic source**

Following are some examples of reference-list entries in APA style. Note that in the reference list, if a work has seven or fewer authors, you must list each one. If a work has eight or more authors, you should list the first six followed by three ellipsis points and the final author's name: for example, "Lam, G. F., Diaz, J. S., Castillo, G., Cooper, C., Reyes, H. N., Thorpe, J. R., . . . Li, B. F."

An Entire Book

Ward, J. (2017). *Sing, unburied, sing.* New York, NY: Scribner.

Note that initials are used instead of the author's full given name or names. Also note the style of capitalization. For book and article titles, capitalize only the first letter of the first word of the title, the first letter of the first word following a colon, and the first letter of a proper noun. For periodical titles, capitalize all key words except for prepositions, articles, and conjunctions. (These rules apply to the APA reference list only. In the body of a paper, all titles are treated according to the rule given here for periodical titles.) Finally, note that in the publisher's name, you should omit unnecessary words such as *Inc.*, *Ltd.*, *Co.*, and *Publishers*, but retain the words *Books* and *Press*.

If you used an electronic version of a book, add a description of the version (if applicable) in square brackets following the title, and include the book's DOI (digital object identifier; if available) or the URL (uniform resource locator) of the site from which you retrieved the book:

Kastrup, H., & Mallow, J. V. (2016). *Student attitudes, student anxieties, and how to address them: A handbook for science teachers.* doi:10.1088/978-1-6817-4265-6

Todd, P. (2014). *Extreme mean: Ending cyberabuse at work, school, and home* [Adobe DRM version]. Retrieved from https://store .kobobooks.com

37b APA

Author   *Title*   Publication information   **Electronic source**

A Book in Translation

Piaget, J. (1952). *The origins of intelligence in children* (M. Cook, Trans.). New York, NY: International Universities Press.

An Edition Other Than the First

Byrne, J. H. (2017). *Learning and memory: A comprehensive reference* (2nd ed.). Cambridge, MA: Academic Press.

A Republished Book

McLuhan, M. (2002). *The mechanical bride: Folklore of industrial man.* Corte Madera, CA: Gingko Press. (Original work published 1951).

A Multivolume Work

Dutch, S. I. (Ed.). (2010). *Encyclopedia of global warming* (Vols. 1–3). Pasadena, CA: Salem Press.

A Chapter or Article in an Edited Collection

Kendrick, W. (2001). Not just another Oedipal drama: The unsinkable Sigmund Freud. In Press, J. (Ed.), *War of the words.* (pp. 137–151). New York, NY: Three Rivers Press. (Original work published 1984.)

An Article in a Journal

Ziser, M. (2010). Bioregionalism 2.0: Global climate change, local environmentalism, and new-media communities. *Western Humanities Review, 64*(3), 81–84.

If you retrieved the article online, include the DOI (digital object identifier) assigned to the article. If the article has no DOI, provide the URL (uniform resource locator) for the journal's homepage.

Author *Title* Publication information **Electronic source**

Sharmai, M., Enosh, G., Machmali-Kievitz, R., & Dvorit, G. (2017). Living in the line of fire: The impact of the exposure to warfare on couple relationships. *Journal of Family Therapy, 40*(3), 349–377. doi: 10.1111/1467-6427.12162

Trust, T. (2018). Screen time, laptop bans, and the fears that shape the use of technology for learning. *Journal of Digital Learning in Teacher Education, 34*(3), 130–131. Retrieved from http://www.tandfonline.com/full/2018.1459100.

A Magazine Article

McLaren, L. (2016, January 11). Workers of the world, commute! *Maclean's, 129*(1), 32.

Hsu, H. (2018, October 15). The rise and fall of affirmative action. *The New Yorker.* Retrieved from http://www.newyorker.com.

A Newspaper Article

Parkinson, D. (2016, April 7). Carbon-tax revenue isn't dirty money. *The Globe and Mail*, p. B2.

Hendrix, S. (2018, October 14). SNL has skewered every president since Ford: All of them reacted the same way—until now. *The Washington Post.* Retrieved from http://www.washingtonpost.com.

A Work by a Government Agency or Corporate Author

North Dakota Career Resource Network. (2018–2019). Architecture & construction: Designing, planning, managing, building and maintaining the built environment. *Career Outlook, 36*, 17–19. Retrieved from http://www.nd.gov/cte/crn/docs/CareerOutlook.pdf.

37b APA

Author   *Title*   Publication information   **Electronic source**

If you accessed the document in print, replace the "Retrieved from" and URL with the city of publication and the name of the publisher (usually the government agency).

A Work with No Identified Author

> The Colors of Money. (2015, November 23). *Forbes, 196*(7), 34.

A Thesis or a Dissertation from a Database

> De Riggi, M. (2015). *Non-suicidal self-injury, online activity and emotional health among adolescents* (Master's thesis). Available from Theses Canada. (AMICUS No. 44230969)

A Music Recording

> Ma, Y. Y., Duncan, S., Meyer, E., & Thile, C. (2011). *The goat rodeo sessions* [CD]. New York, NY: Sony Masterworks.

> Miranda, L. M. (2016). Immigrants (we get the job done) [Recorded by K'naan, Snow the Product, Riz MC, & Residente]. On *The Hamilton mixtape* [mp3]. New York, NY: Atlantic.

A Motion Picture

> Johnson, S. (Director), & Lana Condor (Performer). (2018). *To all the boys I've loved before* [Motion picture]. United States: Netflix. Retrieved from http://www.netflix.com.

A Television Program

> Murphy, R., & Falchuk, B. (Writers), & Buecker, B. (Director). (2017, September 5). Election night. [Television series episode]. In *American horror story: Cult*. Los Angeles, CA: FX. Retrieved from http://www.hulu.com.

Author   *Title*   Publication information   **Electronic source**

A YouTube Video

Concordia University. (2014, June 10). *Jane Goodall at Concordia: Sowing the seeds of hope* [Online video]. Retrieved from https://www.youtube.com/watch?v=vibssrQKm60

Lynch, G. [garrett414]. (2013, July 28). *Marshall McLuhan—The global village* [Online video]. Retrieved from https://www.youtube.com /watch?v=AepP7dNp9YY

A Podcast

Minnesota Public Radio. (2017, May 25). 74 seconds. *The traffic stop* [Audio podcast]. Retrieved from http://www.mprnews.org.

A Blog Post

Geist, M. (2016, February 12). Why journalism is not dying in the digital age [Web log post]. Retrieved from http://www.michaelgeist.ca /2016/02/why-journalism-is-not-dying-in-the-digital-age/

A Tweet

Garneau, M. [MarcGarneau]. (2016, January 25). Air turbulence can be unexpected and stronger than expected. My advice: keep your seat belt on all the time and you'll be fine [Tweet]. Retrieved from https://twitter.com/marcgarneau/ status/691587167945031680

A Post on Facebook or Twitter

Trudeau, J. (2017, June 6). How do we get young leaders to take action in their communities? Thanks @BarackObama for your visit &

insights tonight in my hometown [Tweet].
**Retrieved from https://twitter.com/i/
moments/872271081704267776**

Material from a Website

U.S. Department of Health & Human Services.
(n.d.). About HHS [Online statement].
Retrieved from https://www.hhs.gov/about

In this example, "n.d." indicates that no date of publication was provided. "About" is the name of the web page on which the material appears, and "[Online statement]" describes the format of the material.

Sample APA-Style Research Paper

A sample research papers showing APA style can be found on our companion site at www.oup.com/us/messenger.

 Chicago Style

The note method uses either footnotes or endnotes and a bibliography. The following guidelines are based on the sixteenth edition of *The Chicago Manual of Style* (2010).

Make sure to number notes sequentially in the text. Whenever possible, place a note number at the end of a sentence, after the period. If you need to place the number earlier in a sentence—as you would, for example, when only part of a sentence relates to a particular source— insert it *before* a dash or *after* any other punctuation mark.

Notes—either footnotes or endnotes—should be single-spaced and formatted with either a first-line indent or a hanging indent. Although the note numbers in the text are superscript, the note numbers preceding each endnote or footnote are not. For sources that you've listed in your bibliography, you may use shortened notes that include only the last name(s) of the author(s), a shortened version of the title, and the appropriate page number(s):

Author *Title* Publication information **Electronic source**

1. Brown, *Communicating Design,* 58–61.

2. Kilty, Felices-Luna, and Fabian, *Demarginalizing Voices,* 247–50.

3. Macdonald and Ruckert, "Continental Shift?," 129.

4. Stockwell et al., "Minimum Pricing," 913–14.

For works with three or fewer authors, list each author; for works with four or more authors, list the first author followed by "et al." Note that this guideline applies to both shortened notes (illustrated above) and full notes (illustrated below). If you refer to the same source in two or more consecutive notes, you can use "Ibid." and the page number for subsequent references. If you choose to include full citation information in your notes, do so only the first time you cite a particular source; for second and subsequent citations to the same source, use a shortened note.

List all of the sources you have used—including those you consulted but did not refer to directly—in a bibliography at the end of your paper. Bibliography entries should be arranged in alphabetical order, according to the first letters in each entry.

The following examples illustrate how to treat various types of works in full notes and in the bibliography.

A Book
Footnote or Endnote
For works with three or fewer authors, list each author; for works with four or more authors, list the first author followed by "et al." For works with ten or fewer authors, list the name of each author; for works with eleven or more authors, list the first seven followed by "et al."

1. Nathan Poole, *Father, Brother, Keeper* (Louisville: Sarabande Books, 2015), 6–8.

Poole, Nathan. *Father, Brother, Keeper.* Louisville: Sarabande Books, 2015.

37c CMS

Author *Title* Publication information **Electronic source**

A note or bibliography entry for an electronic version of a book you downloaded from a library or a bookseller should also include a description of the file (for example, "PDF e-book." or "Kindle edition.") at the end. A note or bibliography entry for a book you accessed online from any other source should include at the end the DOI (digital object identifier) assigned to the book or, if the book has not been assigned a DOI, the URL (uniform resource locator) that will direct your reader to the book.

An Edition Other Than the First
Footnote or Endnote

> **2.** Dan Brown, *Communicating Design: Developing Web Site Documentation for Design and Planning,* 2nd ed. (Berkeley: New Riders, 2011), 83.

Bibliography

> Brown, Dan. *Communicating Design: Developing Web Site Documentation for Design and Planning.* 2nd ed. Berkeley: New Riders, 2011.

A Book with an Editor or Translator
If the book you are citing has an editor and no author, give the editor's name first, followed by "ed." If the book has a translator or editor as well as an author, the author's name should come before the title, with the translator's or editor's name following the title.

Footnote or Endnote

> **3.** Jennifer M. Kilty, Maritza Felices-Luna, and Sheryl C. Fabian, eds., *Demarginalizing Voices: Commitment, Emotion, and Action in Qualitative Research* (Vancouver: University of British Columbia Press, 2015), 247–50.

> **4.** Franz Kafka, *The Metamorphosis,* trans. Susan Bernofsky (New York: W. W. Norton, 2014), 52–53.

Author *Title* Publication information **Electronic source**

37c
CMS

Bibliography

> Kilty, Jennifer M., Maritza Felices-Luna, and Sheryl C. Fabian, eds. *Demarginalizing Voices: Commitment, Emotion, and Action in Qualitative Research.* Vancouver: University of British Columbia Press, 2015.

> Kafka, Franz. *The Metamorphosis.* Translated by Susan Bernofsky. New York: W. W. Norton, 2014.

A Chapter or Article in an Edited Collection
Footnote or Endnote

> 5. Teresa Helm Filbert and Nancy Rankie Shelton, "Resisting Colonization in the Intermediate Classroom," in *Literacy Policies and Practices in Conflict: Reclaiming Classrooms in Networked Times,* eds. Nancy Rankie Shelton and Bess Altwerger (New York: Routledge, 2015), 101.

Bibliography

> Filbert, Teresa Helm, and Nancy Rankie Shelton. "Resisting Colonization in the Intermediate Classroom." In *Literacy Policies and Practices in Conflict: Reclaiming Classrooms in Networked Times,* edited by Nancy Rankie Shelton and Bess Altwerger, 100–119. New York: Routledge, 2015.

A Work by a Government Agency or Corporate Author
Footnote or Endnote

> 6. Federal Student Aid, *College Preparation Checklist* (United States Department of Education, July 2016), 21.

Bibliography

> Federal Student Aid. *College Preparation Checklist.* United States Department of Education, July 2016.

37c CMS

Author   *Title*   Publication information   **Electronic source**

An Article in a Journal
Footnote or Endnote

7. Vik Loveday, "Working-Class Participation, Middle-Class Aspiration? Value, Upward Mobility and Symbolic Indebtedness in Higher Education," *The Sociological Review* 63, no. 3 (2014): 571.

If you retrieved the article online, include the DOI assigned to the article. In the rare case that an article has no DOI, provide the URL that will direct the reader to the article.

8. Vik Loveday, "Working-Class Participation, Middle-Class Aspiration? Value, Upward Mobility and Symbolic Indebtedness in Higher Education," *The Sociological Review* 63, no. 3 (2014): 571, **doi:10.1111/1467-954X.12167.**

9. Joanna McIntryre, "Riots and a Blank Canvas: Young People Creating Texts, Creating Spaces," *Literacy 50*, no. 3 (2016): 152–53, **http://onlinelibrary.wiley.com/lit.12080.**

Bibliography

Loveday, Vik. "Working-Class Participation, Middle-Class Aspiration? Value, Upward Mobility and Symbolic Indebtedness in Higher Education." *The Sociological Review* 63, no. 3 (2014): 570–88.

For an article you retrieved online, also include the article's DOI or URL.

Loveday, Vik. "Working-Class Participation, Middle-Class Aspiration? Value, Upward Mobility and Symbolic Indebtedness in Higher Education." *The Sociological Review* 63, no. 3 (2014): 570–88. **doi:10.1111/1467-954X.12167.**

McIntryre, Joanna. "Riots and a Blank Canvas: Young People Creating Texts, Creating Spaces." *Literacy 50*, no. 3 (2016): 149–57. **http://online library.wiley.com/lit.12080.**

Author   *Title*   Publication information   **Electronic source**

37c
CMS

A Newspaper Article
Footnote or Endnote

> 10. David Parkinson, "Carbon-Tax Revenue Isn't Dirty Money," *Globe and Mail*, April 7, 2016, B2.

> 11. Rye Druzin, "Texas Oil Companies Pump More Than $17 Million Into Fighting Washington Carbon Tax," *Houston Chronicle*, October 1, 2018, https://www.chron.com/business/article/Texas-oil-companies-pump-more-than-17-million-13267260.php.

Bibliography

> Parkinson, David. "Carbon-Tax Revenue Isn't Dirty Money." *Globe and Mail*, April 7, 2016.

> Druzin, Rye. "Texas Oil Companies Pump More Than $17 Million Into Fighting Washington Carbon Tax." *Houston Chronicle*, October 1, 2018. https://www.chron.com/business/article/Texas-oil-companies-pump-more-than-17-million-13267260.php.

A Blog Post
Footnote or Endnote

> 12. Melany Hallam, "Volunteer Your Way into a Job," *Career Sense* (blog), April 4, 2016, https://careerlinkbc.wordpress.com/.

Bibliography

> Hallam, Melany. "Volunteer Your Way into a Job." *Career Sense* (blog). April 4, 2016. https://careerlinkbc.wordpress.com/.

A Podcast
Footnote or Endnote

> 13. Earlonne Woods, Antwan Williams, and Nigel Poor, "Cellies," *Ear Hustle*, podcast audio, June 14, 2017, http://www.earhustlesq.com/.

37c
CMS

Author   *Title*   Publication information   **Electronic source**

Bibliography

Woods, Earlonne, Antwan Williams, and Nigel Poor. "Cellies." *Ear Hustle* (podcast). June 14, 2017. http://www.earhustlesq.com/.

A Tweet
Footnote or Endnote

14. Lady Gaga, Twitter post, October 10, 2018, https://twitter.com/ladygaga/.

Bibliography

Lady Gaga. Twitter post. October 10, 2018. https://twitter.com/ladygaga/.

A Post on Facebook or Instagram
Footnote or Endnote

15. Notorious RBG's Facebook page, accessed October 11, 2018, https://www.facebook.com/notoriousRBG/.

Bibliography

Notorious RBG. Facebook status update. Accessed October 11, 2018. https://www.facebook.com/notoriousRBG/.

Material from a Website
Footnote or Endnote

Begin with the title of the web page (in quotation marks), and provide as much additional information as you can: the author, the site's sponsor (if different from the author), the publication date, and the page's URL. If no publication date is given, provide the date on which the content was last modified (preceded by "last modified"); if neither of these dates is available, give the date on which you accessed the site (preceded by "accessed").

16. "In Focus: Myth vs. Fact." United States Department of Homeland Security, accessed October 14, 2018, http://www.dhs.gov/focus.

Author   *Title*   Publication information   **Electronic source**

Bibliography

United States Department of Homeland Security. "In Focus: Myth vs. Fact." Accessed October 14, 2018. http://www.dhs.gov/focus.

Sample CMS-Style Research Paper

A sample research papers showing CMS style can be found on our companion site at www.oup.com/us/messenger.

Checklist for Use in Revising, Editing, and Proofreading

As you begin to prepare a piece of your writing for final submission to your reader(s), it is good strategy to ask yourself a series of questions designed to ensure that you have polished your work to the point where you can consider it finished. What we have listed here are the kinds of questions we ask ourselves in reading and evaluating students' writing. If you can ask and answer all of the following questions in the affirmative, your essay should be not just adequate, but very good.

1. *During and after planning the essay, ask yourself these questions:*

Subject

- [ ] If I am writing a research essay, have I formulated a researchable question? (#33a)
- [ ] Have I limited the scope of my subject? (#1a)

Audience and Purpose

- [ ] Can I clearly describe my purpose and audience? (#1b)

Evidence

- [ ] Do I have enough credible material/evidence to develop and support my topic? (#1c)

Organization and Plan

- [ ] Does my thesis offer a focused, substantive, analytical claim about the subject? (#1d)
- [ ] Are my main ideas arranged in the best order for logic and effect? (#1e)

2. *During and after revising your essay, ask yourself these questions:*

Title

☐ Does the title of my essay clearly indicate the topic and catch the reader's interest?

Structure

☐ Are my subject and thesis stated near the beginning? (#1g.3)

☐ Is my beginning short and engaging? (#1g)

☐ Does my ending avoid re-hashing ideas already presented in the rest of the essay, and does it bring the paper to a logical and satisfying conclusion?

Unity; Development

☐ Do all parts of the essay contribute to the whole, without unnecessary digression?

Emphasis

☐ Is my content particular and specific, avoiding unsupported generalizations? (#14b)

Paragraphs

☐ Does each body paragraph have a topic sentence that connects to the subject of the essay? (#2a–b)

☐ Is each body paragraph long enough to develop its topic adequately to a logical conclusion? (#2d)

Coherence

☐ Do the sentences in each paragraph have sufficient coherence with each other? (#2b–c)

☐ Does the beginning of each new paragraph provide a clear transition from the preceding paragraph?

Sentences

☐ Is each sentence clear and sufficiently emphatic in making its point? (#4e–i)

☐ Have I used a variety of lengths, kinds, and structures of sentences? (#4b–d)

☐ Have I avoided the passive voice except where it is clearly necessary or desirable? (#8h)

Appendix A Checklist for Use in Revising, Editing, and Proofreading

Diction

☐ Have I used words whose meanings I am sure of?

☐ Is my diction sufficiently concrete and specific? (#14b)

☐ Have I avoided repetition and wordiness? (#14f)

☐ Is my level of diction appropriate for my audience? (#14a)

☐ Have I avoided euphemisms, misused idioms, jargon, and clichés? (#14c, #14e–f)

☐ Have I avoided gender-biased, sexist language? (#7e)

Grammar

☐ Are my sentences free of dangling modifiers, agreement errors, incorrect tenses, faulty verb forms, incorrect articles and prepositions, and the like? (Parts II and III)

☐ Have I avoided unacceptable sentence fragments, comma splices, and run-on sentences? (#5a–c, #25a, #25n)

Punctuation

☐ Is the punctuation of each sentence correct and effective? (Part IV)

Spelling

☐ Have I checked all my words—reading backwards if necessary—for spelling errors? (Part V)

☐ Have I used my software's spell-checker to check the essay?

Mechanics, Formatting, and Documentation

☐ Have I carefully proofread my essay in hard copy and corrected all typographical errors? (#1h)

☐ Does my essay conform to all manuscript conventions of set out by my professor (including spacing, margins, font size, pagination, and headers)? (#26)

☐ Have I acknowledged and documented everything required by the rules of my university or college? (#35, #36, #37)

☐ Are all quotations, references, and citations handled properly? (#20, #35, #36, #37)

☐ Have I checked all quotations for accuracy? (#36)

☐ Is my bibliography or reference page complete and formatted correctly? (#37)

The Last Step

☐ Have I read my essay aloud—preferably to another student—as a final check for clarity and emphasis?

APPENDIX B

Sample MLA Research Paper

The following sample research paper illustrates the principles of documentation described in the eighth edition of the *MLA Handbook*. It also illustrates the formatting conventions described online at the MLA Style Center (style .mla.org/formatting-papers/). Before you submit your paper, you should always ask your instructor if she or he has any additional requirements. For example, your instructor might want you to add a separate title page that lists the title of your paper, your name, your instructor's name, the course code and section number of your class, and the date of submission.

Number all pages in the top right-hand corner, and include your last name before each page number. Double-space all lines of text, and indent the first line of all paragraphs, including the first. Set your margins to approximately 1 inch (2.5 cm) all around; in most cases, you can use the default settings of your word-processing program. Do not justify the right margin, and avoid breaking words at the ends of lines.

Begin your list of works cited on a new page at the end of your paper. Each entry should be set with a hanging indent. Arrange entries in alphabetical order, ignoring any initial article (*A*, *An*, or *The*) in entries that begin with a title.

Sample research papers for APA and CMS styles can be found on our companion site at www.oup.com/us/ messenger.

Gabriela Badica

Professor Brown

English 390, Section 2

21 May 2018

"The Story with Animals Is the Better Story":

The Co-Existence of Human and Animal Intelligences

in Yann Martel's *Life of Pi*

The co-existence of human and animal intelligences lies

at the heart of the survivor's narrative presented in Yann

Martel's *Life of Pi*. From its very first mention, the account of

Pi's 227 days of endurance is argued to be "a story that will

make you believe in God" (Martel ix). Martel himself has

described his novel as one that will achieve this task, insisting

on the significance of this central claim (Wood 1). However,

this crucial point becomes significantly more complicated

when the text presents two distinct narratives that explain Pi's

survival in severely diverging ways. While the first account,

characterized by meaningful interactions between human and

animal intelligences, presents a tale of endurance, intelligence,

perseverance, and controlled struggle, the second version, devoid

of any animal intelligences, is a dark account of cannibalism and

human nature at its most savage.

The stark contrast between the two explanations of Pi's

survival immediately makes those on the receiving end of the

accounts question not only which version they believe to be

the truthful one, but also which one they prefer. When faced with the question of which of the accounts is "the better story" (Martel 352), even the novel's most fact-driven and logically oriented characters identify the version with animals as superior. However, is the first account better simply because it is a feel-good story rather than a tale illustrating how even the most religious and idealistic of men can be led to savagery in desperate and dire circumstances? This essay will explore the implications of the co-existence of human and animal intelligences in the first account of Pi's existence at sea; it will also explore the manner in which the connection that is formed between these two types of intelligences is crucial to religious belief and spirituality. While the second version of Pi's survival also holds significant value, especially when considered in conjunction with survivor-trauma theory, the first story is the one that allows for a holistic understanding of the role that religion plays in Pi's life both during and after his shipwreck. Essentially, the story with animals is the better story because it offers the reader insight into the human identity-formation process and highlights the important connection between animality and divinity.

The text highlights Pi's deep connection to animals and religion early in the narrative. As the son of "Mr. Santosh Patel, founder, owner, director" of the Pondicherry Zoo, Pi has "nothing but the fondest memories of growing up in a zoo" (15). He claims that he "lived the life of a prince," with an alarm clock of lions' roars and a breakfast that was "punctuated by the shrieks and cries of howler monkeys, hill mynahs and Moluccan cockatoos"

(15). He anthropomorphizes the animals around him from an early age, recounting such daily routines as leaving for school "under the benevolent gaze not only of Mother but also of bright-eyed otters and burly American bison and stretching and yawning orang-utans" (15). Pi dismisses the frequent criticism that zoos strip animals of freedom through the claim that freedom in the wild, where "fear is high and the food low and where territory must constantly be defended and parasites forever endured" (17), is not something that would be in any way beneficial to animals. As James Mensch has highlighted, Pi describes zoos as artificial Gardens of Eden in which all animals are perfectly content (136).

Zoos are immediately paralleled with religion in this defense, as Pi states: "I know zoos are no longer in people's good graces. Religion faces the same problem. Certain illusions about freedom plague them both" (Martel 21). While Pi does not specifically state what the illusion about freedom that plagues religion is, it is evident that he does not feel constrained by religion at all. On the contrary, Pi has an inherent curiosity for learning about different religions; he becomes a practising Hindu, Christian, and Muslim all at once. Rather than choosing a single religion, Pi clings to his freedom to "love God" however he wants (74). Correspondingly, he asks his father both for a prayer rug and to be baptized. For Pi, embracing religion is a liberating experience. Indeed, along with his connection to animals, religion is one of the main pillars of Pi's identity formation from the early days of his childhood.

Pi's connection to animals undoubtedly informs his initial account of his time at sea. In the confined space of the lifeboat, the species boundary Pi observed in his childhood crumbles, and he recognizes a potent animality in himself. Previously a "puny, feeble, vegetarian life form" (203), Pi must now kill in order to survive. As time goes by, he "develop[s] an instinct, a feel, for what to do" (216). He asserts that he "descended to a level of savagery [he] never imagined possible" (238). As the days go by, his clothes rot away, and he is forced to live "stark naked except for the whistle that dangled from [his] neck by a string" (213). Yet perhaps the most potent moment that crumbles the species boundary is when Pi realizes, "with a pinching of the heart," that he has begun to eat "like an animal, that the noisy, frantic unchewing, wolfing-down of [his] was exactly the way Richard Parker ate" (250). This recognition of his animality becomes crucial to Pi's perspective and his identity.

Nevertheless, although the species boundary is certainly blurred, it is never fully crossed. One of the chief mechanisms that allow Pi to maintain a semblance of his humanity is his devotion to religion. Each day, he carefully says his prayers as part of the schedule that he creates for himself. Additionally, although many of the differences between Richard Parker and Pi collapse over the period of their co-existence in the lifeboat, their reactions to lightning during a thunderstorm illustrate that the species boundary is preserved (Mensch 138). While Pi is "dazed . . . but not afraid" and praises Allah, interpreting the

storm as "an outbreak of divinity," Richard Parker trembles
and hides in fear (138). Thus, the crucial pillar that religion
represents in Pi's identity never falters; as a result, it prevents the
species boundary from completely collapsing. Ultimately, his
effort to understand Richard Parker, a feat that is necessary for
his survival, leads Pi to gain a deeper understanding of his own
identity. As Martel explains, it is in "understanding the other
[that] you eventually understand yourself" (Sielke 20).

The relationship between animality and divinity is explored in
a different manner when it comes to considerations of which of Pi's
accounts is "the better story" (Martel 352). As Stratton argues, the
two conflicting stories highlight the novel's "philosophical debate
about the modern world's privileging of reason over imagination,
science over religion, materialism over idealism, fact over fiction"
(6). The two sides of the debate are embodied in the characters of
Mr. Okamoto and Mr. Chiba, who initially have very different
responses to Pi's story. For Mr. Okamoto, an individual who
exemplifies the view of truth as an objective reality that can be
uncovered and verified by the methods of science (Stratton 6),
the story with animals is "incredible" (Martel 328), "too hard to
believe" (329), and "very unlikely" (332). Mr. Chiba, who represents
Romanticism and its emphasis on spontaneity, subjectivity,
imaginative creativity, and emotion (Stratton 7), favors the animal
version, exclaiming "What a story!" (Martel 345).

While Pi recognizes the importance of reason as a practical
tool, asserting that "Reason is excellent for getting food, clothing

and shelter" and for "keeping the tigers away," he also cautions: "be excessively reasonable and you risk throwing out the universe with the bathwater" (331). The debate comes to a climax when both Mr. Okamoto and Mr. Chiba answer Pi's question about "the better story":

> So tell me, . . . which story do you prefer? Which is the better story, the story with animals or the story without animals?
>
> Mr. Okamoto: "That's an interesting question. . . ."
>
> Mr. Chiba: "The story with animals."
>
> Mr. Okamoto: "Yes. The story with animals is the better story."
>
> Pi Patel: "Thank you. And so it goes with God." (352)

Mr. Okamoto's willingness to recognize the story with animals as the better one demonstrates a change in his own identity, one that Stratton identifies as a development of his imaginative capacity (8). Martel himself has stated that the mechanism of faith uses both imagination and reason (Sielke 25), the principal elements of the story with animals.

However, what is most crucial is the analogy that Pi introduces after having deconstructed the reason–imagination binary. The created link between the story with animals and religious belief illustrates that God's existence occupies the same status in relation to truth and reality as does Pi's experience of shipwreck. In this way, "God's existence is a better story than the one told by those who doubt or deny His being: atheists lack imagination and miss the better story" (Martel 6).

Stewart Cole takes issue with the comparison between believing in the story with animals and believing in God, arguing that it is "problematic in failing to recognize the difference between believing in a story—that is, acknowledging its aesthetic impact—and believing in God" (23). Cole also points out that to conflate these two types of belief is to obliterate the important epistemological distinction between subjective and objective truth, a distinction that he identifies as crucial to discussions of religion (24). However, what this view fails to take into account is that Martel's aim is to justify a belief in God's existence rather than to prove God's existence, and—as with the acceptance of the first of Pi's accounts as the better story—such faith might require a suspension of disbelief.

As Martel has argued, "religion operates in the same exact way a novel operates. . . . For a good novel to work, you have to suspend your disbelief. . . . Exactly the same thing happens with religion" (Steinmetz 18). Martel also asserts that religion works the same way as a novel does in that it makes its recipients suspend their disbelief so that factual truth becomes irrelevant (Sielke 24). He cautions that this does not mean that facts are ignored, but rather that "it's more how you interpret the facts and how much you value facts that affect the totality of your sense experience"; therefore, "to say that the book will make you believe in fiction . . . isn't very far from saying it'll make you believe in God" (24). He also emphasizes that it is acceptable to say that God is a fiction if you understand that "this doesn't necessarily mean that this fiction doesn't exist. It just exists in a way that is only accessed through the imagination" (25). This view parallels the importance of imagination in Pi's first account of his survival narrative. In particular, "empathetic imagination" (25)—the ability to place oneself in another's shoes—is the crux of the story with animals; the co-existence of Pi's human intelligence with Richard Parker's animal intelligence allows Pi to examine and gain a deeper understanding of his own identity.

While the story with animals is the one that presents the enriching facet of the empathetic imagination, the second account and the implications of the first story being untrue have their own value. Several critics have interpreted Richard Parker as the outward manifestation of an internal split. As Robert Rogers notes, an individual suffering from internal conflict often grapples with contradictory impulses by "developing separate personality constellations" (109). Trauma theory explains that severe trauma explodes the cohesion of consciousness, and that "when a survivor creates a fully realized narrative that brings together the shattered knowledge of what happened and the emotions that were aroused by the meanings of the events, the survivor pieces back together the fragmentation of consciousness that trauma has caused" (Shay 188). Therefore, the second account suggests that the first account is Pi's attempt at recovery through the narration of experience and a coping mechanism in light of the trauma that he has suffered.

In a stark comparison to the first version, the story without animals portrays a view of life that is centered on greed, cruelty, corruption, and futility. God is notably left out of the picture, and human beings are completely alone and exiled from the comfort of religion. Thus, the second account demonstrates how even the most pacifist, devoted, and idealistic of men can be led to savagery in extenuating circumstances. While the story without animals contains its own intrinsic value, its lack of the co-existence of animal and human intelligences does not permit for either the fulfillment of the empathetic imagination (Sielke 25) or a connection between animality and divinity, two elements that remain crucial to Pi's identity.

Undeniably, of Pi's two accounts, the story with animals is a feel-good tale of courage, endurance, and intelligence, while the story without animals is a horrifying description of human savagery and desperation. However, this difference appears only on the surface. The facet of the first account that is most significant and most illuminating is that the co-existence of human and animal intelligence is crucial to the process of identity formation and motivation for spiritual belief. Highlighting the link between animality and divinity, an empathetic imagination allows for the ignition of the "spark that brings to life a real story" (Martel vii), thereby representing the key to a holistic understanding not only of oneself, but of all subsequent social interactions that determine identity construction.

Works Cited

Cole, Stewart. "Believing in Tigers: Anthropomorphism
    and Incredulity in Yann Martel's *Life of Pi*." *Studies in
    Canadian Literature*, vol. 29, no. 2, 2004, pp. 22–36.

Martel, Yann. *Life of Pi*. Random House, 2001.

Mensch, James. "The Intertwining of Incommensurables:
    Yann Martel's *Life of Pi*." *Phenomenology and the
    Non-Human Animal: At the Limits of Experience*, edited
    by Corinne Painter and Christian Lotz, Springer, 2007,
    pp. 135–47.

Rogers, Robert. *A Psychoanalytic Study of the Double in
    Literature*. Wayne State UP, 1970.

Shay, Jonathan. *Achilles in Vietnam: Combat Trauma and
    the Undoing of Character*. Touchstone, 1994.

Sielke, Sabine. "'The Empathetic Imagination': An
    Interview with Yann Martel." *Canadian Literature*,
    no. 177, Summer 2003, pp. 12–32, canlit.ca/article/
    the-empathetic-imagination/.

Steinmetz, Andrew. "Pi: Summing Up Meaning from the
    Irrational: An Interview with Yann Martel." *Books in
    Canada*, vol. 31, no. 6, Sept. 2002, p. 18.

Stratton, Florence. "'Hollow at the Core': Deconstructing
    Yann Martel's *Life of Pi*." *Studies in Canadian
    Literature*, vol. 31, no. 2, 2004, pp. 5–21.

Wood, James. "Credulity." *London Review of Books*, vol. 24,
    no. 22, Nov. 2002, www.lrb.co.uk/v24/n22/james-wood/
    credulity.

Index

Note: Page references followed by an "*f*" indicates figure.

Notes on Spelling and Other Issues

Notes on Spelling and Other Issues

Notes on Spelling and Other Issues

Common Mechanical and Spelling Errors

The following list is a quick guide to the sections in this handbook that discuss those mechanical and spelling errors most common in student essays and reports.

14g	Troublesome words and phrases, including commonly confused or misspelled words
26a	Incorrect formatting of an essay
27f	Incorrect abbreviation of Latin expressions
28h	Missing or faulty capitalization of academic courses and languages
28j	Incorrect treatment of abbreviations of proper nouns
28k	Missing or faulty capitalization of titles of written and other works
29a	Missing or mishandled quotation marks for titles of short works and parts of longer works
29b	Misuse of italics for titles of whole or major works
29c	Missing or misused quotation marks or italics for titles within titles
30c	Improper treatment of words referred to as words
31b	Numeral needed or misused for dates
31e	Numeral needed or misused for parts of a written work
31g	Numeral needed or misused for numbers of more than two words
32d	Spelling error due to not knowing when to double the final consonant before a suffix
32i	Spelling error due to confusion with other words
32j	Spelling error due to confusion between homophones and other words that are similar
32k	Spelling error due to a missing or misused hyphen
32-l	Spelling error due to incorrect plural form
32n	Spelling error due to incorrect possessive form